Computer Science and Technology in Schools

Computer Science and Technology in Schools

Edited by:

Adele Kuzmiakova

ARCLER PRESS

www.arclerpress.com

Computer Science and Technology in Schools

Adele Kuzmiakova

Arcler Press
224 Shoreacres Road
Burlington, ON L7L 2H2
Canada
www.arclerpress.com
Email: orders@arclereducation.com

ISBN: 978-1-77407-741-2 (Hardcover)

ABOUT THE EDITOR

Adele Kuzmiakova is a computational engineer focusing on solving problems in machine learning, deep learning, and computer vision. Adele attended Cornell University in New York, United States for her undergraduate studies. She studied engineering with a focus on applied math. While at Cornell, she developed close relationships with professors, which enabled her to get involved in academic research to get hands-on experience with solving computational problems. She was also selected to be Accel Roundtable on Entrepreneurship Education (REE) Fellow at Stanford University and spent 3 months working on entrepreneurship projects to get a taste of entrepreneurship and high-growth ventures in engineering and life sciences. The program culminated in giving a presentation on the startup technology and was judged by Stanford faculty and entrepreneurship experts in Silicon Valley. After graduating from Cornell, Adele worked as a data scientist at Swiss Federal Institute of Technology in Lausanne, Switzerland where she focused on developing algorithms and graphical models to analyze chemical pathways in the atmosphere. Adele also pursued graduate studies at Stanford University in the United States where she entered as a recipient of American Association of University Women International Fellowship. The Fellowship enabled her to focus on tackling important research problems in machine learning and computer vision. Some research problems she worked on at Stanford include detecting air pollution from outdoor public webcam images. Specifically, she modified and set up a variety of pre-trained architectures, such as DehazeNet, VGG, and ResNet, on public webcam images to evaluate their ability to predict air quality based on the degree of haze on pictures. Other deep learning problems Adele worked on include investigating the promise of second-order optimizers in deep learning and using neural networks to predict sequences of data in energy consumption. Adele also places an emphasis on continual education and served as a Student Leader in PyTorch scholarship challenge organized by Udacity. Her roles as the Student Leader were helping students debug their code to train neural networks with PyTorch and providing mentorship on technical and career aspects. Her hobbies include skiing, playing tennis, cooking, and meeting new people.

TABLE OF CONTENTS

List of Figures xiii

List of Abbreviations xvii

Preface xix

Chapter 1 Why Computer Science and Technology Should be Taught in Schools?.... 1

1.1. Introduction 2

1.2. Computer Science Gives Students Vital Skills 2

1.3. How Does Technology Affect Children Development 5

1.4. What Can Be Done To Incorporate Computer Science in Education? 12

1.5. Skills For Successful Computer Science Learner 23

Chapter 2 The Most Important Subjects In Computer Science 31

2.1. Introduction 32

2.2. C Programming Language 32

2.3. C++ Programming Language 33

2.4. Java Programming Language 34

2.5. Microprocessor 34

2.6. Networking 36

2.7. Compiler Design 38

2.8. Operating System 39

2.9. Computer System Architecture 41

2.10. Data Structures 43

2.11. Algorithms 45

Chapter 3 Computer Science In Early Childhood 47

3.1. Introduction 48

3.2. Computational Thinking 48

3.3. Block-Based Programming Languages 64

3.4. Programming Games 67
3.5. Introductory Robotic Systems 70

Chapter 4 Pedagogical Dimensions For Successful Early Childhood Computer Science Education Programs 75
4.1. Introduction 76
4.2. Powerful Ideas 76
4.3. Expressiveness 79
4.4. Low-Floor/High Ceiling 82
4.5. Debugging 85
4.6. Social And Emotional Learning 88
4.7. Guiding Principles For Use Of Technology With Early Learners 91

Chapter 5 Successful Technology Integration In Early Childhood Education 95
5.1. Introduction 96
5.2. The Importance Of Technology Integration In an Early Childhood Education 96
5.3. Types Of Technology Integration 103
5.4. Ways To Integrate Technology Into Your Classroom 124
5.5. Frameworks For Technology Integration 132
5.6. Factors Influencing Integration Of Computer-Based Technologies In Early Childhood 136

Chapter 6 Computer Science In The Elementary School 145
6.1. Interactive Computing 146
6.2. The Main Categories of Educational Use of Computers 148
6.3. Impacts of Computers on The Current Curriculum System 150
6.4. Computers As An Aid To Instruction 153
6.5. The Benefit of Computer Studies In Elementary Schools 156
6.6. Role of Calculators In Elementary School Education 157
6.7. What Preparatory School Teachers Should Understand About Computers? 159
6.8. Primary School Computer-Based Activities 162
6.9. The Cognitive Obstacle 163

Chapter 7 Technology Acceptance of Cloud Computing In Schools 169
7.1. Introduction 170

7.2. Cloud Computing 171
7.3. History of Cloud Computing 172
7.4. Technology Adoption Frameworks 174
7.5. Clouding Computing 191
7.6. Cloud Computing Challenges 193
7.7. Cloud Risks 196
7.8. Cloud Migration 198

Chapter 8 Role of ICT In 21St Century's Teacher 203
8.1. Introduction 204
8.2. ICT Helps Teachers Interact With Students 204
8.3. ICT Helps In Improving Teaching Skills, Helps In Innovative Teaching 206
8.4. ICT Helps In The Effectiveness oOf The Classroom 209
8.5. ICT Helps In Improving Professional Development and Education 211
8.6. It Helps Teachers In Preparation For Teaching 212
8.7. ICT Prepares Teachers For The Use Of Their Skills In The Real Classroom Situation 214
8.8. ICT Is A Tool For Teaching And Learning Itself 216
8.9. ICT As A Popular Tool For Organization And Management In Institutions 218
8.10. ICT Plays An Important Role In Student Evaluation 220
8.11. ICT Helps Teachers To Communicate Properly With Their Students 222
8.12. ICT Helps Teachers Pass Information To Students In A Short Time Frame 224
8.13. ICT Helps Teachers To Design Educational Environment 226
8.14. ICT Helps Teacher To Identify Creative Child In Educational Institution 228
8.15. ICT Helps Teacher To Motivate Students And Grow Interest In Learning 230
8.16. ICT Helps Teacher For Organizational Preconditions (Vision, Policy, And Culture) 231
8.17. ICT Is Helpful For Technical Preconditions (Infrastructure) 233
8.18. ICT Is Helpful For Both Vocational Education And Training Of Future Teachers (In The Teachers Training Institutes) ... 235

Chapter 9 Bridging The Computer Science Education Gap 239
9.1. Introduction 240
9.2. Imparting The Youth With Skills For A Digital Economy 241
9.3. Understanding IT And Computer Science 241
9.4. Filling The Gap For Computer Science Learning 242
9.5. Improving K-12 Computer Science Standards 243
9.6. Computer Science: Things Learners Should Know 244
9.7. Choosing Standards-Based Syllabuses And Teaching Resources 244
9.8. Introducing Elementary School Pupils To Computing 245
9.9. Involving Mid-Grade Pupils In Interdisciplinary Learning 246
9.10. Promoting High School Learners' Appreciation Of Computer Science 247
9.11. Enhancing Enrichment And Investigative Learning Experiences Among Students 248
9.12. Further Actions That Local Governments Can Take 249
9.13. Preparing Competent Computer Science Educators 250
9.14. Obstacles To Educator Certification In Computing Disciplines 251
9.15. Techniques For Equipping And Supporting Cs Educators 252
9.16. Sreb States' Techniques For Equipping Computer Science Educators 254
9.17. Access To Technology And Modern Learning Methods 255
9.18. ICT Planning 256
9.19. Computer Science Investment In Schools 258
9.20. Children's Coding Academies Seek To Fill Up Computer 'Skills Gap' 260
9.21. Interdependence Between Education Technology and Other Systems 261

Chapter 10 Factors Influencing Students' Choice Of Computer Studies In Schools 263
10.1. Introduction 264
10.2. An Overview Of Computer Studies In Secondary Schools 264
10.3. Students' Aspirations On Their Choice Of Computer Studies In Schools 265
10.4. Availability Of Computer Facilities In Schools 268
10.5. Parents' Influence On Students' Choice Of Computer Studies In Schools 270
10.6. Teachers' Readiness To Use ICT In Schools 273

10.7. Prior Computer Training.. 275
10.8. ICT Infrastructure 278
10.9. Internet Accessibility And Computer Usage by School Teachers.. 280
10.10. Computer Competence And Computer Usage by School Teachers.. 282
10.11. The Influence Of Gender Differences On Computer Usage by School Teachers 285

Index 289

LIST OF FIGURES

Figure 1.1. There is a great number of vital skills that a computer science student acquires and becomes part of him/her for the rest of their entire lifetime.

Figure 1.2. Fundamental thinking can be made through dialog expansion, which is where you help your children make sense of how to develop discourses by referencing past experiences or things they've examined.

Figure 1.3. When left to themselves, youngsters regularly utilized home PCs for stimulation as opposed to learning. Grown-up supervision is basic.

Figure 1.4. To implement a computer program, some schools have used computer science as an additional unit of integrating computing concepts into other content areas.

Figure 1.5. In high schools computer science is taught as a subject on its own.

Figure 1.6. Computer skills enable one to have analytical skills since programming involves identifying problems and coming up with solutions to address these problems.

Figure 1.7. In computer science students work on various projects that need a lot of creativity to solve them so that they may eliminate problems, use their knowledge in STEM, and be open-minded.

Figure 1.8. A person with critical thinking skills can be easily trusted to make the companies decide on their own and these decisions are relevant and effective.

Figure 1.9. The main factors that contribute to resilience include a good support system, always maintaining a positive relationship, having a good self-image and having a very positive attitude towards situations.

Figure 2.1. C computer programs represent a simple language to learn.

Figure 2.2. A microprocessor.

Figure 2.3. Computer network.

Figure 2.4. A compiler design overview.

Figure 2.5. The tasks of the operating system.

Figure 2.6. Computer system architecture.

Figure 2.7. Learning data structures is essential as it enables a student to know how to manage large amounts of data efficiently by use of applications such as databases and internet indexing services.

Figure 3.1. Computational Thinking or (CT) is a solution finding process which involves a number of features and dispositions.

Figure 3.2. Understanding maps helps children to develop a mental map in their brains, and therefore they are able to reason conceptually.

Figure 3.3. Block-based coding has been simplified so that younger students can understand its logic.

Figure 3.4. Robotic systems may be used to introduce students to mechanics from an early age.

Figure 4.1. Scratch is a fun and engaging way for students to learn programming.

Figure 4.2. Socioemotional learning is a holistic way of learning that can be adapted into schools.

Figure 4.3. Young children exposed to technology usually develop interest in science and mathematics subjects when they grow up.

Figure 5.1. Above are some self-balancing 3-D figures that were printed by some students.

Figure 5.2. Students are able to do their work on the computer using the help of the internet for research. This makes all the work much easier.

Figure 5.3. Podcasts are a very easy way to keep students engaged with school work.

Figure 5.4. Google docs have made work easier for many different students and companies.

Figure 5.5. There are many different ways in which Facebook can be incorporated into the classroom. These can help in improving student engagement.

Figure 5.6. Virtual trips can allow the students to experience experiences that they would not have been able to go through due to different circumstances.

Figure 5.7. Live streaming in the classroom can help engage students that depend on an audiovisual aid to learn.

Figure 5.8. Using videos and pictures in the classroom can help the students understand certain concepts faster, as well as retain the information easier.

Figure 5.9. Above is an example of an exit ticket that can be integrated online.

Figure 5.10. Above is a visual representation of the SAMR model.

Figure 5.11. This shows how all the aspects of the model have to be integrated for it to work.

Figure 5.12. For computer-based technologies to be successfully integrated, it requires the teachers to have the required knowledge and skills.

Figure 5.13. In the recent studies, it has shown that most math teachers opt to use computers in the learning process.

Figure 5.14. Depending on the type of subjects taught in the school curriculum, with the access to computers they will be able to access e-content that is relevant to the curriculum.

Figure 6.1. Personal computers initially entered the market in 1951 and transistorized computers got well-known from 1958.

Figure 6.2. In business, computer and calculator are the most basic and used tools in working and solving problems.

Figure 6.3. Computer-assisted instruction abbreviated as CAI is the use of computers to give students instructions.

Figure 6.4. Students performing class activities through modern computers.

Figure 6.5. A student proudly shows his elementary coding skills in class.

Figure 6.6. Computer-based activities can help students increase their understanding of key concepts.

Figure 7.1. Cloud computing is the largest generation technology that provides means by which we can utilize the applications and utilities via the internet.

Figure 7.2. Cloud computing has evolved through several phases that include grid and utility computing.

Figure 7.3. Task Technology Fit can be used to measure the effectiveness of an information system.

Figure 8.1. An image of telegram which is used to facilitate interaction in the classroom.

Figure 8.2. An image of a teacher using a computer during class time.

Figure 8.3. An images of students using a smartboard.

Figure 8.4. ICT has also enabled teachers to identify the type of teaching methodologies that would work for them in the classroom.

Figure 8.5. YouTube has been used as a teaching and learning tool.

Figure 8.6. An image of students carrying out a podcast which is one of the method of carrying out student evaluation.

Figure 9.1. Computer science can help expose young girls to STEM subjects in school.

Figure 9.2. Students keenly following a computer science lesson.

Figure 9.3. Schools should make technology accessible to students so as to equip them for the future job market.

Figure 10.1. There are many different reasons why students choose to do computer studies. The main reason has been due to their career options after secondary.

Figure 10.2. A computer laboratory requires to have proper facilities that will help in the maintenance of the computers. These include proper electrical wiring.

Figure 10.3. Parents are an important part of children's lives, and it is important for them to play major role in guiding their children.

Figure 10.4. It is important for teachers to learn how to use computers, so as to allow them to use them in improving student engagement in the classroom.

Figure 10.5. Training is important if the teachers are to be the stakeholders on computer integration in classrooms.

Figure 10.6. ICT infrastructure is paramount in computer integration in the classroom. It is not quite helpful for one to use the hardware without other factors such as internet.

Figure 10.7. Being able to access the internet is important for teachers, considering there any many software's that can be integrated in the school curriculum, and they all mostly require the internet.

Figure 10.8. There are many teachers that do not have the literacy that is required for one to use computers in classrooms. This is up to the government to provide training for the teachers.

Figure 10.9. Above is an example of the demographic that shows the difference between women and men in computer science.

LIST OF ABBREVIATIONS

A	attitude
BI	behavioral intention
BYOD	bring your own device
CRA	computer-related actions
CS	computer science
CT	computational thinking
DMS	database migration service
FAFSA	free application for federal students' aid
GDPR	general data protection regulation
GUTS	grow up thinking scientifically
IF-AT	immediate feedback assessment technique
MICA	my intelligent communication appliance
MIT	Massachusetts Institute of Technology
NCES	National Center for Education Statistics
OO	object-oriented
OS	operating system
PEOU	perceived ease of use
PU	perceived usefulness
SaaS	software as a service
SAMR	substitution, augmentation, modification, redefinition
SLA	service level agreement
STEM	science, technology, engineering, and mathematics
TAM	technology acceptance model
TAs	thinking actions
TOE	Technology Organization Environment

TPACK	Technological Pedagogical Content Knowledge
TTF	task technology fit
UTAUT	Unified Theory of Acceptance and Use of Technology

PREFACE

From a universal point of view, we are living in the world where technology is important. Computer science and technology have the potential to spur production and both fields are increasingly receiving attention in many countries. Technology alone has been touted as the panacea that brings the only available avenue for rising production in different sectors. This volume is going to offer critical information on computer science and technology in schools.

This volume is of great value on numerous levels. First, for those individuals that want to explore different technological issues, the volume will provide significant insights and inspiration for further research. Second, for those researchers that are already doing studies in computer science and technology, this volume has a lot of materials and information that can be used to add extra knowledge. Ultimately, this volume offers important insights for different audience. For instance, this volume has several chapters that epitomize on the issues of computer science and technology in educational sector for the sake of research and business. In other words, this volume is a stepping stone towards enhancing ties between computer science, technology, and education.

The volume has ten chapters, and each chapter discusses about a specific topic: chapter one is all about why computer science should be taught in schools; chapter two is about the most important subjects in computer science; chapter three discusses about computer science in early childhood; chapter four discusses about pedagogical dimensions for successful early childhood computer science education programs; chapter five presents information about successful technology integration in early childhood education; chapter six discusses about computer science in the elementary school; chapter seven offers detailed information about technology acceptance of cloud computing in schools; chapter eight offer information on role of ICT in 21st century's teacher; chapter nine discusses about bridging the computer science education gap; and lastly, chapter ten is all about factors influencing students' choice of computer studies in schools.

These ten chapters were extensively prepared for the readers to have a preview of how computer science, technology, and education relate to each other. The author paid more emphasis on the easiness of the content in order to make the volume clear and understandable to all readers.

It is my hope and trust that this volume will make a valuable contribution towards nurturing many to ride the wave of collaboration in different concepts discussed.

Chapter 1

Why Computer Science and Technology Should Be Taught in Schools?

CONTENTS

1.1. Introduction 2

1.2. Computer Science Gives Students Vital Skills 2

1.3. How Does Technology Affect Children Development 5

1.4. What Can Be Done To Incorporate Computer Science in Education? 12

1.5. Skills For Successful Computer Science Learner 23

1.1. INTRODUCTION

Computer science should be taught in schools now even more than before. There is a lot of debate on whether computer science should be included into the syllabus. Given the rate at which the globe economy is growing, more effective, faster, accurate work task force is needed. That's why more and more school should embrace the fact that we are entering a technological century when almost everything will be automated. The rate of unemployment is growing globally each year. There is a huge demand for computer science graduates and, unfortunately, we can't meet that demand. With each day a new invention is made the more reason to get to teach the computer science in school. Teaching computer science also enables close monitoring of how diseases or other medical emergencies spread. The world is now a global village and it is through this computer scientist work of continuous coding, that we are able to do transactions in various entity: business-wise, in the media, medical field movement and many more the list is endless. Despite that, there is a lot of good that computer science brings with it. Most places around the globe have no access to the study. It is due to this and many more reason's that the countries capable of teaching this study financially to do so as to make the world a better place. Hence it is clear that we can't exist without bringing computer science into our classroom.

1.2. COMPUTER SCIENCE GIVES STUDENTS VITAL SKILLS

Figure 1.1. There is a great number of vital skills that a computer science student acquires and becomes part of him/her for the rest of their entire lifetime.

Source: https://coloradosucceeds.org/network-perspectives/equip-colorados-students-with-vital-computer-science-skills/.

A lot of gratitude is obvious to them for majority of what we have and live with. Reviewing code and accompanying innovative tech arrangements being what computer science student do daily enables the students to acquire these vital skills:

1.2.1. Investigative Abilities

Being a computer science graduate includes recognizing an issue and thinking about a mechanical answer for address it. A lot of research on what has been there and requires change maybe for hundreds of years. This requires having strong illustrative aptitudes that enables the students to understand the issue they are overseeing. The students can then anqalyze different game plans to find the one that best meets their prerequisites (Beauchamp, 2016).

1.2.2. Critical Thinking Aptitude

One of the other key aptitudes for software engineering career's is the capacity to tackle complex issues in a precise and legitimate manner. This is on the grounds that the vast majority of the ventures they will be chipping away voluntarily expect them to take an idea and transform it into a reality. So as to do this, this computer scientist should have the option to think about the best way to deal with execute, how fast and a while later outline the methods expected to finish it (Beauchamp, 2016).

1.2.3. Imagination

Imagination goes connected at the hip with critical thinking and it's one of the other key aptitudes students in the field acquire as a software engineering career. Since coming up with answers for issues is never an immediate strategy, out-of-the-compartment believing is regularly required so as to guarantee that they are conveying the most inventive and viable arrangements.

1.2.4. Basic Reasoning Aptitudes

The basic reasoning is a significant aptitude to have and it is essential for the study of computer science. Students should use it in their entire career live, yet it's particularly significant with regards to software engineering. This is on the grounds that computer science students will be dealing with an assortment of activities and utilizing an assortment of philosophies, so knowing which frameworks to use (and when to use them) is an essential bit of doing what needs to be done. In theory, this understudy furthermore has the choice to assess why certain game plans most likely won't work and to save opportunity in drawing nearer up with the right approach (Guzdial, 2015).

1.2.5. Flexibility

Computer science student knows that one of the key principles in programming (at any level) is understanding that they are in all likelihood going to flop or even fail multiple times before they succeed. Knowing that this has nothing to do with their programming capacities and everything to do with the procedure itself. Programming includes evaluating various components of code until they see the best arrangement and learning as versatile, decided and humble despite different disappointments is a piece of the procedure.

1.2.6. Bounce Back from Disappointment and Move Forward

Computer science understudies wind up having a business outlook. Despite the fact that business majors are our regular foes and there is normally a distinction in morals, having a business point of view is extraordinarily important. Computer science understudy surrender effectively when something doesn't work. They generally have one line it isn't over until they win (Guzdial, 2015).

1.2.7. Peruse and Compose a Great Deal of Code

While it doesn't sound amusing to be experiencing endless floods of code and information, it is an everyday occurrence in the engineering workforce. Computer science graduates are continually focusing on bringing something new or discovering some new information. It is a success when new innovation brings a new software. The engineering vocation will require this innovation and this is why should persistently refresh their abilities to remain focused inside the field.

1.2.8. Quiet in Distressing Conditions

One thing that PC researcher gain is having the option to process a lot of specialized data rapidly. De-stress in most cases causes great damage. This amount to slot of losses some recoverable although at a huge cost some not like in the event of a plane crash due to malfunction of equipment. The PC can be a toy, not only an apparatus. Computer science graduates ought to pick a field where one has a characteristic enthusiasm, and the individuals who tinkering with their PC will most likely be open to working with it expertly. Knowing that the danger there is invade of bad decisions they are taught how to handle all kinds of situation very calmly.

1.2.9. Engage With a Gathering/Group Work

Every individual has a novel comprehension on a circumstance, issue or some other thing. These computer science graduates are constantly educated. In any event, when doing ventures while learning they are given in gatherings. This empowers them to realize nothing creates aptitudes more than staying nearby a gathering of companions who has similar interests. Engaging with a gathering of that bore truly builds up their aptitudes. It's vastly improved to learn with a gathering of companions, learning a similar specialized ability, then it is an educator addressing in a class. What's more, that is the reason no computer science graduate works alone thy consistently look for some organization over to create something more prominent (Guzdial, 2015).

1.2.10. Code Route Navigation

One of the most underestimated aptitudes for software engineering graduates is getting into any code and having the option to discover your way around a task. It isn't permitted to become mixed up in codebases in light of the fact that they haven't rehearsed this expertise enough. Software engineering graduates are urged to discover an undertaking on any stage download its code and attempting to change some essential conduct. It may appear to be a moderately little thing; however, having the option to break down and get what's new with existing code is a significant piece of learning. As such, a computer science graduate is not liable to chip away at an application alone and bosses couldn't imagine anything better than to remain quiet about some work or request help with a portion of the undertakings (Guzdial, 2015).

1.3. HOW DOES TECHNOLOGY AFFECT CHILDREN DEVELOPMENT

Kids in the 21st century are vigorous customers of development – more so than past periods. This phenomenon has incited a ton of thought on the aftereffects of development use, and how this influences children's cerebrums and their socio-enthusiastic, scholarly and physical progression. Regardless of their age, it is evident that everyone has access to technological gadgets either at home or from a friend or any other means, but is it right? In order to answer this question, there is a need to get to know what or how much is exposed to the child as is what will determine if it will have a negative effect on or positive effect on the child development. Education advancement is an ever present worry and the proportion of time we experience speaking with our own development contraptions is simply extending as we need to remain related. Thus, it is very difficult to keep our small kids from likewise wanting these communications (Khine, 2018).

As guardians, we have the right and duty to identify the RIGHT ways for little children to interface with innovation. Furthermore, guardians have to comprehend the manners in which innovation impacts their youngsters, and how to support the correct utilization of innovation. The objective is for tech to positively affect their conduct and advancement, rather than a negative one.

Development, when used viably, can truly have a valuable result on an adolescent's headway. Studies have found that our ability to perceive key information secured inside a gathering of characters and visual redesigns (sees) has extended as advancement has gotten dynamically organized in our lives. Likewise, ordinary interfaces with advancement can incite improved smoothness, playing out different errands, and reaction time. Regardless, when screen time isn't properly controlled, there can be negative effects of development on adolescent advancement.

Lack of measures of innovation time during a kid's formative years is probably going to affect development. Albeit some innovation presentation can be great, here are a couple of territories where a kid could experience challenges because of a lot of screen time (Khine, 2018).

1.3.1. Basic Thinking

Of course, many people gripe that the extension of advancement has incited a decrease in step by step examining. Moreover, it's been battled that in light of the fact that various squares of substance you experience on cutting edge devices are written in not a lot of characters or less, kids are not tried to think essentially, or to build up their thoughts. To adjust this, and bolster fundamental thinking, make sure to set aside time every day for examining where no equipment is accessible.

Figure 1.2. Fundamental thinking can be made through dialog expansion, which is where you help your children make sense of how to develop discourses by referencing past experiences or things they've examined.

Source: https://www.huffpost.com/entry/a-good-connection-girls-s_b_12338336.

1.3.2. Consideration and Imagination

The capacity to focus improvement is influenced by ecological elements. With the different types of innovation accessible, youngsters are regularly increasingly occupied and more averse to concentrate on something different when it is available. Likewise, when there is a lot of visual boosts and an absence of story perusing, this can affect a kid's advancement of creative mind. To neutralize this, it is an imperative that kids have the chance to investigate antiquated innovative play and to let their minds go crazy in storybooks.

1.3.3. Security and Safety

As advances in innovation lead to expanding levels of connectedness, we should consider the impacts that online networking and the web can have on the youngster's psychological standpoint, just as their security and wellbeing. It is critical to comprehend what exercises the youngsters are investigating on the web just as develop an open relationship where your kid feels good talking about any concerning conduct they run over on the web. Kids in these settings can regularly be presented to different degrees of tormenting, which can affect a kid's social and enthusiastic improvement just as their confidence (Khine, 2018). While web-based systems administration can be utilized as a way to deal with brace existing associations, it is basic to offer them the opportunity to practice conversational and social capacities without development. Youths that are constantly using advancement may be hesitant to speak with different children in a social circumstance, which can have negative long stretch effects.

1.3.4. Diminishes Self-Soothing and Self-Regulation

Any individual, who has been brought up as a little youngster, would perceive the greatness of break-in calming a child in a fit. However, gatekeepers today have a tempting interference continually open: development. Additionally, regardless of the way that in the brief giving over a cell phone or tablet may calm? During the time it is found that the interference of PDAs may oppositely impact children's opportunity to make sense of how to self-alleviate and coordinate in those minutes.

1.3.5. Increment in Animosity

When asked, most of the kids consider violent game actress or actors to be their role model. Hence the relationship between mimicked viciousness, regularly found in well-known computer games, and elevated hostility. Presentation to viciousness was found to make youngsters and adolescents bound to contend with companions or educators, and less compassionate and affected by genuine brutality. They try to act as they see in these video games and programs.

1.3.6. Stagnates Physical Activity

A normal youngster spends up to 6–7 hours on tech and a few times increasingly climate it's a TV show or playing computer games. Time contributed with advancement suggests vitality spent sitting. Without a doubt, even with reduced contraptions, the activity itself anticipates that customers should be generally still. Given the colossal proportion of time youths are purportedly proceeding with advancement now, this moreover infers dynamic indoor or outdoor break has now, as it were, been replaced by this stationary development. In incredible cases, children or youths may even manage without other basic activities, likely eating or resting, when attracted with a PC game or other media.

1.3.7. Damages School Performance

Restricted capacities to focus can likewise affect how youngsters act in the study hall. The experienced instructor says that understudies do not have the ability to focus to peruse assignments all alone, because of cell phones and online life. They can't turn into a decent essayist by viewing YouTube or constantly sending messages to their friends. Presently innovation requires a lot of mental switching between different tasks and contexts, which can prompt decreased capacities to focus. Youngsters' minds get are remunerated for hopping to the following undertaking as opposed to keeping focused, which may prompt age of children before screens whose cerebrums will be wired in an unexpected way. A few teenagers concede they incline toward the prompt delight gave by a fast video over toiling through a novel. Some examination recommends the nearness of a PC, regardless of whether planned for instructive purposes, may just fill in as an interruption.

Figure 1.3. When left to themselves, youngsters regularly utilized home PCs for stimulation as opposed to learning. Grown-up supervision is basic.

Source: https://realprogramming.com/.

1.3.8. Lessens Sleep Quality

Research has discovered that youngsters and teenagers who use media before bed were multiple times bound to not get enough rest around evening time. Much further, approaching a media gadget in their dozing condition, regardless of whether the gadget was not being effectively utilized close to sleep time, was additionally connected with a lacking measure of rest. Youngsters younger than 13 ordinarily require 11–14 hours of rest, contingent upon their age. Rest is gigantically significant for youngsters, as it advances development, helps heart wellbeing, influences weight, expands ability to focus, and even lifts learning. In any case, when youngsters don't get the best possible measure of rest every night, these ever-significant characteristics can endure.

While innovation can be incredible, we have to apply some restraint. The issues related with innovation accompany abuse and absence of consideration around how much innovation is "to an extreme." Be certain to control and confine your youngsters' innovation use, and they'll have the option to harvest its beneficial outcomes.

1.3.9. Points of Confinement Interpersonal Interactions

Using a wireless device to occupy children can decrease their social associations. Despite the inhenerent need to bond with other children, if youths are constantly obsessed with technology, they are never ready to be fully emotionally invested in a serious relationship with their peers or family. For progressively prepared adolescents and young people, advancement may fill in as a redirection from upsetting issues: not fitting in at school, gatekeepers battling at home, etc. As opposed to making sense of how to investigate these issues children and youths may find that development can give the dream of refuge – without equipping them with the social capacities expected to investigate clumsy conditions in grown-up life (Sharma, 2002).

1.3.10. Influences Emotional Development

Without a doubt, even in the hands of watchmen and parental figures, development may influence youth progression. Recognition is the fundamental way kids learn, as they check out learn language, watch dialogs, read outward appearances and watch how others investigate energetic conditions. Uncontrolled screen time releases away deliberately, related time with youths that are essential to energetic headway. For more seasoned kids and youngsters, an overwhelming dependence on innovation to impart upsets their relationship building abilities, and may even build up a feeling of separation from others' emotions. For little youngsters, the effect might be felt as screen time replaces time recently gave to play, peer connection and investigation, which are thought to encourage compassion, critical thinking aptitudes, interest, knowledge, and listening abilities. Versatile telephone use may keep kids from creating compassion, social and critical thinking abilities (Sharma, 2002).

1.3.11. Encourages Problem-Solving Skills

Have you at any point knew about the expression "endurance mode? For instance, in the well-known computer game Mine craft, players are dropped into new and various situations and should quickly manufacture safe house and gather things like nourishment, so as to endure and outlast their adversaries. Also, a whole day in Minecraft keeps going only 10 minutes, so players must use sound judgment rapidly.

With these kinds of advancements, kids must work freely to accomplish a particular objective. All the while, they're presented with various kinds of detours and difficulties, which they should figure out how to explore and survive. Thus, they'll be urged to think of their own critical thinking arrangements when confronting genuine issues, for example, schoolwork inconvenience, conflicts with companions, or individual hardship, just as innovation-based impediments.

1.3.12. Creates Future Technological Leaders

It's regular information that our future lies in a significant number of the present developing advances. In the years to come, specialized abilities will be progressively significant in the working environment, just as the developing effect it'll have on everyday life. Perhaps the best advantage of presenting children to innovation is the way that they'll be solid and steady to hop into a pool of accessible, lucrative tech occupations (Sharma, 2002).

With enormous tech organizations like Amazon reliably including several new openings around the nation, acquainting innovation abilities with youngsters at an early age can set them up for a vocation with an uplifting standpoint. Tech occupations are here today. Tech occupations will be here tomorrow. A portion of the present tech will be tomorrow's tech, and a portion of tomorrow's tech will be totally spic and span and something our reality has never observed. Who will be best prepared to fill those positions? The ones who start adapting now.

1.3.13. Helps Build Visual and Spatial Skills

In particular, PC games have been exhibited to help make periphery visual aptitudes. All the more comprehensively, general visual engine abilities (following articles or outwardly looking for something) may improve with innovation use.

1.3.14. Aides Multi-Tasking

At the point when applied properly (instead of driving and messaging, for instance) a well-honed ability to play out different assignments that is speed up with advancement use outfits adolescents with an imperative capacity for present day grown-up life.

1.3.15. Helps Learning

Web clients flex their basic leadership and critical thinking cerebrum works all the more every now and again, and are bound to deal with quick digital ventures well. What's more, innovation may exhibit the accompanying inundation of expert getting ready for understudies who may not prosper in standard educational subjects. Not exclusively is the innovation driven class motivating understudies to appear, it's giving word related learning, and shows a chance to trigger enthusiasm for different subjects. Innovation can likewise bolster instruction in progressively customary manners, withdrawing in games to support vocabularies or through electronic books (Sharma, 2002).

As with about everything throughout everyday life, innovation isn't an issue when utilized with some restraint. Be that as it may, the numbers propose most haven't yet found some kind of harmony, as revealed midpoints are well above Pediatricians prescribes for electronic media. Considering the proposal, no presentation before age 2, and a constrained 1–2 hours out of each day with diversion media, it's protected to state most kids are surpassing as far as possible. We need to look for after a development balance for our children, to benefit by the favorable circumstances and moderate the negative effects of development in youth progression.

1.4. WHAT CAN BE DONE TO INCORPORATE COMPUTER SCIENCE IN EDUCATION?

1.4.1. Implementing Computer Science Classes

With no doubt, it has been proven that it is beneficial for students to learn computer science as it equips them with knowledge and skills. Among the skills being critical thinking, which will help them in other areas of their studies. This is seconded by the fact that computer science on its own is evolving and with the evolvement comes more are and more job employment opportunities ensuring that no one will lack a job opportunity.

This has brought about the need to implement computer science in the education system. This involves implementing computer science into the various education curriculum so that it is taken seriously as a subject. This has led to computer science being taught to the learning of computer science as a subject like any other in schools.

By implementing computer science into the education curriculum, there are various resources that have been purchased to allow the learning of this course. The fact that it is computer-oriented, the schools have had to purchase the computers that would be used by the students in the learning process. This will enable them to get the practical skills that are to be acquired during the learning process. By implementing computer science classes, there are various aspects that come into play. For instance, how the subject will be taught to the students and the possibility of it being tested like other skills (Sharma, 2002).

For some schools, computer science is compulsory for all students meaning that all students will have had to attend classes on computer science but learning on this basis, the students will only get the basic aspect of computer science in other words, they will only get to learn the theory aspect and the practical aspect will be neglected as it has to be taught to all the students. Teachers will have to brush up on their knowledge in order to teach all the students. The other approach is when the computer science course is treated like other subjects in high school.

Here, computer science is taught as a subject and the students who have an interest in it are able to choose it as one of their subjects that will be taught and graded. This is the best approach as the students will be able to attend the classes and they will get in depth knowledge as they will learn both the practical and theory aspect if computer science. By doing so, they are able to get both the knowledge and skills in the line of computer science. By incorporating computer science into classes, it has required that it being a subject, to be packaged as a subject. This means that it has a course outline whereby it is broken down into units, for instance, the students start by first learning the basics then they progress into deeper content as they gradually progress (Guzdial, 2015).

By the end of the learning process, students should have been able to acquire all the principles of computer science. For some, this has influence them to get a major in computer science. For computer science to be taught, the students have been encouraged to take up learning computer science. The schools have had to increase the enrolment opportunities for the students, this encourages many to take up this course and it has been noted that several girls are taking up computer science with their enrolment rates being high in various schools. This improves access to computer education by all students.

Various stakeholders such as the ministry of education are encouraging several schools to take up computer science classes in their schools. Some of them even encourage them by offering to purchase the necessary equipment such as the computers that will be required by the institution leaving them with no choice but to take up computer science into their learning systems. Some countries like India have incorporated computer science into their education curriculum making it mandatory for the schools to offer computer science to the students. The government of India set aside funds in its budget to cater for the learning of computer science in its schools (Guzdial, 2015).

Figure 1.4. To implement a computer program, some schools have used computer science as an additional unit of integrating computing concepts into other content areas.

Source: https://eduscape.com/eduscape-launches-photon-in-u-s-to-drive-computer-science-in-k-12-classrooms/.

Computer science involves the use of mathematical elements like in programming languages and also carrying out various calculations. The mathematical concepts in computer science are at times borrowed from mathematical subjects. Thus, teaching computer science increases the likelihood of the students understanding mathematics and also solving mathematical problems. This has been very beneficial for students who have been encountering problems with math.

Computer science gives them skills such as logical thinking and problem-solving skills. By making the learning of computer science be competitive by giving room for students to come up with projects and various innovations, it challenges them and it also encourages other students to enroll for the computer science classes. As the world is becoming more and more digital oriented, there are plans by various government to introduce computer science classes in primary schools so that children start gaining knowledge on computer science from a tender age. This will greatly impact how computer science is viewed among people as it will be held with high esteem.

Offering computer science classes will be of great importance and will be of great benefit to the society. Being exposed to computer science from tender age helps the individual to easily transits from the various levels of education such that when it comes to getting a major. It will also enable them get the various skills that are required and they will be able to come up with various projects that will assist the society. By incorporating computer science into the education curriculum, it will ensure that all the children will be able to learn computer science (Guzdial, 2015).

1.4.2. Making Computer Science Courses Accessible for All

For computer science to be more widespread among people, people from all walks of life must be able to access it. For instance, in schools, there is no point of introducing computer science into the education program only for it to be taken up by very few students. This is why schools have to expand the student enrolment possibilities so that any student who is interested in computer science can take it up as a subject. The fact that computer science is incorporated into the school curriculum makes it more accessible to the student as they don't have to wait till they finish high school in order to learn computer science. Computer science can be made accessible by first creating an environment that is supportive and engaging for all (Beauchamp, 2016).

This is achieved by first ensuring that there are continuous supplies of computers. Computers are essential; for the learning of computer science to take place. By ensuring that there are several computers available for the learning of computer science, it will increase the accessibility of people in learning computer science as it creates an environment that welcomes people to learn computer science as it has been made available for them. This also attracts people with diverse interests to pursue computer science.

Computer science can be made more accessible by making it easier for students who do not have majors to take up classes in the field of computer science more so in the principals they want to major in. for quite some time, it has been difficult for students who had studied other aspects of computer that were not in close ties with computer science to actually study computer science. For some, they were required to complete the course that they were taking until completion for them to later on take up computer science classes then major in the principles that they were interested in.

This really discouraged several students from taking up computer science. However, in order to make computer science available for all students, education boards came up with strategies to solve this problem. This was solved by allowing students who had majors in subjects such as data science to be able to attend computer science classes without any prerequisites. This has enabled many students to enroll for computer science classes as the barriers they were experiencing were lifted making computer science more accessible for them (Beauchamp, 2016).

For some students, they prefer to take up two majors at once. This is whereby they study two unrelated subjects at the same time. For many years, it was deemed impossible for people to carry out this practice. This led to education boards restraining individuals from pursuing two majors at once. The fact that it was also unheard of, people would have rather completed the major they were taking up then take up another major altogether. It is only until recently where students have been able to take up two majors at one, for instance, engineering and biology.

If education boards were to allow and make it easier for students to take on combined majors, such as biology and computer science it would attract several students. They make it easier by reducing the formalities required. They can also allow students to take on double majors where they can take on computer science and a related or unrelated major. This will be advantageous as it will enable students to get to explore areas that they are interested in and at the same time apply some of the principles of computer science. This will enable them get more knowledge and in the long term make computer science accessible by more people.

Computer science is made more accessible by increasing the number and supply of faculty that teach computing at the intersections of disciplines. In the recent developments in the various fields of work, computer science is being incorporated into the fields in by involving some of the principles into the workplaces. For instance, engineering, in the current trends is involving principles of computer science such as programming into the workforce. This has forced some individuals to head back to learning institutions to get knowledge on computer science (Beauchamp, 2016).

With this in mind, there have been some changes to the faculties so that students learning on biology as a major, get trained on computer science. This means that some computer science classes are incorporated in their timetables. In the end, they get to have training on computer science this has even encouraged tome to get majors in the areas of computer science that they were interested in. some universities are training their PhD students on computer science education so that in turn they are able to offer teaching services in the area of computer science to other students.

This has led to an increase in supply of faculty teaching computer science thereby making computer science more accessible at there are more resource personnel to teach it. Computer science can be made more accessible to students by creating forums that involve computer science such as conference and Tech expos that will enable them get more knowledge and insight on computer science. They will be able to meet people in the field of computer science interact with them and it will be a major encouragement for them to continue studying.

Computer science is made more accessible by removing any demystifying thoughts on computer science. For instance, the thought that computer science is hard or girls cannot take up computer science because it's a man's course should be removed. By giving girls the opportunity to pursue majors in computer science removes one among the various demystifying thoughts. If they get such opportunities, it will be noted that the enrolment of girls will rapidly increase because a barrier they once encountered has been removed. This makes computer science accessible for them. These among others, are some of the ways that computer science can be made more accessible (Beauchamp, 2016).

1.4.3. Improving Teacher Preparation and Professional Development

Improving the teacher preparation can greatly contribute to the incorporation of computer science in education. Improving the teacher preparation can take place in several ways which may be categorized under teacher-preparation programs. The programs have been incorporated so as to bring out more faculty that are well trained to ensure that computer science is well taught to the students. The programs work with an aim of improving quality of education which is achieved by increasing time to practice in virtual and real classrooms. Computer science is a practical subject and for it to be taught effectively, the resource person who in this case is the teacher should have hands on skills (Sharma, 2002).

Previously, individuals would pursue their majors within a short period of time after transitioning from the previous level of education. This gives them a short period of time to gain practical skills which will lead to them having late preparation. The teacher training program should there to provide more opportunities for the students to practice classroom skills earlier. This can be effectively done when students who show and declare their interest in teaching are given preliminary experiences in virtual or real classroom environments.

Some programs provide the teachers with opportunities to work on and improve their professional skills such as classroom management among others. The skills they acquire enable them to determine students who would want to pursue computer science majors as teachers and prepare them to be better and qualified computer science teachers. Improving the teacher preparation can also be done by incorporating new and effective technologies to the classrooms. In the current world, technology is everything.

In the education system mostly in the university level, technology is being used to give instructions to students, monitor them and also asses them. Learning institutions have been given support to integrate and use technology in their classrooms by using equipment such as smart boards in order to manage their classrooms more effectively and also improve the students learning experience. This has created the need of teachers to be well informed of the technology used in the classrooms. The teacher training programs have been improved so that teachers get various opportunities to learn, evaluate and apply the technology in use (Sharma, 2002).

This comes in handy for the computer science teachers as the subject revolves more on computers and technology. By so doing, the teacher will be well prepared to teach computer science to the students. Improving teacher preparation can be done by improving the teacher's education. This entails giving the latest knowledge and skills. They can be acquired by creating workshops and also training programs for the teachers. This should be done more often and more frequently as there is new knowledge every day and for the teachers to remain up to date with the latest knowledge, they require to be frequently updated on the changes. This more so affects computer science as it is more practical and new innovations are made daily.

Apart from improving the teacher preparation, computer science can be incorporated in education by improving professional development. This can be achieved by creating professional development opportunities. This is whereby the teachers are given opportunities to go-to institution of higher learning to pursue computer science as a profession. This has been made possible by some government offering to sponsor the education for such teachers. Some students are awarded loan opportunities to finance their studies, which is a noble goal in their professional development (Sharma, 2002).

It has also been achieved by creating professional development opportunities that encourage teacher collaboration. This is done by creating collaborations with colleagues who are more experienced to a professional level. In the collaboration there is promotion of the culture of trust and knowledge sharing. Through the process, the in-experienced teachers are able to gain more knowledge and sharpen their skills with regards to computer science. This has proven to increase the teacher's effectiveness and the ability to easily adapt to new technologies and innovations.

For the collaborations to work, there must be a common goal that was established during the process of creating the collaboration. It should be oriented towards increasing productivity and creating teamwork among the members. There are actions that are taken to promote teacher collaboration that include promoting peer to peer classroom visits. This enables the teachers to get feedback on how the learning process was, whether effective or not. It also gives room for the professional to give insight on what improvements should be made so that the learning process is effective.

It can also be achieved by creating teacher learning communities. All this work in order to improve the teacher's professional development. Improved professional development can be achieved by providing teachers with ongoing support. Support can be form different areas which include from the administration, instructional support, peer support, supervisory support among others. Recent studies have shown that teachers who receive such kind of support are most likely to easily adapt to the various teaching environments (Hazzan, Lapidot, & Ragonis, 2011).

This happens because they get guidance and feedback from a more professional person and they are able to apply the new skills and strategies that they have acquired. This has led to institutions developing systems for instructional coaching, strengthening school administrations and using the most appropriate technologies. Improved professional development has led to investing in high quality teacher educators. Educators are the personnel that give individuals training so that they can become teachers themselves.

For many years, training colleges and universities were not able to find quality teachers leading to poor quality education among the students. This has been identified as an issue and to solve it, professional individual has been employed to offer teaching and training services to the computer science students. This means that they will be able to equip the future teachers with the necessary knowledge and skills that would be required in the classroom (Hazzan, Lapidot, & Ragonis, 2011).

1.4.4. Allowing Computer Science to Count Toward Graduation

Previously, universities made key emphasis on subjects such as math to count towards graduation. Which the recent advancements that have been made to the workplace that have made it more dependent on technology, there has been a growing demand for graduates who have studied things to do with technology which include computer science. Also, the fact that in future, several job opportunities will revolve around computer science. In order to prepare students for the work environment, most universities are emphasizing on the need to pursue computer science courses with most of them making it a requirement for graduation.

That is not to say that computer science was not offered. Students were allowed to take on computer science courses as electives. This meant it did not count as a core requirement for graduation for courses such as math and science through computer science as a course entails math and science principals. For some institutions, computer science did not fit to satisfy as a requirement for graduation. This is not entirely true as computer science principles are just as any other course and should be given an opportunity (Guzdial, 2015).

This means that if the student has qualified in the area he or she is interested in, but has not done any computer science course, he or she will not be allowed to graduate. This applies to not only in universities but also to high schools. Associations, such as the computer science teacher association in the United States, have been advocating for the creation and implementation of policies that would facilitate computer science being a requirement for students to graduate in math and science courses. This has yielded positive results as many learning institutions have been able to come up and implement such policies in their education policies.

At the university level, it has led to the faculties adjusting their degrees so that the degrees offered are made up of combined principals. For instance, medicine and computer science. This brings about the essence of computer science contributing towards the graduation of the individual. They will be able to learn computer science and it will be incorporated into their schedules. They will have to undergo all the practical and theory lessons. Later on, computer science will be tested and graded like any other unit the student undertakes. This contributes towards making computer science count towards graduation in the university level (Guzdial, 2015).

Figure 1.5. In high schools, computer science is taught as a subject on its own.

Source: *https://news.psu.edu/story/414328/2016/06/10/summer-program-introduce-high-school-students-stem-disciplines.*

Computer science has teachers allocated to teach it and also time is created in the timetables such that computer science is scheduled to be taught at various hours. The students are given both practical and theoretical knowledge and before completing the course, they have to come up with various project that will contribute to the final grade. Just like other courses, it will be tested and graded and its grade will be used to evaluate the graduation of the student. If the student passes, she graduates with a good transcript and if he or she fails, they get a bad grade in their transcript as they graduate.

As computer science is being taken up as a possible requirement for graduation, several universities and high schools have taken up initiatives to make computer science available for their students. Some universities such as Purdue University offered to give introductory computer science and programming classes for free to a high school it collaborated with. This would enable the student to get to experience the programming classes. This has led to high interest rates of students in computer science.

Making computer science to be a graduation requirement has faced some challenges of which some have been solved while others are in the process of being solved. Computer science wasn't considered to be a graduation requirement in several schools due to lack of access to computer science. Though there may be computer science teachers in the schools, they may lack the necessary resources to teach computer science. Resources may include textbooks, reference books or computers which are most essential while learning the practical aspect (Guzdial, 2015).

This creates a barrier for the learning of computer science. To solve this problem, various stakeholders have come into play. Some of them offer to buy and equip the learning institutions with computers to be used during the learning process. Some have made donations of textbooks and reference books to be used during the process of learning. This provides a conducive environment for the students to be able to learn and for the teachers to be able to teach computer science. They will be able to carry out research and get good grades causing computer science to be a requirement for graduation.

Some schools were discouraged from offering computer science classes due to financial and logistic reasons. With support from the government and other partners, this barrier has been removed enabling computer science to be offered in the schools and can contribute towards graduation. Though several employers have emphasized on the need of computer science as the workplace in future will tend to create job opportunities in that sector, several states have not yet created policies that will allow computer science to count towards graduation and the schools that allow it had the decision made by the local school boards. This has derailed the progress of making computer science count towards graduation.

However, various associations have come up with petitions that will champion for computer science being able to count towards graduation. The petitions have been effective in some countries but not in some though there is a lot of work being put so that the policies will be created and implemented. It is only a matter of time until all the countries accept these policies are put in place. The growing use of computer science in the workplace is pushing for the implementation of the policies but until now it is up to the institutions to decide. By making computer science count for graduation, it will facilitate the incorporation of computer science in education (Guzdial, 2015).

1.5. SKILLS FOR SUCCESSFUL COMPUTER SCIENCE LEARNER

1.5.1. Analytical Skills

These are skills that one can apply to a problem and find the most suitable solution for it. As a result, analytical skills are problem-solving skills. Analytical skills are very vital especially in interviewing an individual. This is because managers want people who are equipped with analytical skills such that they can identify a problem look critically into it, come with a suitable solution and communicate it effectively.

Analytical skills exist in various forms but there are 5 major types, which include:

- Communication
- Creativity
- Critical thinking
- Data analysis
- Research

These types are discussed more below to flesh out the concepts.

Communication: It is the ability to pass information effectively without any miscommunication, misinterpretations or misconceptions. When an individual analysis a problem he needs to deliver it appropriately to the others in the organization. It can either be in written or oral. If one lacks the skill of communication it may make information to be distorted in the organization such that the problem may fail to be solved in the appropriate way hence lack of communication skill is a major vice.

Communication skills are shown through how one reports a piece of information, written work of the individual, his oral communication, his presentation, problem sensitivity and active listening.

Creativity: It takes two paths; noticing a problem that others may not notice and solving or finding a suitable solution to these problems. Creativity in an organization applies majorly in budgeting where one should be very careful to notice if a calculation problem arises and be able to solve it. It may also apply in brainstorming, collaboration, optimization, predictive modeling, problem-solving, restructuring, strategic planning and integration. An individual with this skill hence notices problems before they bring destruction to the companies' profits and hence these problems are solved early enough.

Critical thinking: One should have the ability to evaluate information and decide based on their findings so that they can be termed as having the skill of critical thinking. It involves thinking deeply to find as much information as one can get that is related to what one initially had then put them together for evaluation. Critical thinking is what helps one make decisions that help solve a problem in the company. It is shown by diagnosis, dissecting, evaluating, record keeping, data interpretation, judgment, prioritization, judgment, troubleshooting and attention to details. It's a skill acquired by very few individuals since people often look at the upper meaning instead of digging into it.

Data analysis: This is the ability to analyses and understand a certain amount of information or data. It includes; business analysis, SWOT analysis, cost analysis, credit analysis, critical analysis, descriptive analysis, financial analysis and policy analysis.

Research: This is digging into information to get more information or hints to collect more data. It includes; insertion, merits, data collection, data entry, taking inventory and checking for accuracy.

Figure 1.6. Computer skills enable one to have analytical skills since programming involves identifying problems and coming up with solutions to address these problems.

Source: *https://www.thebalancecareers.com/technical-skills-list-2063775.*

1.5.2. Problem-Solving Skills

Problem-solving is the ability of an individual to find a solution to a problem at hand. When a problem arises in an organization, an individual with problem-solving skills looks into the problem to find the cause then comes up with ways to solve the problem.

There are five major steps for problem-solving. They include:

- Analyze the cause of the risen problem
- Generate a set of alternative interventions to achieve your goal
- Evaluate the best solutions
- Implement a plan
- Assess effectiveness

These steps are discussed below for better understanding.

Analyze the cause of the risen problem: This step involves an individual looking deeper to find the cause of the problem. For one to solve a problem there is a need for them to understand what caused the problem from the first place. The problem can be found by gathering and evaluating data, putting aside possible contributing circumstances, and pointing out what needs to be addressed. The skills required for problem-analysis include, active listening, data gathering, data analysis, fact-finding, historical analysis, cause analysis, process analysis and needs identification.

Generating interventions to achieve an end goal: This is the coming up of possible solutions to certain problems. It may be found by one person or by brainstorming of many people. More than one person should be involved in finding possible solutions so that in case the master plan fails other options may be used. The required skills to generate interventions include, brainstorming which is discussing with several people such that each person gives their views to solve the problem, creative thinking, prediction where one foresees the possible outcome, forecasting, project design and project planning. When possible, solutions are invented then they are evaluated.

Evaluating the best solutions: This step may involve the major decision-makers in the company. From the possible solutions that were found, the major decision makers select the best solution that will not only be the most effective but will be cost-effective and will not promote losses. The step can also be done by selected trusted teams or team leads. The required skills include, analysis, discussion, corroboration, teamwork, test development, mediation and prioritizing.

Implementing a plan: This involves applying the solution found so that the problem can be solved.

The skills required include, project management, project implementation, collaboration, time management and benchmark development. This step, therefore, involves solving the problem at hand.

Assessing the effectiveness of the intervention: This step involves checking to see if the problem has been solved and how quickly it is working. If the problem has not been solved, then alternative methods are used for solving the problem. The skills involved include, communication, data analysis, surveys, customer feedback, follow through and troubleshooting. One can improve their problem-solving skills by; acquiring more technical knowledge on the field, setting out an opportunity to solve the problem, do practice problems and observing how others solve their problems. Computer science involves solving very complex and complicated problems systematically and logically. It is mainly applicable to finding solutions during projects that computer science students undertake.

1.5.3. Creativity

This is the ability to discover novel concepts, methods, and ideas in computer science. It is the investion of a new thing. Most employees want employers who can develop a new idea. Creativity involves thinking deeply to come up with something new and different. It involves coming up with new ways to carry out tasks, solve problems and meet challenges. Critical thinking skills include, analysis, open-mindedness, problem-solving, organization and communication (Beauchamp, 2016).

In the analysis, it is where you think about what you want to come up with and examine the information.

In open-mindedness, one should be open to new ideas. They should not be limited to what they know but should be ready to receive new information. they should eliminate bias and assumptions that they may have and look at the thing in a completely different way.

In problem-solving, employers need people who are creative enough to notice a problem and deal with it. This will not only help them to hire a qualified individual but also someone who they can rely on to help them solve their problems (Beauchamp, 2016).

In an organization, one needs to be creatively organized such that they can arrange their ideas logically in a way that flows perfectly. This will help other people to flow through your vision hence they can help you with your findings and correcting you on some areas that you may be wrong.

In communication, one should be fluent and should be able to pass information accurately. It should be both orally and written. one should be able to present his or her work in a flowing manner such that every individual that receives the information get the actual meaning that was intended to be passed.Examples of creative thinking include, Artistic creativity, problem-solving creativity and creativity in STEM.

Artistic creativity is impulsive one and tends to respond to or act on certain current incentives. It may involve designing the company's logo, proposing a new look for a cloth line, devising an engaging lesson plan, designing the packaging of a product or writing an advertising copy. Therefore, artistic creativity involves being creative in the art section. Problem-solving Creativity is coming up with creative ways to solve a new problem. when one has problem-solving creativity, they can come up with new ways to solve problems such that these ideas had not been invented before. it may involve brainstorming and coming up with new ideas (Khine, 2018).

STEM simply stands for science technology engineering and maths. Creativity in the side of STEM involves inventing, designing or coming up with projects that lie in the sector of math's science technology or engineering. This field requires a very creative mind so that the projects created can be working. It needs one to think outside the box on how they will eliminate factors that may lead the project to fail.

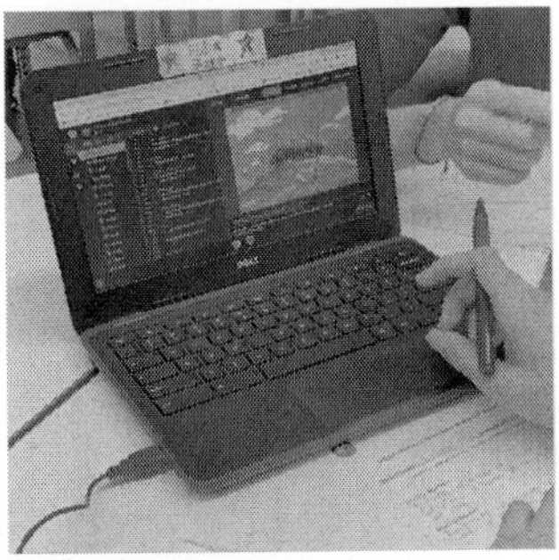

Figure 1.7. In computer science, students work on various projects that need a lot of creativity to solve them so that they may eliminate problems, use their knowledge in STEM and be open-minded.

Source: https://Twitter.com/lolawajs/status/1134177353721102336.

1.5.4. Critical Thinking Skills

It is the ability that one has to analyses some information that he has and being able to make his judgment from it. It includes looking into the facts, data, observable phenomena and drawing your conclusions from them.

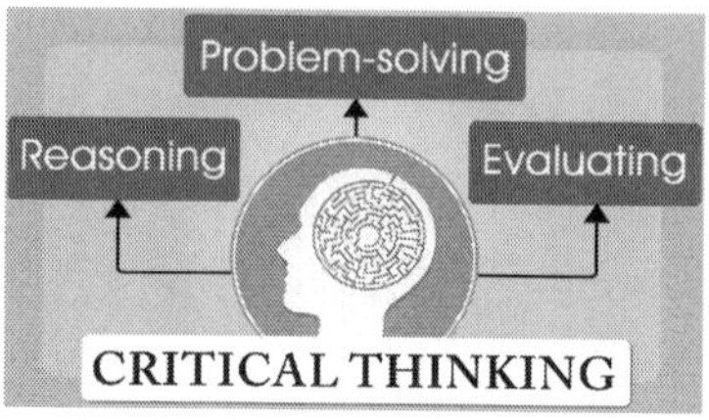

Figure 1.8. A person with critical thinking skills can be easily trusted to make the companies decide on their own and these decisions are relevant and effective.

Source: https://missionself.com/developing-critical-thinking-skills.

Critical thinking skills involve five major steps which include, analysis, communication, open-mindedness, problem-solving and creativity. These are the top critical thinking skills which are discussed more below.

Analysis: It is the capability to examine a set of data, information or a text. A person with analytical skills can look deeply into a piece of information, know what it means by interpreting it then bring it out by explaining to others. The analysis involves asking yourself questions that enable you to dig deep into the information. it requires one to ask themselves several questions related to the topic. It also involves analyzing the data that one has, researching and interpreting. One needs to do more research to find more data then interpret their findings to know if it relates to what they are analyzing.

Communication: As discussed earlier, communication is the ability to share one's information with other people in a way that they will bring a clear understanding to them. Communication assists people to work as a team to come up with solutions. It involves active listening where one listens attentively so that they may not miss any piece of information, assessing the information to check its accuracy and importance, Explaining the information, presentation, teamwork, interpersonal, verbal communication and non-verbal communication. Communication skills not only enable the passing of information but it also promotes teamwork and togetherness in an organization.

Creativity: Creativity involves coming up with new ideas and it, therefore, involves critical thinking where one needs to think deeply so that they can come up with the new idea. It involves flexibility, conceptualization, curiosity, imagination, drawing connections, predicting, synthesizing and vision.

Open-mindness: This is putting aside what we know or think to be open to new ideas without bias. For an individual to be open-minded, he needs to think critically about the new idea to check and confirm if it is relevant or not. It is having a third eye to new opinions and options to make conclusions.

Problem-solving: In problem-solving, one has to think critically to find out the real cause of the problem. It involves paying attention to every detail, clarifying, making a suitable decision, evaluating and identifying patterns. In problem-solving in case, a problem arises, the most suitable way of solving the problem should be applied to ensure that it is solved faster, therefore, an individual should think very critically if the mothed he wants to use if the most suitable to use.

Computer science requires critical thinking skills because in the coming up with projects the individual needs to think deeply so that they can come up with the right approach.

1.5.5. Resilience

It is the process of being able to readjust to changes. If a problem or stress comes up, an individual with resilience skills can adapt well and bounce back very quickly. Most organizations face problems frequently from time to time and only a person with resilience skills can adapt to changes that these problems may bring. An example is in case of the death of a workmate, the employees should be able to overcome this challenge and start working without the presence of the employee. It also applies if an individual loses his loved one or the company faces losses (Sharma, 2002).

A resilient person can easily adapt to a new environment. For instance, if one is required to work somewhere else or is given a transfer, the person should adjust very fast and fit into the new environment to prevent wasting time while adjusting.

The person can cope with difficulty and challenges. This individual must be always ready for anything that comes along the way. He should not depend on things to work in his favor all the time but must have the understanding that things can change at any one time.

A person with resilience must have the skill that enables them to handle stress effectively and positively. Most people often experience a break down since they do not know how to handle stress. Others experience depression but when one can handle stress effectively, they know how to put everything behind them and move forward positively (Sharma, 2002). They should be persistent that is they should always advocate in making things change for the betterment of the organization. In case of a problem, a persistent individual always tries to make issues work out and bring back the organization to stability.They should also understand that not everything they have control of. The individual knows that some things are beyond their understanding for example death and they cannot change them. If they get this understanding then they will be able to cope with any changes on their way (Sharma, 2002).How a person adjusts to a situation is very different from another person because different people react differently to different situations. It should be a person's own initiative to achieve resilience.

resilience
Empowering you
to create change

Figure 1.9. The main factors that contribute to resilience include a good support system, always maintaining a positive relationship, having a good self-image and having a very positive attitude towards situations.

Source:https://www.coventrycitizensadvice.org.uk/project/resilience/.

One can develop resilience by having a plan that includes: recognizing one's signs of stress, building physical hardiness, calming one's body and mind, identifying one's strength, increasing on one's positive emotions daily by being happy more, engaging in meaningful activities, removing unhelpful thinking and creating a caring environment.Computer science instills resilience because some units, such as programming are quite challenging and require one to be ready to fail severally before they pass.

Therefore, studying computer science helps instilling essential resilience skills that employers require.

Chapter 2

The Most Important Subjects in Computer Science

CONTENTS

2.1. Introduction 32

2.2. C Programming Language 32

2.3. C++ Programming Language 33

2.4. Java Programming Language 34

2.5. Microprocessor 34

2.6. Networking 36

2.7. Compiler Design 38

2.8. Operating System 39

2.9. Computer System Architecture 41

2.10. Data Structures 43

2.11. Algorithms 45

2.1. INTRODUCTION

There are numerous concepts and subjects in computer science. This chapter was prepared to offer basic information on these subjects as discussed below.

2.2. C PROGRAMMING LANGUAGE

To comprehend why C is a fundamental language in software engineering, we need to clarify what it is. Specifically, you can utilize C to make in any event of guidelines for a PC to pursue. It has been here for quite a few years and has won across the board acknowledgment. This is on the grounds that it gives the software engineer most extreme control and effectiveness.

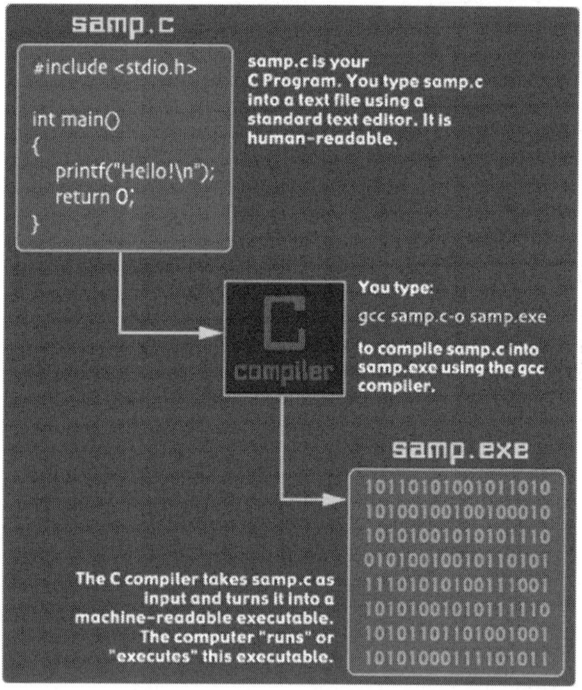

Figure 2.1. C computer programs represent a simple language to learn.

Source: https://computer.howstuffworks.com/c1.htm.

There are numerous dialects yet none is on par with programming language. The C language works at the hardware level in the majority of the cases. You can impart your very own PC equipment with the C language. The best explanation of the C language is that it incorporates low-level access to memory, a straightforward arrangement of built-in capacity and tasks. Because of these qualities, the C language is appropriate for framework programming like working framework and compiler an advancement. The C programming language is the most widely utilized language. Computer programs wrote in C are otherwise called gathered language. Once you have composed your C program, you should run it through a C compiler to make it executable. It is unnecessarily utilized in installed frameworks, even microcontrollers. Therefore, if you are new to programming and wish to learn it, C is the best language to learn. The C programming language has included from three diverse structure languages. ALGOL, BCPL and B language. It utilizes numerous ideas from these dialects and presented numerous new ideas, for example, information types, struck and pointer.

Today, learning the C programming language accompany offers several advantages: –

It uses many present day programming dialects: You can build up your very own Linux form by altering it. Likewise, you will have the option to actualize distinctive working framework activities. Overall, you will have the option to assemble compiler of various dialects which can take contribution from different dialects and convert it into low-level machine language.

Learning this language is fundamental as it is a base for other languages: Learning C programming language is simple and requires less exertion. Learning this language makes it simpler for one to learn other programming languages. This is on the grounds that at the programming language like Java, Python, JavaScript PHP are comparable in a way. It is incredible language as it requires less PC memory space. This functions as a preferred position since it doesn't slow the PC (Beauchamp, 2016).

2.3. C++ PROGRAMMING LANGUAGE

This is another essential subject that everyone who does software engineering as an understudies must do. C++ is a broadly useful programming language. With it, you can make anything with programming. It very well may be utilized to make little, utility projects or huge scale disseminated frameworks. It assembles to machine-language, the quickest way that product can be executed by a computer. C++ differs from numerous other mainstream dialects in a few different ways:

Incorporates to machine language: C++ programs get "changed over" to machine language, the local language of a PC when they're arranged (transformed into something the PC can really run). When running a C++ program, the PC doesn't need to transform the program code into something other than what is expected, it just runs it. Numerous other programming dialects command to a transitional language, which the PC needs to re-compose into something it can really do. It is Object-Oriented. C++ enables projects to be written in an item arranged way, yet doesn't uphold it. Progressively, present day dialects—C Java—authorize Object direction (they can't uphold great Object Oriented) by the manner in which they're planned. C++ considers it; however, you can even now compose programs in C++ that are not question arranged.

Execution is quicker: This is C++'s essential quality. Since C++ programs accumulate to straight machine language, a C++ program's execution speed is unrivaled.

2.4. JAVA PROGRAMMING LANGUAGE

Java is viewed as the best designer language. It is increasingly a comprehensive, versatile and convenient language. Its code runs the equivalent in each working framework as long as the device has Java runtime environment.

This shifts on each gadget relying upon the specific sort of gadget, yet basically it runs a virtual machine, or condition, that makes an interpretation of the code into an application or program. It is likewise an object-oriented programming language. It is the one being used by most programmers in these advanced days.

2.5. MICROPROCESSOR

A microprocessor is a very crucial subject in computer science as it contributes to the very existence of computers. In terms of the generation of computers, it was used to provide processing power for the fourth-generation computers. It is a very crucial subject as it is used to explain the architecture of computers. The microprocessor in a computer carries out the incorporation of functions of a central processing unit onto the integrated circuits.

Figure 2.2. A microprocessor.

Source:https://blog.adafruit.com/2018/12/05/the-gigatron-a-ttl-microcomputer-without-a-microprocessor-vintagecomputing-8bit/.

This allows the computer to work efficiently as it processes data at a faster rate. The microprocessor is efficient as it is multipurpose, register-based, clock-driven and it allows data to be entered into the computer in binary form. Microprocessors have been integrated into the computer science syllabus as it is beneficial to the students in understanding computer architecture. It is also advantageous in that it enables the understand various concepts of low-level machine assembly language as well as controlling the hardware devices making it very essential. The fact that it uses low level machine language, means that it is programmable making it suitable to carry out arithmetic and logical operation to produce information as required by the user (Guzdial, 2015).

This is essential for computer science students as programming is one of the principles of computer science. It will enable them learn how to program and they can be able to transition from the low-level language to high level language that is being recently used such as Java and JavaScript. They get to interact with knowledge of clock speeds of different microprocessors in which the fastest is the 64-bit microprocessor. In order to understand the architecture of a different computers, they interact with different types of microprocessors.

For instance, the explicitly parallel instruction computing which facilitates the parallel usage of compliers. It is known to carry out complex instruction using low clock frequencies as it encodes its instructions into the 128-bit bundle. The learning about microprocessors consists of the following outline:

- Introduction to microprocessors which entails the learning about CPU, the various buses, input/output devices and internal data operations
- Introduction to microprocessors is followed by microprocessor instructions which entails the classification, formatting and trimming, the various instruction set which includes 8 and 16-bit instruction, debugging and programming.
- After that is microprocessor interfacing which involves the various types of chips and their extensive applications and the memory, keyboard and display interface
- Next is the microprocessor architecture and instruction set that entails the architecture of the processor as well as the instruction set. Instruction set involves instruction format and discussion on instruction set among others
- Later on, they learn the computer architecture and the types of memories. The learning of microprocessors has been o great challenge to most of the students more so those who lack knowledge on programming. This is why it is advisable for students who want to pursue computer science to have basic knowledge on computers,

2.6. NETWORKING

Computer network is the link between computers that facilitates the sharing of data between the linked computers. The link can be between two or more computers according to the preference of the user.

Figure 2.3. Computer network.

Source: https://www.completemyassignment.com/subjects/computer-network-assignment-help/.

Networking is an important aspect of computer science as it helped with the revolutionization of the internet which has been used to connect various computer systems. Networking has its own advantages. For example, it facilitates technical support where a person from a distant country can offer technical support to a person in the other side of the earth.

It also facilitates efficient sharing of data in different formats from one person to another despite the geographical distance. It has facilitated the sharing of hardware resources, such as storage space and processor. It has enabled easy sharing of software where software is easily transferred from one computer to another. It has facilitated easy communication to develop different ways of sharing information which includes text and video chatting (Guzdial, 2015).

It has also been used to decentralize data processing which makes it easier to secure, control and manage the data to be transferred. While learning computer science, the student will learn about different types of network which include the local area network, the metropolitan area network, and the wide-area network. The local area network is used to link computers within a premise with the largest distance being 200m. This type of network is usually very fast as it is able to transmit data with a high bandwidth hence the high-speed connectivity.

This network involves the interconnection of devices. The metropolitan area network covers a larger area compared to the local area network. It is known to cover a city which may be referred to a metropolitan area. This type of network transmit data at a lower bandwidth compared to the local area network making its processing speed to be lower than that of the local area network. The wide area network is used globally as it covers large geographical areas across the world.

Due to the fact that it is used globally, it transmits data at a lower bandwidth hence the speed of connectivity may be slow. It therefore has the lowest speed connectivity compared to other networks. This type of network is usually provided publicly by the government agencies to the citizens. Other types of networks include the personal area network, wireless local area network, campus area network, storage area network, system area network, passive optical area network, enterprise private network and the virtual private network (Guzdial, 2015).

Computer science students are required to learn about various networks. As networking is a principle of computer science, if the student has key interest in networking, the student can be able to major in networking.

2.7. COMPILER DESIGN

A compiler is a type of software that is used to convert programs that are created in high-level language to low-level language or vice versa. In most cases, they are used to convert computer language to the assembly language.

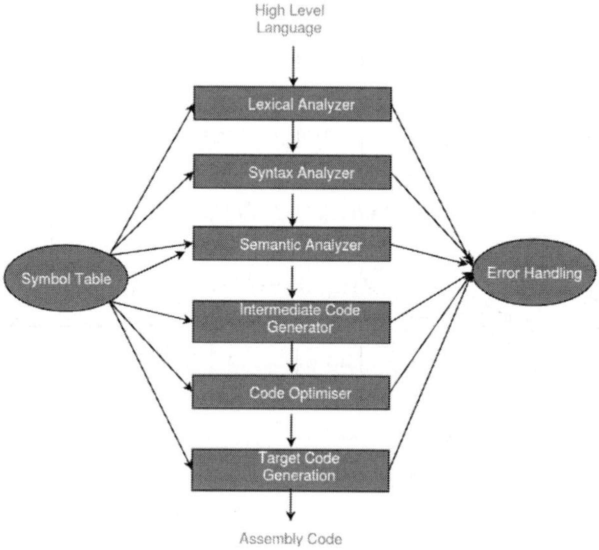

Figure 2.4. A compiler design overview.

Source: https://www.geeksforgeeks.org/introduction-of-compiler-design/.

The computer compiler subject is used to equip students with knowledge and principles that can be used in the design of any compiler. For instance, the formal language theory is used to solve problems such as analyzing source programs. While studying computer science, the students learn about different types of compliers.

They include cross compiler, which is capable of creating a code for a platform other than the running compiler. The other is source-to-source compiler, which translates source code of the original programming language to another source code of another programming language. They also learn about the phases of a compiler in which there are two major phases the similarity is that each of them takes input from the initial level and they work in a well-coordinated way. They get to learn about the two types of phases which include the analysis phase and the synthesis phase (Hazzan, Lapidot, & Ragonis, 2011).

The analysis phase involves an intermediate representation that is generated from the allocated source code. It houses lexical analyzer, syntax analyzer, semantic analyzer and intermediate analyzer whereby the lexical analyzer divides the given program into tokens, the syntax analyzer is used to identify sentences in the program with the use of syntax language, semantic analyzer used to identify static semantics for each of the constructs and intermediate generator is used to create an abstract code.

The synthesis phase is a program that is created from intermediate representation and it contains two parts which are code optimizer and the other code generator. Code optimizer is used to optimize abstract codes while the code generator is used to translate abstract intermediate code into the machine instructions. Learning computer science is essential for computer science students as they are able to learn programming languages which is a compulsory for all the computer programmers. This is important the students with theoretic and practical knowledge required to implement programming languages.

Compilers use algorithms and data structures which equips the students with knowledge on algorithms. This, in turn, will make it easier for learning algorithms which is a subject on its own in computer science. Compilers are generally used to model applications. This is because the applications are created with the existence of compilers. It therefore gives them knowledge on designing real world applications. Compilers are also used in software developments. As they deal with assembly languages, they knowledge on compilers will enable them to create computer software (Hazzan, Lapidot, & Ragonis, 2011).

The study of complier design is not usually offered in most universities that is why the students are urged to tell their universities to offer it as a subject as it contains information that is very useful in the long run therefore enabling the computer science students to do a variety of tasks.

2.8. OPERATING SYSTEM

Operating system is a computer software that is used to perform basic task that include file management, memory management, process management, handling input and output and controlling peripheral devices. It is generally referred to as the brain of the computer. It manages both hardware and software resources (Donohue, 2014).

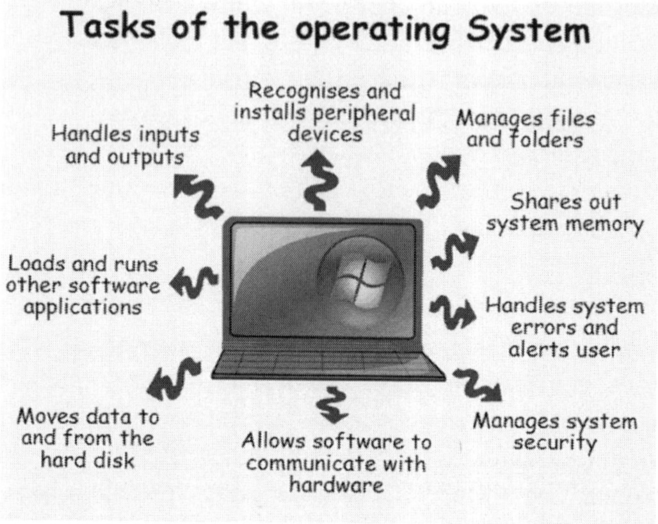

Figure 2.5. The tasks of the operating system.

Source: https://www.ictlounge.com/html/operating_systems_new.htm.

Basically, all computer programs require the operating system so that they can function. In memory management, the operating system keeps track of the status of the memory in the computer whether it is inbuilt or it is an external memory. It plays a role in the allocation of memory among the competing processes.

While managing peripheral devices, the operating system handles the translation requests between devices. It also decides where data that has been processed is placed before being displaced and where information which include incoming messages will be stored by stimulating the sleeping devices to wake up to store or retrieve data. While managing hardware interfaces, the operating system also facilitates communication between devices when connected with interface such as wires and sockets. In terms of storage allocation, the operating system deals with the allocation of ownership and permissions so that the user can access information. It can be used to identify area of the disk where the information is stored (Donohue, 2014).

Multitasking between programs. The operating system is able to carry out a multi-user system whereby the programs are allocated with a given time to process information according to the time allocated to each user. This is usually referred to as a time-slice which is referred to as the amount of time given for processing of data. There are various types of operating systems which include Linux, OS X, windows, IOS, Android OS, Google chrome OS and play station OS among others. Knowledge of these types of operating systems is essential for the computer science students because it will enable them identify the type of operating system to use when carrying out various tasks.

Several aspects come into place for the selection of the type of operating system to use,. This include the number of users that the operating system can handle and the processing speed among others. The operating system usually provides the essential tools that are used in managing the operating system which are often called the utilities and system tools. This gives information on how the operating system is managing different resources such as the memory and the hardware devices among others.

The course syllabus contains the overview of operating systems, characteristics and functionalities, hardware concepts related to the operating system, the concept of a process; operation on processes and processes states among others, UNIX process control and management, interrupt processing, job and processor scheduling, problems of concurrent processes, mutual exclusion, semaphores and its uses, inter-process communication, deadlock, memory organization and management, virtual memory, file organization and file and directory structures (Donohue, 2014).

Knowledge of the operating system is useful for the computer scientists as it enables them to understand processing functions and is applied in creation of computer networks among others.

2.9. COMPUTER SYSTEM ARCHITECTURE

Computer architecture is a science that deals with how computer software and hardware are joined and interact so as to bring about the efficient working of a computer. It is used to determine the technologies the computer is capable of handling.

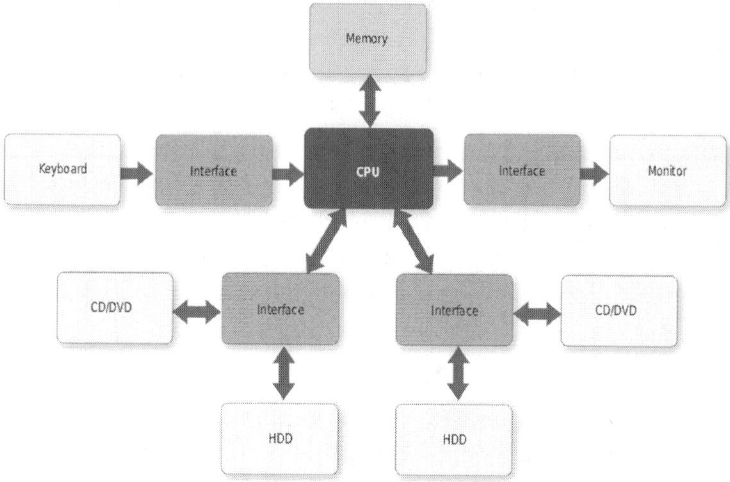

Figure 2.6. Computer system architecture.

Source: https://en.wikibooks.org/wiki/File:Computer_system_architecture.svg.

architecture involves building a computer and all the devices that go into the creation of a computer system. In the syllabus, the students get to learn of the three categories of the computer architecture which include system design, instruction set architecture and microarchitecture.

System design entails the hardware resources of the computer such as the memory controllers, CPU and direct memory access. It is mostly referred to as the actual computer system. The instruction set architecture involve the functioning of the CPU and its capabilities, the data formatting, the CPU's programming language and the processor registers among others. It mostly involves the software applications that aid the running of the computer. It includes software such as windows which is mostly used among the users among others (Beauchamp, 2016).

The microarchitecture entails the data processing and storage elements, the data paths and how they can be rightfully implemented into the instruction set architecture. The elements work together to ensure the efficient working of the computer. This makes it an important subject for the computer science students. The objective of the subject is to ensure that the students are able to identify basic elements of the hardware and how they work together to form an architecture.

They are able to explain the representation and manipulation of data stored within the computer system. They are able to identify the functions of the operating system. They are able to explain how the computers interact through the various networks as they are given knowledge on the on the computer networks in the designs of the computer's architecture. The students also learn the layers of computer architecture which include hardware, software, operating system and users. The hardware layer deals with the tangible components of the computer. Software layer deals with the intangible applications of the computer used in its running. The operating system deals with the control of the functioning of the computer and user layer is the platform that enables the user to interact with the machine (Beauchamp, 2016).

They also learn about the different types of computer architectures, which depend on the purpose of the computer. They include embedded CPU architectures, microcomputer CPU architectures, server CPU architecture which is generally referred to as work station CPU architecture, mainframe CPU architecture and the mixed-core architectures. All of this is vital knowledge and will enable the students to design various computer architectures. This is crucial because the students need to know where to put the various elements such as the memory, registers, command interpreters and the arithmetic unit among others (Beauchamp, 2016).

Together with this, they learn the complex instruction set which execute various low-level operations while addressing various modes with the use of single instructions set in the computer.

2.10. DATA STRUCTURES

Data structure is basically the organization, management, and storage of data that facilitates efficient access to data so that we can easily modify it. It entails the collection of data values, creating relationships among the data and identifying the operation that can be applied to the data. Data structures create a basis for the abstract data types which are usually the form of the given data type. Therefore, the data structure is used in implementing the physical form of the data type. Depending on the type of application, the data structures are designed specifically to suit the application.

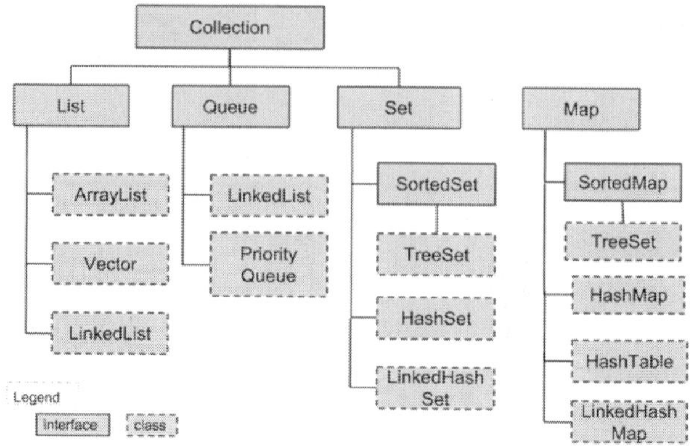

Figure 2.7. Learning of data structures to a computer science student is essential as it enables the student to know how to manage large amounts of data efficiently by use of applications such as databases and internet indexing services.

Source: https://www.toolsqa.com/java/data-structure/.

Data structures are used in designing algorithms among others. The knowledge is used in the organization and retrieval of information stored in the different types of memories present in the computer. Examples of data structures include Float, Boolean and Char among others.

There are different types of data structures, which include the linked list, tree, graph and stack among others. They facilitate various operations to be done on data. Therefore, the data structure is selected according to the type of operation that is to be carried out. For the easy learning process of the student, the data structures are usually divided into characters which include linear, nonlinear, homogenous, static and dynamic characters. For the linear data structures as the name suggests, the data is usually arranged in a linear sequence example include the array data structure (Sharma, 2002).

For the nonlinear data structures, the data is not in any sequence and it entails the tree and graph data structures. Homogenous data structures deal with data items that have the same elements and an example includes the array data structure. The no homogeneous data structure is the opposite of the homogenous data structure in that the data types usually have different elements. They include the structures. Static data structures are those that use the size of the data to determine whether the data is to be stored permanently or temporarily in the memories. It therefore decides the type of memory that will be used an example is the array data structure.

The dynamic data structures are those that either expand or reduce depending on the type of program required and the execution of the operation. They also affect the location of data in the memories and they include the linked list data structures. The learning of data structures is important for computer science students as it equips them with skills such as translating data into a variety of applications, for instance, displaying related data in a binary tree. For the students who decide to major in programming, they will be able to use programming languages to create data structures that will be useful in creating organized code and information in a digital space making it advantageous for them (Sharma, 2002).

2.11. ALGORITHMS

An algorithm is basically a set of instructions that are written in a given order that are used in executing a certain predefined task. This is basically a solution to a type of problem experienced. For instance, if two computers are sending information in a server-based network and they send information at the same time, there is a message sent to the server so that later an algorithm is produced, so as to solve the problem. In this case, the algorithm may be to adjust the time-lapse of the computers so that each computer sends information at its own time.

Learning algorithms is essential for computer science students because it entails solving problems. This is the key role for computer science. Throughout the learning process, students will realize that their algorithms must satisfy certain requirements and properties. They include input that may be supplied externally to the algorithm. Alternatively, there could be more than one output obtained from the algorithm. On the same note, definiteness which requires that every step of the algorithm should be well and clearly defined (König, 2012).

Other properties include finiteness and correctness. Finiteness refers to the finite number of steps taken in solving the problem. Correctness refers to the fact that every step in the algorithm should be able to generate correct output. An algorithm that has all these properties may be rendered efficient as it will be fast and will consume less of the memory space. The students should therefore have knowledge on how to measure the performance of an algorithm. The performance is measured on the basis of time and space complexity. Space complexity is the amount of space that the algorithm will require during the process of its execution (Blake, 2009).

Space is a key factor as a computer that has several users may be limited in storage capacity. An algorithm requires to store its elements which include the instruction space that stores the programs that are to be executed, the data space that stores the variables which may be temporary or permanent and the environment space which contains information required in resuming a suspended function. Time complexity basically refers to the time taken by the program to run until it completes its tasks. The use of step when solving problems show the relationship between algorithms and programming which brings about programming algorithms.

This outlines the procedure that is taken by the computer in solving a problem. It generally instructs the computer on the steps it should take so as to solve the problem. The learning of algorithms for the computer science students is beneficial as it encourages them to be critical thinkers when they have to come up with the solutions to various issues and various algorithms may be used to solve the same problem enabling them to identify the best. The fact that they also learn on the software and its developments, it enables them as software developers to come up with programs that are error-free and efficient when in use (Blake, 2009).

Chapter 3

Computer Science in Early Childhood

CONTENTS

3.1. Introduction 48
3.2. Computational Thinking 48
3.3. Block-Based Programming Languages 64
3.4. Programming Games 67
3.5. Introductory Robotic Systems 70

3.1. INTRODUCTION

Before applying computers to solve complex any problems, we should comprehend its methods. Computational thinking systems help with instilling these skills and ways of thinking. This procedure allows people to take a complicated issue, learn what the difficulty is and create possible solutions. Consequently, these solutions can be delivered in a means that a computer or person can comprehend.Basically, computational thinking entails taking a complex matter and dividing it down into much smaller and manageable parts. Every one of the smaller bits may then be addressed personally, remembering how similar issues have been solved beforehand and concentrating only on the essential details, whereas ignoring immaterial information that may also be there. Afterwards, basic steps or policies to solve these smaller issues can be developed. Ultimately, these simple procedures or rules are applied to code the computer or assist in solving complex issues in a simple way.Nevertheless, thinking computationally doesn't involve programming. It's also not about reasoning like a computer, since computers don't, and never, think by themselves. Simply said, programming shows a computer what it needs to do, including how this should be done. It permits you to determine precisely what to command the PC to do. For instance, if you consent to meeting someone at a place you've never visited before, you will certainly plan your journey before stepping out of the home. You may ponder the routes present and which one is 'best' to follow – this could be the path that's shortest, fastest or most convenient to use.

3.2. COMPUTATIONAL THINKING

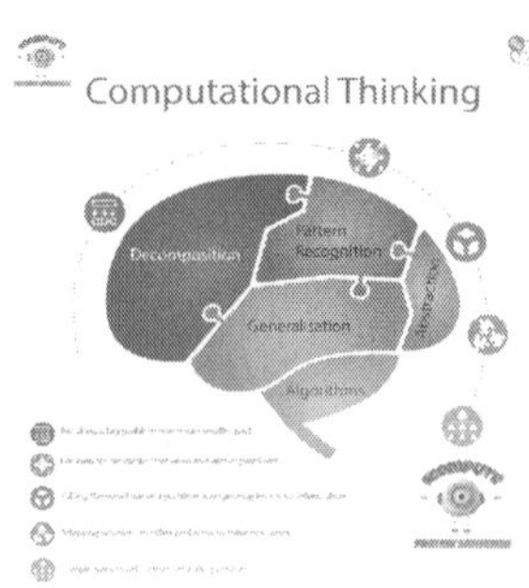

Figure 3.1. Computational Thinking or (CT) is a solution finding process which involves a number of features and dispositions.

Figure: http://www.icompute-uk.com/news/computational-thinking-2/.

This program is necessary for the creation of computer applications, though it can further be used for supporting problem-solving solutions in various disciplines, including humanities, science and mathematics. Students that learn CT all across the syllabus may start to see a connection between school subjects, including between life within and outside of class.

The field in which you use CT may be any subject discipline or topic, including the discipline that you specifically teach as an instructor. These styles of thinking may be applied anytime you seek to develop a procedure or algorithm for solving a problem. You may realize in the process that there are some lessons which include programming code. Nevertheless, CT doesn't always end in utilizing a programming language, despite being a great way of determining what's possible (Khine, 2018).

3.2.1. History of Computational Thinking

The background of computational thinking goes back roughly to the 1950s, even though some of its concepts are much older. This model involves concepts like abstraction, information representation, and rationally organizing data, and these are also predominant in other forms of thinking, like scientific thinking, mechanical thinking, structural thinking, design philosophy, model-based philosophy, and so on.

Neither the concept nor the phrase is recent. In fact, they are preceded by words like algorithmizing, technical thinking, algorithmic process, and computational understanding brought about by computing innovators like Donald Knuth and Alan Perlis. It wasn't until 1980 when Seymour Papert used the word computational thinking, then later again in 1996. Computational thinking might be applied to algorithmically unravel complicated issues of scale, plus is often applied to realize significant progresses in efficiency. The term computational thinking was officially introduced to the computer science training fraternity in 2006, coming from an ACM Interaction thesis on the topic by Jeannette Wing. The thesis suggested that reasoning computationally was a vital skill for everybody, not only computer scientists, further arguing for the significance of incorporating computational thoughts into other topics in school. The scale of computational thinking inquiries in education vary from K-9 calculation for kids to skilled and continuing education, whereby the test is how to pass on deep principles, adages, and styles of thinking among experts (Khine, 2018).

3.2.2. Application of Computational Thinking

Computational thinking is essential in the modern century as it is applied for communication, collaboration, critical reasoning and creativity. It consists of tools which generate models and visualize information. Furthermore, computational thinking is relevant across various subjects beyond technology, science, math and engineering, also known as (STEM) subjects. The discipline is applicable in language arts and social sciences. Scholars can participate in activities whereby they detect sequences in grammar and sentence structure, while also using prototypes for studying relationships.

Since its foundation, the Cs mentioned above have progressively gained approval as vital components of many learning institution syllabi. This invention triggered an adaptation in contexts and directions like inquiry, course-based, and more insightful learning across various K-12 levels. Several countries have also introduced computer reasoning among their students. For instance, UK has been incorporating CT within its nationwide school syllabus since 2012, whereas Singapore considers it to be a "national capability." Similarly, other nations such as Australia, New Zealand, China and Korea started endeavors to introduce computational reasoning in schools (Khine, 2018).

In America, former President Barack Obama developed this program, naming it Computer-Science for All in order to equip the current generation of learners in the U.S with the appropriate computer science expertise needed to thrive in the digital economy. Computational reasoning means discerning or solving issues like computer scientists. The procedure points to thought processes needed to understand problems and framing solutions. The process involves logic, valuation, patterns, mechanization, and generalization. Also, career readiness might be incorporated into learning and training environments in different ways.

3.2.3. Philosophies of Computational Thinking

All around the globe, instructors are being encouraged to help their scholars get ready for a future in a progressively computational globe. Combining computational intellect into school activities, modules, and curricula not just supports development of fresh skills, but also boosts learning and commitment in every field.

Nevertheless, there are still various educators who don't feel contented with computational reasoning ideas than the ones who do. To solve this dilemma, some organizations lead workshops with multiple teachers from different scholarly disciplines to familiarize them to computational reasoning practices (Khine, 2018).

Borrowing from both educational sciences research and response from educators, this framework is developed to support instructors in determining where their pupils can leverage computational reasoning. Within these mentioned concepts, instructors of science, mathematics, linguistic arts, social studies, plus art have discovered connections with what their learners are anticipated to know including how to do certain activities.

These main philosophies of computational reasoning are categorized into two groups: which are practices and foundations. The latter are cognitive systems vital for writing computer programs. Meanwhile, practices comprise of the foundations, extra skills and knowledge required to solve a practical problem, whether the ultimate result is a computing program, improved understanding of the biological environment, or an improved appreciation of how people's migration patterns match with geographical landscapes (Khine, 2018).

Incorporating computational thinking isn't simply another add-on, instead it can be an actual value-addition for instructors in any discipline area. Nowadays, there are also organizations that recognize teachers for developing learning experiences whereby learners can develop certain abilities with these practices.

The credentials are built around computational reasoning practices, since the extent to which learners have established foundational abilities can't be measured until they are demonstrated through the functional practices. To earn recognition from these organizations, teachers provide evidence of pupils work from daily class activities where they've actively applied computational thinking practices, including documentation of course planning and reflection (Khine, 2018).

However, there's still some debate going on plus tasks to be completed within the practical sciences research fraternity concerning how to describe computational thinking, advantages of this work, plus how these abilities can be transferred.

Similarly, driven by shifting societal and learning policy priorities, instructors in K-12 are being encouraged to incorporate computational thinking, plus to adopt fresh standards which particularly call out computational reasoning as skills and activities to learn.

3.2.4. Four Skills of Computational Thinking

Pattern recognition: When decomposing complex problems, we usually find sequences among the lesser problems we create. These patterns refer to similarities or features that a few of the problems have in common. Pattern recognition is among the primary foundations of Computer Science. Basically, it involves determining the relationships or patterns among trivial, decomposed problems which can help people solve more complex issues more efficiently. In computational thinking, similar characteristics in an object are referred to as patterns. Upon knowing how to define one object, it's would be much easier to describe others just by following the already established pattern.

Establishing patterns is quite important. They make our work easier. Problems are much simpler to solve if they share patterns, since we can apply similar problem-solving patterns wherever the arrangement exists. The more similarities that can be found, the simpler and faster our general work of problem-solving shall be (Sharma, 2002).

Suppose we hadn't checked for patterns in an object. It means every time we needed to solve it, we would require to stop and figure out the issue first and this would have slowed us down. We could still arrive at a solution – and they shall still be relevant – though each problem-solving process will take way longer to conclude. This can be quite inefficient, and a wrong way to go around solving the problem at hand.

Additionally, if we don't check for patterns then we may not notice that all tasks available have certain central similarities.

To discover patterns in issues we must search for matters that are similar in every problem. It could turn out that there aren't any common characteristics existing among problems, though we must still look. Patterns exist among diverse problems and even within particular problems. To find patterns between problems we search for factors that are alike for each problem.

For instance, delving into the task of preparing a cake, there would be need for the baker to recognize all the answers to a set of smaller issues such as; what type of cake is being baked, the ingredients needed and quantity of each, number of people who would consume the cake, when each ingredient needs to be added and so forth. Once patterns have been identified in the above example, then the baker can work towards finding common solutions among the problems (Sharma, 2002).

Simply put, pattern recognition refers the procedure of approaching an issue in a systematic way and developing and expressing an answer, so that it may be performed by the computer. However, you don't have to be a computing expert to reason like a specialist. As a matter of fact, students from all fields of study are encouraged to register for this course. A number of quantitative and data-based issues can be resolved through applying computational thinking, plus a comprehension of computational thinking shall give you the foundation for resolving problems which have real-life, social impact. Pattern recognition is a computational thinking pillar that can help you engage better with the problem, and arrive at a positive solution (Khine, 2018).

Creating and using algorithms: Algorithmic thinking refers to the application of algorithms, or procedural sets of guidelines, to finish a task. Teaching pupils to use algorithmic reasoning prepares them for innovation. Algorithmic thinking is closely linked to computer science, as well as mathematics, since algorithms form the backbone to completing series of code or breaking down big issues into smaller, more manageable parts.

They utilize computers' decision-making procedures to do certain matters at specific intervals. Instead of claiming that the solution is permanently "red," an algorithm describes rules which lead to that response being a regular conclusion.

Certain algorithms are pre-formed. For instance, the quick sort algorithm forms an effective technique for grouping items into a list. Other systems aren't so simply defined. Case in point, what's the ideal means to go from A to B? The cognitive map you envisage might take diverse factors into account. You may need to consider that you must drive through a particular store in the journey. These choices factor into the "route finding" algorithm that you create (Khine, 2018).Nevertheless, understanding what an algorithm is may be quite different from reasoning algorithmically. This is the point of variance between learning a formula and building your own. It's about understanding conditional accounts and loops, then using logic to solve the problem and develop procedural writing.

What is algorithmic thinking? This is a means of finding solution by the clear description of the steps required – nothing occurs by magic. Instead of arriving at a single response to an issue, students instead form algorithms. These are instructions or sets of rules which when followed accurately, whether by an individual or computer, provide solutions to the original as well as similar problems (Khine, 2018).

For instance, we all study algorithms for accomplishing multiplication tasks at school. In case we follow the established rules, then we were told specifically we can get answers to any multiplication issue. When we master the algorithm then we don't need to work out ways of doing calculation from scratch each time we encounter a fresh problem.

There are several benefits of algorithms as present below:

- It's a procedural representation of a finding to a particular issue, which makes it simpler to understand.
- Algorithms apply a definite procedure.
- Each step required in an algorithm features its own rational sequence, such that it's simple to debug.
- Through using algorithm, the issue is divided into smaller bits or steps thus, it's simpler for the programmer to adapt it into the actual program.
- It's not reliant on any coding language, therefore it's simple to understand for everyone even without any programming background.

Algorithms are closely linked to computer science. By using step-by-step programming chunks, this allows for more complex and robust courses, plus the ultra-personalization of media depend on algorithms. Moreover, there are algorithms which are proprietary, like the software behind Google's searching algorithm.

These systems have received quite a lot of media exposure lately, particularly from the inherent prejudice that they can receive from their coders up to the notion of daily algorithms. Understanding conventional algorithms has always comprised a portion of the computer-science course.

Decomposition: Decomposition is described as the procedure of subdividing an issue into its sub-parts. While most descriptions of computational thinking cover decomposition by itself, others break down the entire decomposition process beyond a mere description. Being among the first phases in the computational reasoning process, it's essential to better comprehend the different methods in which decomposition happens, the most effective methods, and within what conditions.

For a better comprehension of the decomposition procedure, the evidence of decompositional practice can be applied in a range of disciplines. Decomposition refers to a style of thinking about issues, algorithms, artifacts, procedures, and systems with regards to their constituents. The different sections may then be understood, resolved, established and assessed distinctly. This makes otherwise complicated problems simpler to solve and bigger systems simpler to design (Khine, 2018).

For instance, when developing a computer game, different people may design and formulate the different levels individually provided certain vital aspects are agreed upon in advance. By decomposing the original task, it means each component can be designed and assimilated later into the process. A basic arcade level may further be decomposed into multiple parts.

The following are real life examples:

- Women are naturally good at multitasking, therefore as a cook gets more confident they begin to overlap a few of the roles, determining what to perform next while mixing the pot probably, or leaving the sauce to boil while cutting the herbs. Computers perform more or less similar things.
- It is a fact that technology changes society. Whether it is the invention of fire, wheels, ammunition or skyscrapers, they all made massive contributions to the way that we labor, live and play. Computing is rapidly fast-tracking the change and bringing whole new matters which society has to adopt into.

Decomposition is a vital step in various problem-solving procedures and is utilized in various fields. For one to better appreciate decomposition, it's imperative to analyze case studies coming from different research disciplines in order to understand how decomposition functions and is measured. Following a brief investigation, for instance, scientists were able to detect relations between some STEM subjects with concepts of foundational theory like Philosophy, Design and Anthropology. For purposes of adding to the theoretical comprehension of de-composition being a problem-solving method, scholars searched for relevant publications in these theoretical disciplines for information which would improve their comprehension of decompositional procedures in non-STEM subjects (Beauchamp, 2016).

Some common methods of decomposing the computing problems witnessed in computer science are to subdivide the issue into its structure, role, sequence, and dependence factors. Structural decomposition involves breaking down the issue into mini-components and resolving each part separately. On the contrary, functional decomposition subdivides the problem down depending on which roles are performed and which bits of the system, subdividing them such that each section can be examined separately (Beauchamp, 2016).

Understanding abstractions: Abstraction is among of the key foundations of computer science. It entails filtering out the factors that we don't require in order to focus on the ones that we do. Likewise, it is the sieving out of particular details from which we form a basic representation or idea of the item we're seeking to solve.

This technique allows us to develop a general concept of what the issue is, and practical ways of solving it. It instructs us to take away all specific detail, plus any patterns which won't assist us in resolving the problem. As such, it helps us to construct an idea of the issue commonly known as the 'model.'

In case we don't abstract then we might end up having the incorrect solution to the issue we're seeking to solve. Basically, abstraction is a means of making problems or structures simpler to contemplate. It basically involves hiding detail and extracting needless complexity. The knowledge is in determining the specific detail to conceal so that the issue becomes much easier, and without compromising anything that is significant (Beauchamp, 2016).

Typically, abstraction is applied as a means of making it simpler to develop complex algorithms, including whole systems. A vital aspect of abstraction is in determining an ideal representation of a structure. Different contexts make different tasks simple to do.

For instance, when playing cards, we typically utilize the word 'shuffle.' Each player realizes that 'shuffle' means placing the cards in some random order (Khine, 2018). This term is an abstraction by itself. The same form of abstraction applies when programming. Effecting 'shuffle' in a computing game simply means providing a means of randomizing the cards. Here, we can connote to shuffling throughout the project and comprehend what is intended without needing to think on how it's really done by the program. Basically, all that's required is that the package does include a definition somewhere of exactly how shuffling is performed.

While a computational thinker isn't similar to a Computer-Programmer, programming through abstraction promotes creativity, rational thought, accuracy and problem-solving, plus helps in fostering the individual, learning and intellectual skills needed in the current school curriculum. Equally, programming provides concrete, physical form to the notion of "abstraction," plus repeatedly displays how practical it is in whichever discipline (Khine, 2018).

In abstraction, data structures point to a method of storing "stuff." Same as we can place "objects" in stacks, piles, bales and buckets – the same arrangement applies to data (information). One popular example of a record structure, in real life, is the popular Pez Dispenser. It uses 'stacks' to stock and dispense candy. In the absence of structure all the available "stuff" can't be applied as information for solving various issues.

In addition, sorting algorithms is an important aspect of handling data. Sorting is, basically put, organizing objects in a logical manner, regardless of what that particular item is. Maybe you could sort a pile of cards or categorize your groceries. This same principle applies to computational thinking. In the classroom context, students will learn concrete systems of sorting plus will learn to relate these techniques to matters that are intangible (Khine, 2018).

3.2.5. Teaching Computational Thinking in Early Childhood

Approaches on the practicality of technology in promoting early childhood education tends to be rather divided. On one hand, we have those that believe we must safeguard kids from technology, due to the potential risks of exposing them to excessive screen time, as well as unsupervised internet.

On the other hand, we have those that believe youngsters will benefit from applying the latest technology from an early stage and regularly, so they can grow to be savvier and sharper than the preceding generation.

Early childhood tutors experienced in both conventional constructivist learning and advanced computer science syllabus development can be cautious and inventive in the ways that they introduce kids to technology, while teaching them more about computer science (Khine, 2018).

Computational thinking training in early childhood: Out of the four recognized groups of computational thinking—which are pattern recognition, using algorithms, decomposition, and comprehending abstractions—there's just one category which can't be effortlessly incorporated into the early childhood syllabus. Abstractions is an especially high-level thinking ability which most youngsters aren't capable of mastering in preschool. The model of child development envisioned by Jean Piaget shows us that youngsters learn through their basic senses, which are movement, and through manipulation of physical objects. This is applicable in almost every learning move, ranging from the tangible to the conceptual, from the actual to imagined, and concrete to abstract (Sharma, 2002).

Case in point, we are able to count to ten by feeling and stretching the fingers on both hands. Later on, we can envisage the model often in different ways—as a number, digit or decade. That's why block play is vital in early childhood. For the most part, computational thinking arises from the pre-school block corner. As youngsters create towers, pathways, fortresses and bridge with blocks of standardized shapes and dimensions, they gather experience recognizing and producing patterns using qualities like shape and size. Whenever a kid seeks to copy another youngster's building project, in essence they're forming and using algorithms.

If the block structures ultimately tumble and they scatter all over the floor, the kids learn decomposition since they apply their own tiny hands to subdivide the blocks into stacks and put them back onto the shelves. Block building, nevertheless, isn't abstract.

The kids are touching, lifting, handling, balancing, and, in most cases, hitting over physical, concrete objects. This is the real and practical beauty of the entire experience. By participating in block play, kids are literally establishing the framework for computational thinking. Youngsters need to have these tactile and kinesthetic experiences handling real-life objects in the actual world, so as to better prepare them for theoretical and virtual experiences which they'll need to learn to operate and program PCs and robots (Sharma, 2002).

Building spatial reasoning in youngsters: A child playing with LEGO or wooden blocks today shall be programming and utilizing computers in a dynamic future that people can barely imagine or predict. So, what can adults teach kids now, when they're still young, to help develop a foundation of aptitude and knowledge that shall assist them in becoming innovative problem-solvers? Computational reasoning provides the solution. But still, how teachers assist kids in making the skip from actual problem-solving in the physical world to theoretical problem-solving within the virtual world is debatable. The resolution to these questions may, in part, be offered by tiny plastic robots (Hazzan, Lapidot, & Ragonis, 2011). Spatial thinking refers to the ability to reflect on the way items exist and travel through space. The focus on spatial thinking during early childhood is crucial in planting the seeds for computational thinking. Comprehending how robots, blocks, plus their own bodies travel through space, circumvent obstacles, and match with other objects, can help kids learn to broaden their reasoning from the physical to the abstract.

Using, developing, and conceptualizing maps: The significance of spatial thinking in the creation of computational reasoning can be illustrated, plainly, through kids' use of charts in playing and learning. When youngsters build a small town in the class corner through LEGO, they have basically developed a 3D map. When kids make a simple robot to travel from one spot to another, they use their minds in the same way as a grid map. Though moving around a toy may seem playful, it actually involves the use of problem-solving abilities involve the application, making, and conception of maps. For early childhood educators with a sharp interest in blocks, maps and robots, it's significant to understand the fascinating ways in which spatial reasoning in kids opens opportunities for computation thinking (Orit Hazzan, Tami Lapidot, & Noa Ragonis, 2011).

3.2.6. Begin with Spatial Reasoning

Spatial reasoning refers to a sub-group of reasoning ability that allow students to visualize spatial pictures in their heads and rationally manipulate them. This skill helps people to think about items in 3D, and make implications about those items from the basic information available. Basically, this logic involves tracking the location and moving of items, either cognitively or materially, in space. It's not a single skill or process, rather it refers to a significant number of models, tools and processes.

Testing for spatial thinking: Spatial reasoning exams assess the student's capacity to think on items in both 2 and 3D, drawing conclusions to those items from limited information. Learners will have to perform assembling and dismantling of various objects, images, and revolve and watch them from different angles. The non-verbal aptitude tests, commonly referred to as spatial cognizance tests are typically applied by teachers in psychometric testing processes. A student with great spatial ability is also capable of thinking about ways in which a particular object shall look once rotated. These abilities are applicable in many real-life situations and may be enhanced with practice. An aptitude test is among the many available tests in IQ exam training. Spatial thinking tests prove useful in evaluating a candidate's ability to interpret 2D and 3D shapes. The teacher will determine their student's capacity to detect patterns or associations between these shapes.

Games and activities for improving spatial reasoning skills: The good news on spatial reasoning among children is that it may be improved through certain activities. Below are a few games which can be introduced to kids to assist them in building their spatial reasoning ability.

- Master-builder game: This game involves two players only, who are the master and builder. Without both players seeing each other, masters develop a design or sequence with objects, such as LEGO blocks. The master consequently is required to provide the builder with verbal directives to reimagine the design. As a tutor, you must always encourage the application of real-time spatial language whenever probable. Research has shown that youngsters who've been taught spatial ability perform better in spatial duties compared to their peers. Some common forms of spatial words are the words tied to location, expanse, positioning and direction, such as left, right, above, below, central, parallel, short and tall. Games such as Master-Builder are helpful for developing spatial skills.
- Sliding block: The objective of this game is moving the blocks freely so as to release the red slab. You might already have realized that this is quite similar in design to Rush Hour, whereby the objective is freeing the red vehicle from the traffic grid. Apart from promoting spatial reasoning through helping kids conceptualize blocks on a network, Sliding Block further encourages problem-solving as kids determine how to move the blocks to release the red one. This helps them in learning how to analyze and think with 2D shapes plus their attributes.

Spatial thinking tests: Spatial reasoning tests comprise of various questions linked to dimensional reasoning. The number of accurate answers shall form the student's score. Following that, the results might be compared with the outcomes of other exam-takers or the normative group. This refers to a group of students who've already proven their understanding for certain activities. The variety of questions available will assess how well one can use their imagination and thinking to derive conclusions about certain objects (Khine, 2018).Students shall have to cognitively process the 2D and 3D images available, so as to find out the answer. Basically, spatial reasoning test covers queries based on items pictured in multidimensional levels. These questions may consist of mirror images, perspective-based pictures, bi-dimensional shapes as well as spatial reasoning cubes.

These tests measure the student's multi-dimensional thinking. They will receive images of some items and must have to process these in their mind, in order to arrive at a solution for the question. The learners' performance shall determine how well they have mastered spatial reasoning skills. Generally, practicing is the most ideal way to attain the best outcomes in spatial thinking tests (Khine, 2018).

Important spatial abilities for kids

- Reading – kids must know that certain forms, like "m" and "w" and "9" and "6," may have different implications based on how they're moved on the page.
- Calculation – trigonometry and calculus need the ability to visualize an object revolving in space.
- Sporting and physical activity – in order to capture a ball mid-air, kids must assess its speed and distance in flight and alter their motion accordingly.
- Daily activities – these include functions like using the mirror to comb hair or tying up their shoelaces.

3.2.7. Using, Making, and Imagining Maps

Figure 3.2. Understanding maps helps children to develop a mental map in their brains, and therefore they are able to reason conceptually.

Source: https://www.pbs.org/parents/thrive/why-children-still-need-to-read-and-draw-maps.

Cognitive maps are really essential since they give people the freedom to navigate anywhere they want to go, even amidst roadblocks, detours and other obstacles.

Parents should start early to introduce mental maps to their children. Even in pre-school youngsters have the capacity to understand the association between a chart and the real world, but still require some form of guidance—preferably a teacher to introduce them to maps plus teach them on the essentials of how they operate (Guzdial, 2015).

Developing maps skills in youngsters: Spatial thinking permits students to understand and analyze matters relating to the venues and spaces around them—including at angles from which they're able to touch and experience a room or neighborhood up to a global map or worldwide. This form of reasoning is among the most significant skills that learners can develop since they learn environmental sciences, Earth and geography. It also amplifies and gives a greater grasp of history to learners, apart from being closely linked to achievement in mathematics and science. Youngsters also grow their language skills since they cooperate and communicate concerning spatial relationships. Pupils who build robust spatial reasoning skills shall be at a benefit in the progressively global and technical society. It can never be too early to train youngsters on spatial awareness. Training kids these skills may begin when they are still young. Training basic map skills may be realized through reading publications on mapping, or from practical mapping lessons.

Importance of teaching kids to read maps: For quite a number of adults, it's sometimes incomprehensible to imagine that there existed a period when we didn't know how to read maps. However, for others reading a map is as instinctive as reconstructing an event in our brain from the points on the page which constitute a photograph. As a matter of fact, the capacity to "read" maps, even the seemingly basic one, is an ability which must be learned plus can require significant time and effort. Even though nearly everybody acquires the fundamental map reading abilities by completion of primary grade, this doesn't minimize the scale of these achievements for youngsters. Just as reading and mathematics, learning how to comprehend a map is the foundational ability that's a vital prerequisite for consequently building a diverse set of knowledge and ability.A brief assessment of the media which kids watch in their schools, residences, and communities shows how regularly maps are applied to pass important information and relations. In recent National Educational Assessment studies, it was found that around 58% of 4th-grade instructors mentioned that they apply maps or classroom globes in their training at least once per week (Guzdial, 2015).

For this purpose, any delay in learning how to read charts or low proficiency in understanding maps may be an impediment to scholarly and intellectual progress. Regrettably, map skills aren't taught as reliably across the U.S. as they ought to. Nor do a majority of primary grade instructors have the teaching materials or knowledge to teach mapping skills. For these reasons, stakeholders in the education industry have launched several initiatives to enhance the training of mapping skills in the early classes. This endeavor is aimed at providing educators with the knowledge, talents, and resources they require to coach their students.

Henry's Map: Portrayed as "An exciting introduction to charts through the perspective of a delightful pig," Henry's Map is intended for preschoolers – and 2nd graders between ages 4 to 8 years. In this book Henry is a finicky pig residing on a farm. He is upset when upon looking outside the window he sees lots of mess. Henry then goes off on a trip to draw out his farm, in such a way that every creature gets back to the position they should be. He uses a map to direct the hens back into the coop, horses into their stable, and sheep in the wood-shed (Beauchamp, 2016).

This book offers children a nice introduction to the idea of what really a map is, including why individuals create maps. When the primary concept of what makes up a map has already been introduced, the following step is practically producing a map of some small area like your kid's room or house yard. This map may either be drawn by hand or through an online program like a mapping application. As the youngsters become more proficient, they can be encouraged to develop maps of imaginary locations or places found in their preferred books.

3.3. BLOCK-BASED PROGRAMMING LANGUAGES

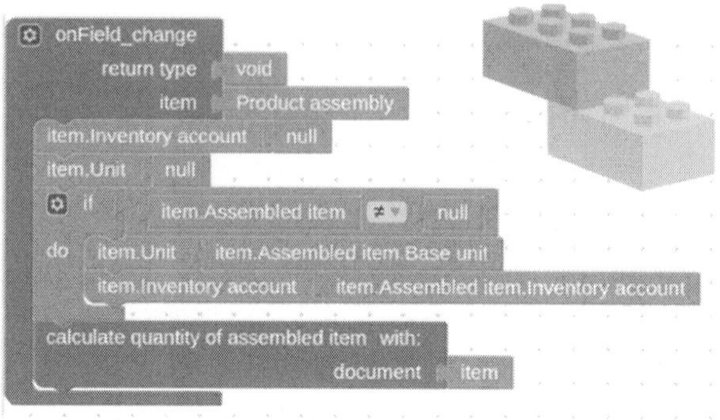

Figure 3.3. Block-based coding has been simplified so that younger students can understand its logic.

Source: https://www.codejig.com/fi/block-based-coding/.

In comparison to text-based programming, the block-based coding refers to programming system and IDE which divides executable functions into modular parts called blocks. The blocks are normally represented with signs which can be ticked or drawn to reorder them. Modifiable fields, such as drop-down menus, permit users to offer increased input. This detailed representation of programming can showcase the procedure to new operators who might be unacquainted to programming. Block-based coding may be simpler to understand compared to traditional text-based coding languages, such as Java or Python. Nevertheless, block programming is a lot more limited compared to text languages that need more specific guidelines from the coder to complete certain actions. Block-based coding is typically used to assist kids in learning how to develop basic programs plus start to understand coding (Beauchamp, 2016).

3.3.1. Blockly Programming Languages

Blockly is an archive which adds a pictorial code modifier to internet and mobile apps. This editor applies interconnecting, graphical slabs to represent code models like loops, variables, and logical expressions among others. It further allows users to employ programming philosophies without needing to worry about structure, or the inconvenience of a blinking pointer on the center line.

From the user's viewpoint, Blockly is an instinctive, optical method of building a program. From a developer's viewpoint, Blockly is an available UI for developing a graphical language that produces syntactically accurate user-generated program. Blockly can transfer blocks to multiple programming languages, such as Python, PHP, JavaScript, Lua and Dart. Factors that go into developing a Blockly app:

- Incorporate the Blockly editor. This app in its basic form consists of a toolbox for storing block types, plus a workspace for assembling blocks.
- Develop your app's blocks. Upon installing Blockly in your system, the next step is forming blocks for users to program with, then include them to your app's toolbox.
- Construct the remaining of the app. Blockly is simply a way of generating a code. The core of this app is in determining what to perform with that code.
- Add attribution to Blockly. If you want to let people realize that you applied Blockly for building your app, simply use an in-built Blockly badge that is available.

Benefits of Blockly: Blockly is among the fastest growing visual coding systems. Determining which one to apply in your application is a crucial step, therefore below are some few of Blockly's greatest strengths in helping you make a better decision:

- Transferable code: Users can extricate their block-based systems to common coding languages and easily swap over to text-based coding.
- Open source: All Blockly operations are completely open: meaning you can divide it, hack it, or use it for your own software and Android apps.
- Extendable: Blockly can be amended to fit your requirements by including custom blocks into your API, or eliminating unnecessary blocks or functionality.
- Highly versatile: Blockly is not a toy. It can be applied to implement complex programming roles like determining standard deviation from a single block.
- Global: Blockly has been interpreted to more than 40 languages, as well as right-to-left editions for Hebrew and Arabic.

3.3.2. Scratch Programming Languages

It is a block-based graphical programming language and virtual community targeted mainly at kids. Operators of the app can develop online projects through a block-based interface. This service is built by MIT Media Lab, and has been converted into more than 70 languages, plus is used in various parts of the globe. The app is taught and applied in after-school institutions, schools, and universities, including other public knowledge centers (Willmann, 2017).

By 2019, community data on the language's formal website show that well over 40 million programs shared by more than 40 million users, plus almost 40 million website visits each month.

Scratch derives its name from the technique applied by disk jockeys known as "scratching," whereby vinyl records are cropped together and operated on a turn-table to create different sound effects as well as music. Just as scratching, the app allows users to mix together varying media (such as graphics, acoustics, and other programs) in innovative ways by "remixing" files (Willmann, 2017).

User interface: The Scratch interface comprises of three main sections which include: a stage zone, blocks palette, plus a coding zone to place and organize the blocks into practical scripts. The podium space features the results, such as, animations, turtle graphics and so on, either in a minor or normal magnitude, with a whole-screen option also accessible) plus all sprites thumbnails getting listed in the base area.

The point uses X and Y angles, with coordinates 0:0 being the platform center. By having a sprite designated at the base of the staging zone, blocks of commands may be included to it by moving them from the slab's palette into the programming area. The Costumes label allows operators to change the appearance of the sprite, so as to form different effects, such as animation. On the other hand, Sounds tab permits for linking sounds and music onto a sprite. When forming sprites and backgrounds, operators can design their own sprite physically, select a Sprite from an available library, or put up an existing image.

Unreal Engine Blueprints: The Blueprints Visual Programming system in Unreal Engine is essentially a holistic gameplay scripting structure, which is centered on the model of applying node-based interface for creating gameplay components from within the Unreal Editor. Just like with most common scripting languages, it is applied to describe object-oriented (OO) courses or items in the engine. While using UE4, you'll regularly find that items described using Blueprint are largely referred to as only "Blueprints." This program is highly flexible and powerful since it gives the ability for inventors to use practically the whole range of concepts plus tools, typically only accessible to programmers. Furthermore, Blueprint-specific markup accessible in the Unreal Engine's C++ operation allows programmers to develop baseline systems which can be improved by designers.

In their core context Blueprints are visually written additions to your app. By attaching Nodes, Events, Roles, and Variables onto Wires, it is possible to develop complex gameplay components. Blueprints function by using diagrams of Nodes for different purposes – product development, individual functions, plus overall gameplay events – which are particular to every case of the Blueprint so as to actualize behavior and other functions (Willmann, 2017).

3.4. PROGRAMMING GAMES

Nowadays, various popular Visual Programming apps like Scratch and Tynker from MIT Media Labs are applied to engage and train students on programming theories (Hazzan, Lapidot, & Ragonis, 2011). Through programming games such as these, pupils can have an enticing and engaging experience whereas learning computer science modules like loops, provisional statements, variables among many others. Programming games aren't just for potential coders; they also help children get a better foundation in computational reasoning and problem-solving needed in their respective occupations in the future.

In some of the programs, students are taught how to direct the robots through easy puzzles and projects. These activities introduce learners to computational reasoning through models like algorithms and binary numbers, detached from the distractions as well as technical aspects of having to operate computers. Notably, no coding is needed for engaging with these concepts. Throughout the workshop they'll learn the primary concepts of coding such as events, conditionals and loops among others. Ultimately, students will move from simply playing games on smartphones and PCs to comprehending exactly what happens behind the game devices they've been using (Hazzan, Lapidot, & Ragonis, 2011).

3.4.1. Code Master

It's a free online programming game that's established off the Code Master Coding Logic Game. The virtual version has a starter and advanced levels. The player is required to control the explorer or "Avatar," in order to gather crystals while roaming to a mysterious temple. Code Master is among the newest games to be released by Think Fun, a "STEM puzzle" firm that ran the highly successful Kickstarter operation for Robot Turtles. Basically, Code Master asks players to put a limited amount of direction tokens in series to successfully transfer a game component around a path.

Eventually, the result is roughly equivalent to the roles that constitute a program. Meanwhile, your avatar—a figure that evokes the voxellated Minecraft visual— must gather small plastic crystals and prevent trolls. The only contest is the game by itself, which notches the difficulty upwards over 60 levels (Khine, 2018).

The commands are rather simple, though the gameplay may be challenging. Essentially, you need to find out how to move from venue A to B using different maneuvering puzzles. The pictorials are retro but still fun. This makes Code Master a great game for younger children, though can challenge older children and grownups as well.

Player must think carefully, since at every level, just one particular series of actions shall result in success. Upon collecting all the Crystals then landing at the Portal, eventually you win. Playing this game won't just train students on the basic ideas behind programming, but also develop planning, sequential thinking and problem-solving abilities.

After going through the initial easy stages, Code Master eventually begins to run as a series of Sudoku-form puzzles—this is to mean also that the replay ability of every puzzle is practically nil. That varying puzzles iterate mostly on a similar Code Scroll, allows for ingenious economy of game properties, and there are familiar aspects of coding like looping paths and consequently conditional functions (Khine, 2018).

3.4.2. Minecraft

Ever since its release in 2011, Mine-craft has captivated the minds and attention of today's youngsters. Moreover, with the recent launch of Minecraft EDU class version, this famous game is quickly becoming the most significant educational app of our generation plus is now applied to teach reasoning, problem-solving, and geometry.

Whereas many teachers apply Minecraft to train on project-style learning and other progressive arts topics, others don't understand that Minecraft is among the best techniques to train students on computer programming. Below are a few reasons why Minecraft is ideal for training kids on coding:

It motivates students to try coding: Getting children to like computer programming is remarkably easy. Having them engaged, nevertheless, is a totally different thing. While youngsters will quickly acclimatize to the fresh stimuli, they seldom take the journey towards becoming gurus of this new, although complicated skill. However, in terms of this popular game, children are often more fascinated than most adults can imagine. By gradually introducing mods, adults can engage their kids by allowing them to modify their own game. In fact, "Mods" is simply a short form for modifications, and points to changes to the game which add to its characters, features and maps out new and amazing characteristics. For a player to "mod" their game, they should learn to program so as to make significant changes. When children are able to envision and program their unique custom mods, they eventually become motivated and engaged.

Modding trains students on real java: When youngsters are ready to move their programming abilities to the next stage, Minecraft Modding through Java can present them to actual programming. Among the most interesting byproducts of Minecraft's liberal makeup is that it permits operators to utilize Minecraft's Java program code to virtually form anything they can envision (Khine, 2018).

While modding using Java, children learn to develop their unique custom pickaxes, game enemies, or even new dimensions. Likewise, they can apply Java programming to give their inventions special properties plus try out their invention in the game which they like to play.

The discovery moment when a kid plays with their mod in the Mine craft game is definitely a sight to see, besides once youngsters experience it, oftentimes they seek to learn more. Generally, modding provides kids additional inspiration and persistence needed to overcome various glitches in programming –such as bugs, omissions, and other technical faults (Khine, 2018).

It provides visual block programming options: Looking for the correct buttons on a keyboard may be infuriating for young students. As a remedy, some brilliant teachers established drag-and-drop graphical block tools which allow children to perform event-based programming, using Lego-like utility blocks.

In 2016 Microsoft released a Minecraft drag/drop programming platform. Visual blocks signify important computer coding functions like Loops and If Then statements, among others, plus can help younger pupils learn the basics of computer science within a visual context. Therefore, visual block programming in some aspect is similar to the training wheels found on a kid's bicycle.

It can help initially in learning how to balance, but is ultimately intended to be outgrown. As for the early learners, nevertheless, it allows pupils to concentrate more on concepts instead of syntax, plus provides another great means of using Minecraft as a programming resource (Khine, 2018).

3.5. INTRODUCTORY ROBOTIC SYSTEMS

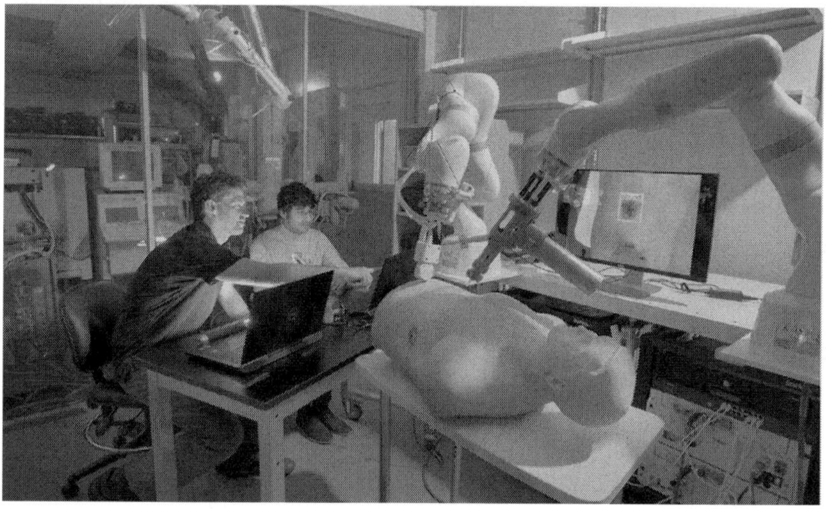

Figure 3.4. Robotic systems may be used to introduce students to mechanics from an early age.

Source: *https://www.wevolver.com/article/a.sense.of.purpose.enables.better.humanrobot.collaboration.*

Robotic systems may be broadly defined as machines which provide intelligent solutions and information through coordinating with their environment and human beings, through the use of special sensors, activators and human interfaces. Physical properties of a robotic structure might significantly vary and comprise mobile robots, manipulator robots, robot house, pet robots and humanoid robots (Guzdial, 2015).

Similarly, the extent of robotic unit applications may be quite broad, including though not restricted to communication and play robots, rescue robots and transportation robots among others. Ultimately, robotic systems should address the technological fields including matters of different complexities like hardware management, intelligent algorithms, data processing and dispatching, security, reliability and so on.

Many experts agree that modularization of robots and calibration of robotic technology modules can greatly help moderate the creation and integration rate of robotic structures. As such, efforts are being made towards future regulation efforts in the fields of interoperability and reusability of robotics systems (Guzdial, 2015).

3.5.1. Key Components of Robotic Systems

Manipulator: Same as a human arm, robots have a manipulator with multiple joints and links. As the name suggests, this device is applied to manipulate objects without actual physical interaction by the controller. The manipulator was originally applied for handling biohazardous materials, through the use of robotic arms, or for reaching otherwise inaccessible places (Donohue, 2014).

Robotic manipulators may be subdivided into two parts, each playing a different role, which are the Body and Robot Arm. Both of these are applied to transport and set up parts or objects within a working site. They are built from three joints fused together by large links. Most robot manipulators are developed from a series of attachments which fuse the axes or joints. These axes are the flexible parts of robotic manipulators, which cause comparative motion between adjacent links.

The mechanical parts used to develop the robotic arm adjuster comprise of 5 primary forms. A pair of the intersections are linear, whereby the virtual motion between adjoining links is non-rotational, while three are rotary forms, in which the virtual motion comprises of rotation between links. Likewise, the arm-and-body segment of robotic manipulators is centered on different configurations. Every anatomy provides a unique work casing and is suitable for varying applications (Donohue, 2014).

End effectors: In robotics, the End effector is an appliance that's linked to the edge of a robotic arm, where otherwise the hand should be. This component is the section of the robot which directly interacts with the ecosystem. The configuration of end effectors and the form of programming and firmware that runs it relies on the work the robot shall be performing.

The bottom of the manipulator usually is attached to bottom support, while at its other open end, the End effector would be attached. This End effector is required to perform roles normally done by the hand and finger systems of a typical human arm (Donohue, 2014).

Also referred to as End-of-the-Arm Tooling, these devices are intended to be used as robot wrists which manipulate the surroundings. In robotics, arm can perform only certain roles without changes to the end effectors' auxiliary hardware or programming. In case a robot wants to pick an object up, a special kind of robot hand known as the gripper is a highly practical end effector. In case a robot should be able to fasten screws, nevertheless, then the robot should be fixed with an end-effectors which can spin.

The Locomotion Part: For The power for movement of arms, palms and the fingers are delivered by muscles. In case of robots, the ability to move or locomotion is delivered by the motors. These motors which are used for promoting movement in robots are available in three forms based on the energy source, which are Hydraulic, Electric or Pneumatic.

For a robotic equipment to traverse through different geographical landscapes, a platform with multi-terrain maneuvering function is needed. There are various forms of designs accessible in the markets that make the robotic appliance capable of maneuvering through multiple terrains, though their proficiency and performance is often a challenge because of variances in design arrangement for varying natural landscapes. The legged movement in hilly regions is preferred in recent times, though the structural framework and energy efficacy is typically a challenge (Blake, 2009).

Robot locomotion is among the most significant roles of the robotic appliances, which helps the unit in passing through rough terrain; handling and interacting in real human settings. Even though wheeled movement is more common, secure, power efficient and highly controllable, still there are other movement alternatives available like bi-pedal, track belt, sliding and other forms.

- Two-legged or Biped Robot: Commonly known as Humanoids, they are among the most popular robots to be released during the past decade. There are various examples available, from which the most renowned and successful robot is the acclaimed HONDA ASIMO. This is a humanoid machine, measuring 130 cm in height and weighing roughly 50 kg. On average, this biped robot has a walking pace of roughly 2.7 KPH, and running pace of 7 KPH. It uses a TOPIO 3.0 processor and is further fitted with artificial neural networks, and the camera operating at a speed of 200-fps (frames per second).

- Three-legged or Tripod Robot: The three-legged or tripod robot isn't common since they generally don't have biological counterparts. Researchers from the Romela Lab have built a Self-running tripedal vibrant experimental robot called STriDER. This particular tripped robot has two legs that act as stance, whereas the third one works like a swing. The robot's stability comes from its distinctive model of actuated passive flexible locomotion, plus it can also shift its path while walking.

The Sensors: Sensors are another part of robots which are used to feel and measure the symmetrical and physical properties of items in their surrounding areas, such as position, alignment, velocity, speed, distance, size, impact, temperature, radiance and weight. Overall, sensors are categorized into two groups which are internal and external sensors. The inward sensors include position, velocity and acceleration sensors which acquire data about the machine itself, whereas external sensors include cameras, direction sensors, force and proximity sensors which gather information about the surrounding environment.

Chapter 4

Pedagogical Dimensions for Successful Early Childhood Computer Science Education Programs

CONTENTS

4.1. Introduction..76
4.2. Powerful Ideas 76
4.3. Expressiveness 79
4.4. Low-Floor/High Ceiling 82
4.5. Debugging...85
4.6. Social And Emotional Learning 88
4.7. Guiding Principles For Use Of Technology With Early Learners.........91

4.1. INTRODUCTION

Introducing computer science to young children is a very important activity. This can be done through enrolling children in early technological education programs that include computer science lessons. This chapter provides vital information on successfully childhood computer science education programs.

4.2. POWERFUL IDEAS

Incorporating computer science-based activities into early childhood curriculum isn't a departure from conventional norms of developmentally suitable practice. Instead, computer science (CS) promotes play-based pedagogy, supports what teachers are already doing in the classrooms, and guides young students to identify, name, and identify how programming shapes their world. Through this early computer science exposure, kids can be prepared for the wider K–12 frameworks later on. CS is suitable for early childhood schooling as it provides a learning environment whereby youngsters can learn useful skills while playing (Guzdial, 2015).

4.2.1. Onset of Computer Science in Schools

Most high schools in the US and Canada began offering computer science courses as early as during the 1960s, though they remained scarce well into the late 80s. These machines were largely focused on upfront business applications like basic data processing and bookkeeping. By modern standards, these early classes may be categorized as computer literacy—or subjects concentrated on doing basic tasks. Nevertheless, beginning from the mid-70s, as state funding to colleges increased, computer science courses thrived across campuses, therefore pushing up demand for secondary school curriculum up to the elementary level.

4.2.2. Powerful Ideas in Pre-K CS

The K–12 CS Framework derives ideas from Seymour-Papert's "powerful ideas" in articulating certain computer science ideas and activities for the K–12 school environment. Generally, four powerful concepts are captured within the central content fields of mathematics, literacy, and science, including the fifth—which is social and emotional knowledge—simply understood as a wholesome frame for every early childhood learning practice. Additionally, these powerful notions are covered by the pedagogical foundation of early schooling environments. The five ideas are mentioned below and present CS as a normal extension that develops upon what teachers are already doing in their day-to-day practice.

- Social and emotional knowledge: Kids usually develop group and emotional abilities through playful contacts with peers and grownups, besides research continually indicates these interactions may have considerable impacts on kids' learning and development milestones. The solid affective, behavioral, and mental competencies that come with socio-emotional learning offer the foundation for effective learning and growth. Within the CS classroom, students are taught how to work and interact with others through different perspectives. Instructors can foster a comprehensive computing setup by giving opportunities for learners to share, cooperate, and support each other. The best products are developed by teams comprising of members with various backgrounds who take heed to and respect each other's opinions. Furthermore, computer science entails more than simply creating objects; it further involves efficient communication through verbal and visual cues which are built through classroom interactions.
- Patterns: Patterns assist us in making sense of the surrounding world by forming objects and information through common features such as color, shape and size. In CS, patterns allow students to lessen complexity by simplifying and applying answers to multiple situations. Knowledge on patterns during the early years may establish a basis for developing and applying abstractions, for instance, defining and naming procedures, resolving computational problems more efficiently, and make inferences like using models and replicas to draw out conclusions. Among the key aspects of forming and applying abstractions is the capacity to classify items and recognize general attributes centered on those categories, or "abstract" out rather general patterns for describing the categorizations.
- Problem-solving: Young kids naturally participate in problem-solving practices in their day to day lives while exploring and interacting with their surrounding world. Tutors can assist in making problem-solving "popular" by asking questions for

uncovering children's thinking and reasoning processes, plus offering structured techniques to scaffold kids' problem-solving. One such technique is the iterative learning process. It involves detecting a problem; formulating and testing solutions; assessing the results; and reviewing and redoing in order to get the best solution. For some part, computer science can be described as the detection of glitches, problem-solving processes, and finding solutions which result from these processes. Participating in problem-solving activities from the onset can help students set the basis for recognizing and describing computational problems, participating in testing and improvement strategies, and building and assessing computational solutions to real-life problems.

- Representation: Any dialect that features a print edition is a good example of how dialects can be represented. For the situation with English, the dialect is represented by certain words or word structures, which symbolize sounds and meanings. Likewise, computational languages are signified by integers, text, and symbols. Learning representation in the initial school years can develop a basis for understanding how PCs represent data and mimic the behavior of objects, these aspects both important for creating and using abstractions. Furthermore, the development of computational artifacts entails making simulations and visualizations which require a comprehension of how PCs represent data, plus effective communication around computing includes presenting data through visual representations, such as storyboards and graphs.
- Sequencing: Kids often learn about sequencing through formative literacy and math classes. For instance, youngsters learn that stories oftentimes follow a structure of beginning, middle and end. Likewise, sequencing is monitored through ordinal numbers which are first, second, third, including size and magnitude which vary from the least to largest. In CS, sequencing is a vital basis for algorithms that are accurate sets of instructions which computers follow to realize a specific task. It's essential that users give guidelines in the correct sequence, since computers do precisely what they are preset to do. In case the instructions aren't well sequenced, then it means the algorithm won't attain the desired result.

Understanding sequencing in the initial schooling years can develop a basis for learning either of the 5 core models of the computing framework mentioned above. Furthermore, Algorithms and Programming—which are key concepts in abstraction, computational problem-solving and artifact building can be nurtured through sequencing.

When integrated into the classroom setting, computers can be bearers of creativity and powerful ideas, which shall prove useful for the youngster's future career development. In the 21st century, computers will be applicable in almost every aspect of society, and therefore it's advisable for parents and teachers to give youngsters a head-start by exposing them to these machines early in their lives.

4.3. EXPRESSIVENESS

In computer programming, children can learn that there's a great need for preserving strong communication skills, since the task of computer coding isn't only restricted to programming but also handling various situations effectively. For instance, it could happen that one student is stuck in solving a programming problem, and requires assistance from others in order to resolve that particular situation. This way students can learn teamwork, while finding a solution at the same time.

Furthermore, there could be a requirement for conveying development in the coding procedure, or including various other options or accounts to the existing structure. Moreover, the corresponding development might be a cause for bringing changes accordingly, thus that the system may meet the requirements arising from different programming issues or suggestions. For whichever reason, both oral and text communications skills are essential. When learning computer programming, students must understand the problems and relevant issues so as to offer help and assistance in a form as required. This helps in encouraging cognitive skills and critical thinking abilities among learners (Guzdial, 2015).

Critical thinking refers to the capacity to select a belief or activity in a clear yet balanced way. It encourages creative problem-solving, develops self-expression, and promotes cognitive flexibility. It's believed that coding and computing is among the best tools for teaching critical reasoning with a real, physical-world approach.

Similarly, software development entails various stages, including, investigation, inquiry, design, construction, operation and maintenance. For the activities relating to each phase to be effective, all the main players involved in the project must maintain effective communication, which is what ultimately leads to the projected success.

While studying CS, kids will learn the significance of having solid communication skills which can't be underestimated. Good communication is a practical way of performing various duties and responsibilities effectively. It allows computer programmers to interact with computers which helps them stand out in the modern-day job environment. Additionally, early programming further enables students to enhance their experience levels ultimately promoting professional development in this field if they would want to pursue it later on in life (Guzdial, 2015).

Yet another benefit is that students learn to react to different situations appropriately and communicate even complex messages without generating conflict or diminishing the trust of other peers.

Other ways computer-science promote expressiveness among students:

4.3.1. It Can Be Used to Share Personal Ideas

Recent studies reveal that using computer technology can motivate imagination and promote creativity, especially in the classroom. For instance, social media apps and online platforms provide students with an outlet for sharing project ideas and fostering opportunities for mutual collaboration, interaction, and response from their peers. With the Internet, pupils are now writing frequently outside the classroom plus are able to freely share their projects with a wider, more diverse audience. As a result, they grow more self-assured in not just their writing skills, but also their thoughts and opinions.

4.3.2. Promotes Artistic Expression

New technological inventions like gesture control now allow creative authors to add computing devices to their list of art supplies. For instance, the Intel Real Sense app shall soon make it practical for users to open apps directly from their laptop or tablet, make drawings in virtual space using bare hands, and get the results directly on their screens. Through this app, students can easily channel their inner artistic side. Additionally, if a student's preferred medium of expression is photography, computer technology can provide a boost in this field as well. A program like Intel Real Sense photo utilizes three different lenses to snap your pictures. This depth-sensing permits you to adjust the angle of your photos following the snapshot, switching the photo's viewpoint, or adjusting coats of color. From one shot, you can produce a series of images to reveal your personal perspective (Hazzan, Lapidot, & Ragonis, 2011).

4.3.3. Expression of Style

Long gone are the years when putting wearable technology meant bulky watches, wristbands, and odd glasses. Technology companies are currently teaming up with designers to develop wearable's which value both style and function, therefore, students can remain connected while displaying their individual style. Recently, Intel released MICA (My Intelligent Communication Appliance), in conjunction with Opening Ceremony. Made with deluxe finishes such as sapphire glass, these smart computing devices can perform functions like syncing your calendar, texts, notices, and more. However, since they look more of a jewelry than a technological innovation, students who use them will be able to convey their personal style as well.

4.3.4. Communicating With the Computer

It may initially sound like science-fiction, but indeed new technology is allowing people to communicate with their devices instantly, without using a mouse or keyboard. Three-dimensional cameras fixed in your computer can monitor facial movements, meaning your device can essentially understand your emotions. With just a basic smile or frown, children can express their love for an app they're using or express frustration with the instructions that they're reading and so on. The computer will then adjust accordingly to capture the expressed feeling.

4.3.5. Making of Music

For students who are into music, technology makes it conceivable to express themselves through sound without having to be good at piano or vocals. This is possible via two ways. First, there are simple-to-use apps and software to help learners compose songs of their own. Second, the computer's gesture regulation functions also make it practical to play a musical instrument without necessarily having to take a lesson. Equally, inventions in headphone technology now allow users to listen to their favorite mood-setting tune anytime, anywhere—plus with no cables or charging involved. Older students can synchronize their headphones together with a fitness tracker in order to stay in-tune with your body health needs. In addition, CS technology makes it possible for students with cognitive and physical incapacities to connect with their surroundings in ways which hadn't previously been imaginable. Recent research has found that portable technologies increase communication, social, and mechanical skills for students on the autism scale. In particular, digital storytelling and individual-centered projects inspire youngsters with autism to showcase their thoughts, ideas and talents just like other normal children.

4.4. LOW-FLOOR/HIGH CEILING

Computer science education has lately been getting lots of attention from government departments. Various institutions like the Information Technology Advise Committee, and Association for Computing Mechanism have been formed to promote the strength of existing educational activities in computer science. For the greater part, most of what computer-science was a few years ago is still the anchor of what constitutes it now, with terms like bytes, bits, Pascal and Assembler still being popular (Blake, 2009).

Nevertheless, computational concepts may still be taught nowadays in a much simpler way by applying the latest introductory tools for computer learning, built by remarkable research institutes like Massachusetts Institute of Technology (MIT). Some of these tools concentrate on the creative ability behind computation by reducing the minimum level which allows learners to get remarkable results. In addition, interesting visualization products have also been developed recently to assist students in comprehending some of the complex aspects of computational science like algorithms.

4.4.1. Scratch: Programming Environment for Learners

The programming system of Scratch certainly is essential young students. Any non-programmer may begin coding Scratch without even realizing that programming is happening. The user platform of Scratch is simple: essential menus and only a few icons. Nevertheless, all the significant aspects are visible: from the cat sprite at the podium on the right-hand corner, to a collection of shaded slabs on the left-hand corner.

Figure 4.1. Scratch is a fun and engaging way for students to learn programming.

Source: https://www.udemy.com/course/programming-for-kids/.

It's normal to try and choose one of the shaded slabs and check that the result of what's written on the slab immediately relocates to the stage sprite. All the slabs are noticeable in the left panel, neatly arranged in logic classes such as movement, look, pen, sound, control, sensing, variables and operators, with each recognized by a different shade (Blake, 2009).

Another factor that makes Scratch great is its capacity to model every "instruction" or colored slab in a rather natural wording, which makes it easier for students to understand such as "adjust score by 1," "go 10 steps," and "direct towards mouse-pointer." Students don't need to recognize in advance the coding dialect or its syntax. Every block indeed is accessible in the block depository on the left-hand direction. The way that blocks can merge together is reserved by their contexts: only when the white halo shows around an open slot can the dragged block attach onto the other blocks. This, in turn, prevents syntax errors.

Therefore, students just have to pay close attention to the semantic meaning of whichever activity they're doing. Moreover, a Multilanguage Programming Dialect Scratch, the semantic and the user-face, is available in a total of 50 different dialects spoken globally, reducing the benchmark for non-English talking individuals, who typically must learn a foreign dialect like English while also learning a new, official way of conveying their knowledge (Blake, 2009).

The above-discussed features considerably lower the floor, with regards to base knowledge, which a non-programmer must reach when faced with programming: plus only minimal knowledge is required to get the desired results, in comparison to typical programming languages. Various problems like unknown formalism, syntactic errors, awkward syntax and unknown user interface can easily be avoided through thoughtful design.

Furthermore, variables, which are among the most complex elements of coding languages, are typically not required in Scratch. The general sprite properties such as position, direction, size, costume and volume of sprite's "voice" are largely available as "monitors," circular blocks whose values may be immediately displayed on the stage through clicking their checkboxes. As mentioned above, the format of the guidelines of the Scratch coding language (Scratch blocks) is indicative of the form of Lego slabs. Scratch is a useful drag-and-drop coding language that can be used by students of any age (Khine, 2018).

The blocks may be snapped together through dragging and dropping objects on the middle grey area, the "Script" zone. The script zone is where Scratch coders develop their projects. Scratch's sprites are generally like actors which perform on the stage through following the scripts availed by the programmer. To operate the scripts, it's necessary to click upon them or choose the green flag icon at the upper right side of the Scratch frame. With a Reasonably High Ceiling in spite its basic interface, Scratch may be applied to develop various interesting projects very effortlessly.

Even if Scratch didn't have 3D capacity and the pace of its transcription is slow, with an embedded photo editor, a webcam capturing tool, sound recorder, and possibility of merging projects over meshes, for sending to and receiving texts from other sprites, it still makes a flexible learning app for computer science learners. Another interesting feature of the Scratch app is that it's inspiring to learners who have the opportunity of publishing its projects concerning the Scratch website only by choosing the "Share the project" button found at the top left side of Scratch's interface. Projects are thereafter immediately usable virtually inside the Java applet, or even in form of a versatile Flash application (Khine, 2018).

As of now, Scratch 2.0's future is believed to be in the mobile world. Moreover, the outstanding port to iPhone, new programming system and player are being presently fully rewritten in Flash. Besides, new editions of Scratch executed in JavaScript plus for the Android OS and Nintendo DSi appliances are presently under development. Being programmed to help individuals to get accustomed to computational ideas, Scratch inventors have ensured the Scratch dialect is as basic as conceivable on purpose. Therefore, lots of interesting factors that may be done by applying the extraordinary Scratch user face are scarce.

Even though Scratch doesn't have the capacity to describe new blocks, read or write files, in order to gain full control of the components of the tool. It's still a reliable tool for teaching youngsters programming skills, catalogs and string elements have further been included into Scratch recently to make it more versatile. Besides, Scratch is an open source, meaning its language and tool may be improved by skilled programmers from Smalltalk, the coding language applied by Scratch's inventors. This has caused the formation of a whole range of Scratch extensions, known as "mods," which offer Scratch coders a lot of varying features (Khine, 2018).

4.5. DEBUGGING

A great part of knowing to program is "debugging", which stands for finding and fixing errors in the code developed so that it operates as preferred. Debugging is testing. It needs patience, diligence and a nearly scientific methodology—skills that aren't simple to impart in only one class. Debugging is especially challenging for youngsters who are inspired by the ultimate product, like a game. They frequently don't observe the transitional debugging phase as an opportunity for learning; they simply want to remove the bug and carry on!

It's also not simple to teach, either. Therefore, requiring teachers to be at their ultimate best. Instructors must use the appropriate ratio of scaffolding to prod learners from waiting for the solution, to fixing the problem on their own.

Debugging is fundamentally a problem-solving skill, since students often debug when the software isn't working. Regardless of how proficient a person is in programming; they will always encounter situations where the code isn't performing what they want. As a matter of fact, almost by design, the initial run of a program fails to work, plus it takes several repetitions of debugging to eventually get the functioning codes (Khine, 2018).

It's essential for children to understand that debugging is a vital component of coding. It typically requires more time to debug than even writing codes from scratch. The process can be tiresome and therefore requires patience and strong critical-reasoning ability from learners.

4.5.1. Procedures for Debugging

Stage 1: Typically, the initial step in searching for "bugs," is looking for typos. In most real coding, it's quite common to see a learner miss a semicolon, closing quotation mark, or even misspell a particular word. Typos are a common error in coding that can open doors for bugs to enter your computer.

As a teacher, you can request students to figure out the typo mistakes then correct them. It's significant to ask youngsters if they have done similar faults themselves. This shall help them realize making mistakes in programming is quite common, and great programmers are those who are proficient at finding mistakes, fixing errors, and solving problems (König, 2012).

Stage 2: If after fixing the typos the system still isn't working, then it's advisable to check the code by sections. It's yet another reason as to why it's significant to subdivide a large chore into smaller bits. Upon arriving at some well-defined steps, where you recognize what the finish point of every step is, you may need to check up each step individually. When, after running the code for the first step, the finish point of your initial step isn't what's expected, you will know there are errors in the initial step. However, if the finish point of the initial stage is what's anticipated, but the finish point of the second step isn't, it means then that the errors are in second step (König, 2012).

An example of a programming game that can be used to train kids on bug detection is Morning Routine. Here, the child is expected to use a digital figure to visit the bathroom, wash their hands, brush the teeth and return back to the bedroom. If any step is missed during this process then the kid can't perform the next phase, which is getting dressed.

As can be seen, the main checking stops are the End Points of every step. By going through this process, they'll be able to detect the portion of the code which contains errors, then concentrate on examining that particular part, plus rectify the mistake once they discover it. For activities such as these, students can be presented with a set of accurate codes as reference.

Stage 3: After fixing the problematic bugs, you should next re-run the code to see whether it functions this time. If this works, great. But if it doesn't, then the student should return back to Debugging in Step 1. Ultimately, there is a lot to learn if one wants to become good at debugging. For youngsters, the goal is realizing that coding isn't an activity which you perform once and assume it to work well straight away. Inspection and debugging are crucial parts of coding. Even if the program isn't performing as anticipated, just remain cool, since it is normal for programs to act this way. In case this happens, all you need to do is simply commence the debugging process.

Oftentimes, teachers are ready to step-in and provide help but this isn't recommended since it discourages personal growth and learning. After all, it's not just the students who need a quick fix; instructors want to provide the solution too so that they can carry on to the subsequent concept or program. Usually, class-time is restricted and there are additional lessons to be completed (König, 2012).

For teachers with a whole class load, it is easier to rush by and swiftly assist those that are stuck. Nevertheless, this isn't just the wrong method; it's impossible to execute. Every learner can have a particular bug and fixing every one individually may take time, that's limited to say the least. Most significantly, teachers lose the chance for the pupil to learn how to code independently by directly intervening.

Among the solutions is encouraging struggling pupils to get assistance from other students. This, however, still has its own pitfalls. Depending on classmates to provide the answer can create a dependency association. Peers aren't skilled teachers and therefore won't give hints, describe or train on the debugging process. Instead, they will simply give the imagined solution, or directly fix it before going back to their original project (König, 2012).

Experienced instructors can provide the correct amount of help plus use the bug since a teachable moment, possibly clarifying some misinterpreted concept in the procedure. By moving in and providing the correct amount of support, instructors can sensibly manage the learning journey for each pupil. They can lessen frustration among newbie programmers, build confidence and embolden them to go past the current basic programming class to more advanced courses.

Additionally, in the "skill of teaching" CS. There's never one particular answer for all pupils. Some succeed on the debugging test and can continue so for long durations of time, others however, require more time to grasp the concepts (König, 2012).

4.6. SOCIAL AND EMOTIONAL LEARNING

Figure 4.2. Socioemotional learning is a holistic way of learning that can be adapted into schools.

Source: https://blog.shapeamerica.org/2019/06/why-i-integrate-sel-into-my-hpe-classes/.

Social-emotional learning refers to the ability of students to manage their emotions, interact with others, plus apply compassion and understanding to appreciate the needs of peers around them, establish strong relationships and arrive at good decisions. Even though concepts defining socioemotional learning have been changing with time, the term first came into public usage during the early 90s when an organization called CASEL was established, for the purpose of bringing together teachers, psychologists, kid welfare advocates and scientists to promote socio-emotional education in schools. It was also at this pivotal moment that the works of Daniel Goleman's, on the relationship between Emotional Intelligence and IQ, was launched and improved the levels of awareness among scientists, researchers, instructors, and parents (König, 2012).

4.6.1. Application in Real Life

In North America some schools are piloting an innovative computer science initiative where kindergarten learners pass through a set of tools which help them understand computer-programming skills.

The objective is providing students with a number of STEM resources for giving them a solid foundation in CS, and encouraging them to remain in technology-based careers even when they mature. Even though these programs are still in the pilot stage, students can still learn a lot about computing skills. They will be able to learn how to cooperate and develop solid socio-emotional learning, as well as problem-solving abilities (König, 2012).

Nobody really knows what type of jobs modern generation kids will have when they eventually become adults, plus the kind of workforce which would be needed in the future. Nevertheless, it's known that technology shall have a great impact, and it's just going to improve more over time. Based on research from Tufts University, the more exposure kids have to how PCs, programming, and robotics operate, the more prepared they'll be going into the future.

When caregivers express concerns on their kid spending lots of time on technology, they should realize that it's really not about the device, but rather what they're doing with it. For instance, a student can use technology to learn how to recognize patterns, work together and communicate with peers on how to solve problems. They are the skills which help students to develop a solid ground for computational thinking (Beauchamp, 2016).

Machines can help make children more human: While kids are developing valuable computational thinking skills, concurrently they're addressing their socioemotional development. There are many examples of kids who considerably grew socially by using robotics. By sharing the roles of controlling robots with other classmates, students are not only sharpening their computer programming abilities, they're also working on other social skills—such as sharing and collaborating with others—which shall assist them just as notably in the future.

Furthermore, when handling robotics, students often develop some problem-solving skills that contribute towards promoting socio-emotional intelligence. Case in point, if they reach a point in the work where they feel overwhelmed, or things aren't working out the way they would want to, then they can consult with their peers and in this way socio-emotional intelligence is built (König, 2012).

Likewise, students will develop the perseverance and grit for overcoming any obstacles that come their way. For example, in a kindergarten class where teachers provided a hokey-pokey lesson through robotics, where students were introduced to the essentials of robotics and programming. It was found that as student pairs struggled to program the movement they needed to see, they were required to communicate with each other and cooperate on different concepts. Students who show each other ways of adjusting the machine's barcode reader to check the appropriate block, or repeat a scan in case the robot didn't complete the dance correctly eventually develop better rapport with their peers. While some pupils struggled with sharing in their lesson, the levels of collaboration and mutual functioning together developed over time.

Teachers never tire of watching a kid discover something inventive about their world. The laughs of excitement heard after students have successfully coded a robot to perform a particular command never gets old. Early computer science courses show that indeed pupils can build soft skills together with CS skills, eventually becoming active and involved participants of the 21st-century technological world (König, 2012).

4.6.2. How to Foster Socioemotional Learning in School

- *Create intervention programs:* These programs have been applied in middle school, where youngsters enter the classroom with some basic explanation provided by the teacher on kid development and social feedback, in order to work on mid-schoolers' empathy abilities. The programs may have huge successes in getting teenagers to get past their self-entitlement behaviors, and start to think about the society at large. Organizations like CASEL now provide listings of evidence-centered programs on their website, which teachers can use to train socio-emotional skills.
- *Provide affirmative words:* On the typical daily scale, classrooms can encourage good social-emotional abilities by building positive 'rules' and endorsing pro-social behavior. For instance, in a situation where one student is helping the other solve complex problems, as a teacher you can comment that you like how they are supporting each other to find a solution to the problem. This will help promote teamwork and cooperation among the students.
- *Concentrate on process:* By fostering problem-solving, creativity and critical thinking instead of only searching for the correct answer, educators help learners to appreciate that the procedure is equally as vital as the eventual outcome. This is a message which isn't emphasized much in modern-day classrooms, where there normally can be excess focus on uniform test scores.

Despite the grade level, providing materials for promoting social-emotional learning is critical. Early programming books, for instance, can be read out loud by students in class to foster cohesion. Furthermore, teachers are encouraged to welcome their students warmly, making eye contact and direct face-to-face communication as much as possible. Additionally, calling students out by name can help them realize that they're appreciated and seen by others around them. Ultimately, this awareness fosters a culture of compassion and support, while reminding learners that their behavior whether good or bad affects the society in some way. Students will therefore grow to become responsible citizens within the community (König, 2012).

4.7. GUIDING PRINCIPLES FOR USE OF TECHNOLOGY WITH EARLY LEARNERS

Figure 4.3. Young children exposed to technology usually develop interest in science and mathematics subjects when they grow up.

Source: https://www.nytimes.com/2014/09/11/fashion/steve-jobs-apple-was-a-low-tech-parent.html.

The reasonable application of technology by caregivers and early trainers can occupy kids in key abilities like play, individual expression, and computational reasoning which shall support future success across various scholarly disciplines and assist in maintaining young kids' natural curiosity. There's wide-held belief that guidance must reflect the reality which concerns families and early trainers having access to apps, video chatting apps, virtual books, games and various other interactive technologies which can be applied with young kids. Even as fresh technologies emerge, there's still need to regulate how children interact with them (Chao, 2012).

4.7.1. First Principle: When Used Correctly, Technology can be an Instrument for Learning

Age appropriate usage of technology may help youngsters to grow and learn, particularly when families and childhood educators play a key role. Early learners might use technology to discover new worlds, promote belief, and actively engage students in fun and complex activities. The students can learn more on technology and innovation tools and apply them to play, resolve problems, and even role play.

Early trainers should remember the various developmental levels of kids when applying technology for preliminary learning. Meaning, they first must consider what's ideal for vibrant child development, then determine how technology may assist early learners in attaining positive learning outcomes. Ideally, technology shouldn't be employed only for technology's sake, but instead be applied for learning and reaching developmental goals, which can comprise being applied as an implement during play (Chao, 2012).

In situations where technology is applied in early education settings, it must be incorporated into the learning course and applied in rotation together with other learning equipment, such as art supplies, writing materials, play resources, and books. Additionally, it should give pupils a chance for self-expression without substituting other class learning materials.

There are various considerations for teachers to contemplate when technology is applied, like whether a given device can substitute interactions with instructors or peers, or if a device has attributes that can distract from learning. Similarly, early educators must consider the general use of innovation throughout a kid's day and week, plus adhere to suggested policies from Let's Move movement, in close association with families. Furthermore, if a kid is qualified for services as per stipulations of IDEA, Section 504/Title II, they may need particular technology to guarantee that the learner can access the guideline material (Guzdial, 2015).

Same as other educational equipment, school-aged kids must be taught skills on how to accurately handle and maintain technological devices. These abilities and the usage of technology must generally not be imparted as a different rotation or class, instead incorporated into the learning goal of the lesson. For some cases, nevertheless, individualized instruction can be applied for meeting the particular needs of a kid. As youngsters grow older, they must continue building on this basic ability with courses in digital citizenship.

4.7.2. Second Principle: Technology Must Be Applied to Promote Access to Education Opportunities for All Youngsters

If correctly used by children, technology can supplement or promote learning in methods not easily attained otherwise. For instance, technology can introduce kids more openly to cultures and environments outside their community. While youngsters might have access to various print amenities from libraries, still technology can improve the quantity of reference information directly accessible to them on any given topic, plus provide them the room to ask questions regarding people out of the class setting. Moreover, within a youngster's own community, technology must be culturally responsive (Beauchamp, 2016).

Kids themselves might be inspired to participate in generating this content. Technology may help kids fashion their own materials plus stories, and even share real-life encounters with others, growing the ratio of diverse, culturally significant, and community-based material in the classroom. Moreover, for low-income kids who don't have easy access to instruments or the web at home, preliminary childhood education can offer opportunities for students to learn ways of using available tools more actively (Beauchamp, 2016).

4.7.3. Third Principle: Technology Should Be Applied to Reinforce Relationships among Families, Caregivers, Early Instructors, and Young Children

Technology may be applied to build up relationships between childhood teachers and family members. Case in point, digital content documenting student progress through pictures, audio, and video tapes allow instructors to share what kids are learning within the classroom with families regularly and more casually than is imaginable in conventional school-based conferences.

Technology allows caregivers to track their kid's progress in school, provides increased opportunities for teachers to validate their kid's efforts and achievements, and opens up doors for the caregivers to engage their youngster concerning the learning in order to emphasize or supplement it. Apart from using e-mail, texting and social media for driving communication between teachers and families, technology may also be applied to avail information and training to caregivers in order to strengthen at home what's learned in school (Willmann, 2017).

In addition, it can be applied to improve relationships between kids and adults, or between youngsters when distance and other obstacles like health inhibit in-person interaction. Although video chatting may be performed at any age, fresh evidence reveals that infants and children may attend to and participate in joint communications during video-chat talks, but perform so more efficiently after about one and a half years of age plus with parental support.

Additionally, video chatting isn't limited to connections between caregivers and kids or grandparents and their children, though it's also useful when youngsters communicate with peers. Even though technology has the ability to close the physical rift between kids and dear ones in the methods described, it shouldn't be applied to substitute meaningful face-to-face communications (Willmann, 2017).

4.7.4. Fourth Principle: Technology Becomes More Impactful for Learning When Grownups and Peers Cooperate or Co-View with the Youngsters

Majority of research available on kids' media usage reveals that kids absorb more from content in case their caregivers or early educators observe and interact with the children, inspiring them to make practical connections regarding what they're viewing both when they're watching and afterward.

Although technology like tablets and smartphones have been formed to be hand-held and avail themselves to personalized rather than shared experiences, youngsters may benefit immensely when caregivers are actively engaged while kids use such devices. Adults are advised to always supervise the technology their kids are using to ensure it's beneficial for them (Willmann, 2017).

Chapter 5

Successful Technology Integration in Early Childhood Education

CONTENTS

5.1. Introduction 96

5.2. The Importance Of Technology Integration In an Early Childhood Education 96

5.3. Types Of Technology Integration 103

5.4. Ways To Integrate Technology Into Your Classroom 124

5.5. Frameworks For Technology Integration 132

5.6. Factors Influencing Integration Of Computer-Based Technologies In Early Childhood 136

5.1. INTRODUCTION

Technology is applying scientific knowledge especially in a particular area either in industries or our daily lives or a set of tools that help make work easier for solving problems.

To integrate technology into our day-to-day lives, we can combine many things into one concept. As a result, technology integration is the applying of technology in a certain field to yield positive results. Contextually, technology integration in early childhood education has allowed students to apply computer and technology in learning and problem-solving specifically though the use of technology tools. These technology tools include an overhead projector and PowerPoint presentations, internet, stimulators, graphing calculator software and geometer's sketchpad (Donohue, 2014).

Steps of effective technology integration include getting to know if the technology being integrated has advantages that will affect learning process positively. Next, you determine the objective of the technology being integrated by asking yourself what will the students be able to achieve at the end. You then design instructional strategies by keeping in mind the students' readiness alongside their physical and affective needs. Ensure that the learning environment is suitable for new technology for example availability of power if the technology requires it. After the technology has been integrated you analyze to ensure that positive results are being achieved.

Integrating technology gives students a better understanding of broad topics but they require constant maintenance and repair and infrastructure. The importance of technology integration includes an increase in academic skills, reduced school dropout rates, eliminate racial divide in academic performance, increase SAT scores and making the lives of teachers' easier. These advantages will be discussed below:

5.2. THE IMPORTANCE OF TECHNOLOGY INTEGRATION IN AN EARLY CHILDHOOD EDUCATION

5.2.1. Increase in Academic Skills

Academic skills are a collection of study habits, learning strategies and time management skills. Technology has increased academic skills in various ways:

- Technology presents subject material in a simplified format that students can easily comprehend some core subjects like mathematics, sciences and reading. According to Garcia and Rose, (2007), computer technology created collaborative learning opportunities.
- Students who use technology in their studies are known to perform better than the ones who have little knowledge of technology. Technology enables students to research areas where they do not understand perfectly. It also enables the students to save time on their research since they can get information faster unlike when they have to research without technology (Donohue, 2014).
- It has been proven that computer-based applications like visualization, modeling, and simulation are powerful tools for teaching scientific concepts. When these concepts are integrated study becomes clear and better understanding is achieved.
- The use of technology also enabled students to understand rather than getting the main point or basic concept in the study. The student can visualize and come up with a picture and hence can easily recall without difficulty.
- In the olden times teaching of mathematics, students were required to apply basic knowledge like multiplication, division, subtraction and addition however, nowadays people use mathematical skills to reason about uncertainty. Using technology to prove if an equation is correct is faster than writing on paper.
- Technology can also be seen in the area of language arts by application of literacy programs and word progressing systems. When one is writing a report or an assignment using technology like the computer can spot errors of spelling or punctuation hence elimination of errors. Also, the computer counts the number of words one has written to prevent undersized essays.
- Technology gives students a wide scope of information as they can access virtual libraries and obtain information that the school may lack.
- Communicating through the internet or emailing also improves on the language and language skills of the students.
- Technology integration makes learning interesting to the student as the use of the computers not only provide information about any topic but they develop an interest of the students to learn more.

- Students can access revision material which assists them in their study unlike reading books only. In places where revision material may not be offered, students can browse for these materials and acquire them easily. They can also work out online tests to improve their understanding.
- Students improve on their ability to pronounce words correctly and improve their spellings when browsing since the browser offers spellings and pronunciation of words. This enables students to be more eloquent when delivering their work and be accurate hence improving their academic performance.
- Students can improve their thinking capacity and skills hence allowing them to use real-world situations to solve problems due to technology integration. This is because they are opened to a large scope of information hence, they are not limited to a little information.
- We, therefore, see that technology integration brings about positive results in improving the academic skills of the students.

5.2.2. Reduce Dropout Rates

School dropouts have been experienced over the past few years at very high rates. Challenges that bring about school dropouts are often systemic and will take a collision of teachers, school leaders' political leaders, parents and many more.

Among the many ways to curb school dropouts is the use of technology. In our current world children are addicted to their mobile phones and other devices and instead of battling with them to put them away they can be used to help reduce school dropouts.

Educational technologies are the use of both physical hardware and software to facilitate learning. EdTech products have been formed on this account. These EdTech products include,

CLASS DOJO: It is a classroom behavior app that assists teachers to keep track of positive and negative behaviors for each student. It was founded in August 2011 in San Francisco, California. It allows students, teachers, and parents to connect support and develop skills. The teacher can track positive and negative behaviors for each student. Teachers first register to obtain a free account and then create "classes" with their students. Also, merits and demerits are given to ensure that students maintain their morals. Merits are the good things that are done while demerits are the negative things that are done. When the students perform a good task, they are awarded merits and if they do something wrong, they are awarded demerits. This enables the teachers and parents to help their students with issues on disciplinary affairs (Willmann, 2017).

HERO K12: It is a student behavior management application that rethinks traditional behavior and discipline policies building programs that positively recognize students. Their main goal is to recognize the students that do-good deeds or those who show positive behavior. It was founded by BV investment partners on October 30th, 2017. It is a powerful app and can be described as transformative. It encourages kids to attend school when they realize they have a voice which can be heard.

ISTUDIEZ: It is an award-winning app that enables students to remain focused on their goals and organized. Students can track their grades assignments and classes. This app mainly assists those children who are working to support their families and may drop out so that they can focus on one thing, it enables them to keep track of their lessons as they work. For the students who are not working it enables them to experience education as fun and in case they do not understand a certain concept, they can go back and review. It should be noted that it became a free app to download and is still a free app up to date. Many students use this application and they have proven to show positive results. These applications affect not only the students but also the teachers and parents. It makes learning an interesting process interesting, improves the behavior of students and enables parents and teachers to keep track of the students' general performance. Improvements in technology are still being carried out to ensure as many students as possible remain in school and hence reduce school dropouts.

5.2.3. Eliminate the Racial Divide in Academic Performance

Several efforts have been made to address racism. Racism is simply bigotry and prejudice. It has different levels and implies that a certain group of people is superior to another. The source of racial divide is an unconscious limited condition of a society who determines who is right and who is wrong by looking only in the physical based on whatever views and ideas we have been brought up to accept without questioning.

The most effective way of curbing and maintaining adequate racial diversity is to use a large racial preference to admit a great number of black and brown students than would get in based on how they perform. The black academic achievement is very low and disappointing and it is far behind one of Asian Americans' and whites. Racial gaps make it hard to improve in how the blacks perform thus the solution is a racial preference in college achievement (Willmann, 2017).

The racial divide in technology is caused by relatively low rates of internet, especially in African America and Latinos.

In the olden days, the racial divide was prominent in academic performance such that students learning in African or Asian continents lagged than those in the other continents. It has been proven that proper use of technology by students increases their academic performance outcomes. The ability to have technology is highly dependent on socio-economic factors

The use of technology in teaching and learning is dated long ago in the American history of education. It is dated as early as the 1970s before the invention of the first personal computers. Research has proven that the use of this technology improved the academic results significantly (Willmann, 2017).

The digital divide has been eliminated by technology in the following ways:

- Students are most likely to have access to a computer either at home or at school and access to internet services hence academic improvement has been noticed.
- A white poor child is more likely to have internet access as a black child on the same level hence the growth of academic is fair to all of them.
- A wealthy Asian family is likely to own a computer as a poor black home hence equality in academic results.
- A child from a dual-parent family which is white has internet access as a black child hence reducing racism.
- Therefore, it is proven that the disparities in access to telephones, computers and the internet exists still and has widened significantly.
- Since deeply racialized systems are expensive eliminating racial divide may underpass outcomes and increase life chances for all groups since the use of a systemic approach will enable both white and black to graduate. Also, impropriation in common criminal justice will decrease and voting will be done fairly.

- The aim is not to just eliminate the gap between white people and people of color but to increase the success for all groups goals and results that will result in improvements for all groups in academics hence a worldwide growth.

5.2.4. Increase in SAT Scores

SAT score is the sum of two scores math and evidence-based reading and writing. It has a total of 1600-point scale. Technology as improved learning as it provides a lot of information hence saves students the stress of having to go searching in encyclopedias' hence saving them time. This enables students spare time for extra studies and hence improve their scores (Willmann, 2017).

Technology has helped the teachers though the use of the learning management system to act as a force multiplier. Students can access resources online and hence their study materials increase.

When a student has internet access, they can access revision resources online and also assignments and hence they can keep the pace of their peers in case they are slow. Also, students can have revision material hence they can study more and improve their SAT scores.

For those parents who are extremely busy and lack time to check their children's assignment or even to meet up with the teachers, technology has enabled them to hold meetings online through web conferencing with the teacher and discuss on the performance of the child. They can also keep up with the academic results of the child by viewing the report online hence enables them to encourage their children appropriately. If the parent is far away, he can communicate with his child through emailing or skype and still keep up with the performance of the child (Willmann, 2017).

Technology-based projects enable the students to think and hence improve their memory. These projects inspire them to think and collaborate as opposed to memorizing. it also helps them to know the technology skills hence improve their scores.

Students can access information that may not be found in their school libraries or given by their teachers. This improves their understanding of the topic since everything they need is found on the internet. In case the student did not understand a certain concept in class they still can understand by going through the information on the internet.

Technology has assisted students in their revision as it offers past papers and even answers to the questions so that the student can evaluate themselves. This enables the student to know if the concept they have gained is the actual concept or if they have not yet understood so that they may review once more.

Teachers can also discover resources from the internet that they can incorporate in their teaching and hence the student can gain a better understanding of the topic. The teacher can also be guided on the best way to approach the topic and hence the student gains more from the lesson and his scores are boosted.

Technology has made learning an interesting and fun activity for it can help students learn concepts in a playful, interactive manner. Watching the videos also creates interest and since some videos have been animated it makes learning more enjoyable.

Lastly, technology has improved communication among teachers and students where teachers post assignments to the student, change classrooms, post discussion questions and ask students questions more hence improve the students score.

5.2.5. Makes the Life of Teachers Easier

Teachers are the most important people when it comes to learning. They are the ones who interact more with the students when it comes to academics. They should, therefore, ensure that what they offer the students is of good quality and will make the students get most of what they are taught. For this reason, teachers spend most of their time figuring out the best way to approach a certain topic so that their students can understand. Technology has therefore assisted the teachers immensely in many ways hence making their lives easier (Blake, 2009).

Technology has helped teachers collaborate more with the students through emailing file sharing to document editing. It enables teachers and students to collaborate on projects writing assignment and more.

Teachers can manage the behavior of the students. This is made possible by the introduction of applications like the class dojo or hero K12 that enables teachers to keep track of students' behavior. Teachers give merits and demerits to the students and help ensure the students remain disciplined. This has assisted the teachers because they can learn the behavior of the student faster with the apps than it would take them to know one student at a time.

Technology has enabled parents and teachers to be in constant communication. Teachers send the reports of the students to the parent and the general performance of the child and hence the parent can evaluate the student. They can also hold meetings online and discuss on how to improve the child's performance hence this saves time. In case of the sudden illness of the child, the teacher can contact the parent using the telephone and immediate actions can be taken (Blake, 2009).

Since it is difficult to access and document students' progress, technology has helped the teachers to review the students' progress easily. Through the use of audios and videos, teachers can access the pronunciation of the students. This enables the teachers to understand each child and their capacity hence they can approach each of them correctly.

Technology has enabled teachers to get many resources and information that is beyond their reach. This makes them save on time that they would have spent searching for information. It also helps ensure the teacher has adequate teaching materials and information for their lesson hence makes reading enjoyable and fun.

Lastly, technology has assisted teachers in their planning and preparations for lessons. It provides teachers with alternative ways of approaching a topic and provides them with resources for teaching. This has ensured that teachers deliver the lesson in the most effective way and hence students gain more from the lesson. Technology is, therefore, a great aid when it comes to lesson preparation (Blake, 2009).

5.3. TYPES OF TECHNOLOGY INTEGRATION

Technology integration exists in different types as shown in the following subsections.

5.3.1. Online Learning and Blended Classrooms

Online learning are correspondence courses that are offered over the internet. They are delivered to students through the internet using their computers. Online learning is also called distant learning.

Online learning is of great help to those who are working but studying at the same time. Distance learning helps students organize their time for work and study, therefore, they do not have to drop one class to focus on another. It is accessed via the internet. It can be offered by the school itself or other institutions. Apart from those students who are learning while working, the online study also helps those students who are slow in learning to keep up with their peers and hence perform well too (Blake, 2009).

The main difference between online learning and traditional learning is that online learning does not involve students going to school every day and being present in class. Apart from this, there is no other major difference since the course is the same as the one offered in schools.

Online learning can be given or delivered in a certain way or a combination of all of them. These methods include 100% total online education where the student does not visit the school at any one time but undertakes all his studies in the comfort of his home. The other method is hybrid where it is a combination of online and on-campus learning where the student can undertake both. Another type is the online courses which are certain courses that are taken online on their own to master a certain skill. Finally, there are online courses which are delivered as online classrooms where as many as ten thousand people are in attendance.

No matter the choice of the online method of education used, all of them are very effective and yield good results.The most popular degree courses offered online include business courses, nursing, accounting and early childhood education.Gaining this important skill means that one can study at the comfort of their homes, one can work and study at the same time or stay home with their children. It also brings certain flexibility because it does not limit students to the institutions near their residence. It also saves a lot of time since the students do not have to travel to school and back every day and it enables students to take tests at the most convenient time to them. Apart from this online study also helps students to learn at their own pace hence gain a better understanding and study the career faster (Blake, 2009).

The main challenge of online studying is the lack of one on one interactions of the students and their teachers. It can also breed procrastination and it can be boring to study alone. Hence, a student is limited regarding the possibilities of making new friends.

To solve this problem, solutions to connect students to the peers and teachers have been discovered. These services include online message boards and chat rooms, video conferencing and web-based forums.

To enroll for online studies is very simple as it only involves five easy steps. First, they contact the chosen school, get copies of online transcripts, fill out the college application form then fill out the free application for federal students' aid (FAFSA) form and studies begin (Blake, 2009).

Blended classrooms are those classrooms that use online information as the integral aspect of instructions. It is the combining of e-learning with traditional classroom and independent study to come up with hybrid learning. It can be referred to as hybrid, integrated or mixed. It may include adding computers to the classrooms for study (Blake, 2009).

This method is commonly used as it is very effective and efficient.

Blended classrooms contain three primary components; classroom activities are foreseen by a trained teacher, online learning materials given by the teacher and study time of the students which are guided by the materials provided by the teachers and the skills they gained and experiences.

The facilitators in the blended classrooms have some roles which include,

- Developing both online and offline content of the course, guiding the learning experience of the specific individual students, facilitating communication with and among students and assessing and grading the student just like the teachers do.
- Technology is the main learning tool by students and the major classroom and data management tool by teachers in the blended classrooms.

5.3.2. Project-Based Activities Incorporating Technology

Project-based learning was invented as early as the 1900s. It includes students discovering and choosing a certain topic to study, carrying out extensive research, collecting data, putting data collected and presenting results as reports or poster. This type of assignments is called projects.

It involves posing a challenging question to students mainly about issues affecting the world and the students are required to carry out extensive research and provide solutions to the problem.

Projects hence assist students to think over the issues affecting the world and come up with appropriate solutions to these problems.

Project-based learning is commonly used because it has been identified to promote learning in the following ways;

- It promotes combining of two skills for different subjects such as mathematics and science. It is also known as a cross-curricular approach.

- It also promotes collaboration between the students to each or students and teachers hence ensuring team building and growth of students together as they boost each other.
- It also enables the students to carry out extensive research and undertake a lot of inquiry.
- It encourages the students and motivates them to the learning process as it eliminates boredom and monotony in learning hence making learning a fun process.
- It also enables students to make decisions on their own and choices because they undertake the project on their own without the help of the teachers hence self-directed learning is enabled.
- Projects enable students to discover the best way they understand and gain knowledge and skills.
- It promotes critical thinking because the student is required to analyze, interpret, evaluate and make conclusions on the project.
- It also promotes creative thinking as the students are required to imagine, think and come up with new ideas to solve a problem.
- Lastly, it enables technology integration since projects require students to integrate the use of computers in their research hence technology-based learning is enabled.

In the process of projects, technology is widely used in the following ways:

- To acquire information on the topic. The student uses the internet to acquire a broad array of information about what he is working on.
- To organize the information. The student uses the computer to identify how the information he has acquired flows so that he can arrange it appropriately.
- To demonstrate. In case the project cannot be demonstrated physically due to equipment being unavailable, the student can demonstrate with the aid of the computer by showing videos that were done by people in the past.
- Lastly, it enables the students to present the project. They can present using PowerPoint presentations or printing a piece of hard copy information.

The benefits of using technology in project-based activities include:

- Accommodates different styles of learning.
- Enables students to get information on the project.
- Promotes critical and creative thinking.
- Enables students to present their information in a logical manner.
- Promotes collaboration amongst students.
- Simulates problems that enable students to come up with new ways to solve them.

Ways to integrate technology for effective project-based activities include,

- Training both students and teachers to use of software
- Using whiteboard animated videos to explain certain concepts to students that they may not understand.
- Assigning points to students based on the completion of the course.
- Communicating learner's data to parents, students, and teachers.
- Integrating videos at the end of the lessons to enable the students to understand concepts in greater depth.
- Using the flipped learning system.
- Using the learning management systems for teachers to communicate with the students about the course and send information to their students.

The project-based learning activities include:

Social service and community-based projects which involves students researching on issues affecting the nation, current affairs and finding solutions to these problems. They are given different topics according to the age and level of understanding of the student.

Arts and performance projects which are based around artistic work. In these projects, students can be told to weave a mat or make a mat. It is mainly applied to students in kindergarten and the more complex ones given to the older students.

Integrative learning projects which bring together different skills and assist to improve the performance of the students. Students are required to read extensively about what they learn and write down a summary of their understanding of it.

Project-based learning is a very important skill since everyone could be studying the same skill but by using project-based learning, students can notice their abilities, talents and interests.

5.3.3. Game-Based Learning and Assessment

Game-based learning is the use of educational games to promote the success of the students. Educational games are games that are designed to enable students to understand concepts, acquire skills, improve on language, expand concepts, reinforce development and understand a historical event or culture.

The coming up of kindergarten was based on play in the 19th century. It was based on the fact that kindergarten students could not retain a lot of information therefore they were taught through games.

Game-based learning includes putting children together to compete against each other hence they gain the required motivation to learn, using video games, cards and board games (König, 2012).

Game-based learning enables students to have fun while studying, remove boredom, helps students learn from their mistakes and it motivates them to learn.If a teacher wants to incorporate game-based learning in his lessons he should follow certain steps the first one being, determining why he should use the game-based learning. The teacher should identify the use of adding the game to his lesson. in case the students are facing difficulty in understanding a certain topic the teacher can incorporate a game to boost understanding. Also, if the teacher wants to instill a certain skill like being able to remember things learned, the teacher can use a relevant game-based activity.

The teacher should then do a pre-test of the game to see if it will achieve the desired goals. He should play the game himself to see if it will help the children to obtain the information he wants. It also helps the teacher to be fully prepared for his lesson because he will know exactly what the game entails and how to play it (König, 2012).

The teacher then ensures the game meets the expectation of parents. The use of game-based learning should not be an affair of students and teachers only but the parents should also be engaged. The teacher may send a letter to the parents signaling them about the game-based activity that the students are using so that the parent may also be of help in ensuring that the child gains the required skill from the game. This helps indulge both the parents and teachers in the academic performance of the child.

Next, the teacher should create time during the lesson to play the game with the children. They should include it in their lesson planner as they plan for their lessons. This ensures that the teacher will be able to explain how the game works and how the children can play it. The teacher can also give rules to the game and ensure the children understand what they are supposed to do (König, 2012).

Lastly, the teacher is supposed to access the progress of each of the students as this will help them know the weak areas of the children and hence, they can rectify them appropriately.

Technology is integrated into game-based learning by mainly incorporating video games into the study. Video games are computer games designed to entertain children. Some video games are majorly for entertainment but others can be educational. Some video games can be downloaded and others can be accessed online. Prodigy is an example of a video game that enables the improvement of math up to the eighth grade.

The advantages of game-based learning include:

- Increasing the child's memory capacity. Just as the child can recall how to play the game, they will be able to remember what they are taught.
- Students will be able to know how to operate a computer and hence boosting computer fluency. Living in a world of technology students are required to know how to utilize this technology, using video games, students can know how to use the mouse and the keyboard appropriately.
- Helps students think and find solutions fast since while playing these games, they are required to think very fast of their next move to prevent them from losing.
- It also helps to develop hand and eye coordination since students use both their hands and eyes to play the games.
- Lastly, it helps students build their skills for example map reading since most video games involve adventurous that require the reading of maps to prevent getting lost. Other skills include managing finances and money-making skills. also, children can learn how to save and the advantages of saving.

It is, therefore, necessary for game-based learning to be used but students should be carefully followed up to ensure they do not misuse their time playing these games.

5.3.4. Learning with Mobile and Handheld Devices

This is the use of smartphones and smart devices in learning.

Smartphones provide features which are used can be used in the learning process. These features include video, audio, and multimedia content.

Mobile technology enables students to be able to air their views hence students become engaged in the learning process. A good example is the students' response system where students can air their views about their teachers and hence this enables students to be acknowledged in the learning process (König, 2012).

Learners can communicate fast with the teachers hence giving information and obtaining feedback. Students can access the internet using their mobile phones hence they can research their phones anywhere.

The advantages of mobile phones include, they are portable because of their small sizes; they are also very easy to use hence convenient to any ender and they are affordable as a mobile phone can range as low as five hundred. There are several limitations in using mobile phones which include network problems, wireless communication problems and they are highly prone to theft.

The use of mobile phones for learning has improved learning because; they are easy to be obtained due to their cheap value and they are easily available, unlike the computers which are not easy to obtain hence mobile devices are widely used (König, 2012).

Mobile phones are very easy to use and a student can carry out research easily. One hardly needs a manual to be able to operate a mobile phone hence this makes them efficient.

Mobile phones connect people and hence enables communication through social media platforms.

One can install educational applications on their mobile phones as many software have been developed to assist students in their studies. These apps can enable boost the performance of the students by offering topics of study, revision questions and past papers.

By incorporating mobile phones in education, students can use their devices more beneficially rather than misusing their time doing unbeneficial things with them.

Using your mobile phones one can access the following:

- Students can obtain documents from the internet that enables learning. This saves time since the student does not have to go to the library to obtain these documents. It is also cost-efficient since students do not have to buy their documents.
- Learners can access quizzes and revision questions which enable them to evaluate their understanding of the topic. Most of these questions have the answers hence the student can confirm if they have the right answers.
- Students can also participate in lessons and tutorials. Since the mobile phones have access to the network, students can watch lessons and tutorials that enable them to understand sectors they had not understood. The leads to giving them new understanding if a topic, correcting misinterpretations and ensuring they have a wider view of the topic.
- It also enables the student to present their work for example they can type their work and present it or make a video of the process. This enables students to be able to present information in a logical manner.
- Lastly, students can access audio libraries hence enables them to read more without difficulty.
- The disadvantages of having mobile phones in a classroom include:
- They may distract the children from learning where the students lose concentration as they stare at their mobile phones during class time.
- Students can use mobile phones to cheat during their examinations since they can easily obtain information. This is unfair to the students who use their knowledge during the examination.
- Having mobile phones may promote stealing in schools as students compete to have better than the other students. A student may fail to be contented with his device hence steal another person's mobile phone so that he can have the best phone.
- Having mobile phones may put children at risk and hence make them insecure. This is because students can easily be tracked by thieves and kidnappers through social platforms. Also, they can know the whereabouts of the child hence plan accordingly to invade their premise.

- Lastly, mobile phones have promoted the growth of the gap of social classes among students. It is very easy to spot a rich child from the phone he carries from a poor child. This has created a lack of equality in schools as the rich kids want to be regarded higher than the other children.

To solve these problems, many schools have abolished students having phones in school or have regulated the use of phones in school.

5.3.5. Instructional Tools like Interactive Whiteboards and Student Response Systems

There are many different tools that are normally used in schools so as to help in supporting the teaching and learning of students. These options vary from options with high technology, and those that are traditional. Some of the options include posters, student response systems, posters, whiteboards, 3D printing, etc. One can choose from the options depending on the goals and outcomes that are expected form course learning. Teachers are able to choose from the options so as to improve the learning and teaching experience and environment for the students. Some of them include:

Audience Response System – So as to ensure efficient support of student learning, it is important to have feedback methods that are formative. Using student response systems can help the teachers get feedback on the concepts that the students have been able to understand, in real time. This can also allow the teachers to come up with strategies that make sure that the students maintain classroom engagement, using the course material by manipulating it to be more engaging.

Using Posters in the Classroom – Using posters in the classroom as a tool that promotes a visual aid helps in promoting the learning of students. Using visual aid is supported by cognitive science as it is normally useful. Posters have helped to give students and opportunity to have learning in visual terms, as they also use textbooks and lectures, as well as homework. Students should be asked to create posters as a course project, for the development of research, or even as a presentation to the class.

Use of Note Cards in the Classroom – This is also called an index and it help in supporting student learning in the classroom. They facilitate this by assisting the teachers in gathering names, having knowledge beforehand, misconceptions, etc. Through activities that have been planned in a proper and effective manner, teachers are able to collect feedback that is informative on the progress of the students, so as to promote improving the learning outcomes, and also so that they are able to gather important information about their students.

Open Educational Resources – These include video content, lesson plans, textbooks, modules fo the classroom, and also any other media that can be accessed for the classroom, has undergone licensing, is able to integrated and adapted for the use by students. Open educational resources have helped in providing many new and different approaches to teaching. There are many different open education resources that are available, allowing the teachers to choose from a wide variety, allowing them to look for those that are able to provide more resources, cost efficient, and also be easily adapted by the students.

Using Google Tools for Collaboration – There are tools that are provided by Google such as Docs, Slides and Drives, allowing the students to use collaboration to share and work through content and activities, even when they are researching for their school work, which can promote a healthy and effective learning culture. These tools are able to promote sharing of content, brainstorming and even live video chats.

Utilizing Immediate Feedback Assessment Technique (IF-AT) Scratch Off Forms – These forms are utilized in higher education to help in student engagement in term of assessment. It works like a ticket, where the student is able to choose a question and an answer and he/she is able to scratch off the answer as if it was a lottery ticket, until one gets the right answer. These forms allow the students to finish the lesson and leave the classroom while already aware of the answer to the questions. These forms have been proven to reduce anxiety that is accompanied in tests and exams.

Utilizing 3D Print Models – Teachers in higher education have greatly adopted 3D Printing in their classroom. This allows the students to see features on objects provided by the teachers, that are in 3D. They are also able to view artifacts that have been replicated, that are not accessible to them, as well as art work. They are also able to design their own models. Research has proven that when teachers integrate both verbal and physical learning, it helps in enhancing student learning while also lowering the cognitive loads on the students.

Figure 5.1. Above are some self-balancing 3-D figures that were printed by some students.

Source: https://www.trendhunter.com/amp/trends/3dprinted-models.

Virtual Reality – These help in creating 3D environments that allow one to interact with situations that are real or not real. These help students to interact with an environment that allows them to create in the environment, engage in learning that is considered meaningful, etc.

Use of Applications and Canvas Features – This normally has a variety of features and applications that are used to promote student engagement through different forms of communication, as well as building up the community. It can also help in promoting an inclusive classroom community by using the applications to have discussions that are held online.

Whiteboards and Chalkboards – These are the most common interactive tools used in classrooms. They are considered the easiest mode of visual teaching which helps students learn better. In addition, it helps in brainstorming activities which help students come up with new ideas and also learn in an interactive manner.

Wikipedia and Open Source Writing – This allows students to write and edit on a platform that is public and also digital. This platform aims at reaching an audience. Open source writing helps in developing certain traits in students, including: the ability to appreciate the construction, access and preserving of knowledge, skills for collaboration, etc.

5.3.6. Web-Based Projects, Explorations, and Research

Web projects involve the development and creation of websites, and certain actions in the network that aim at a goal that has been defined initially. This network can be accessed by anyone who would want to access as in the internet, or only for a few specific people as an intranet. Web projects aims at transferring content that is both static and dynamic in a direct manner to those who will use them, and also in an indirect manner through certain specific interfaces.

Web projects are normally based on the technology of Transfer Control Protocol and Internet Protocol. This helps in the transference of content that is either static or dynamic. There are many aspects that play a part in a web project. These include development of the software that accompanies it as well as programming, network administration together with web server, web business, developing and administrating databases, constructing interfaces, management of projects and also ensuring quality, optimization of the search engine, ensuring that the data in the management of the content is maintained (Blake, 2009).

There are a couple of markup languages (e.g. HTML) that can be used to program web projects. Scripting languages such as JavaScript and PHP can also be used. There are also programming languages that are much more complex such as Java which can be used.

When one is hosting a Web Project, they are required to provide the appropriate hardware and software infrastructure, and assure others that they will provide the most effective, efficient, reliable and available service. For people who are interacting with the website, there should be an assurance of high quality that is offered by the graphic design for the web projects. Modern web projects are managed using agile project management, so as to help in responding to any changes that are required by the customers, and any hardships during progression of the project. Project managers are meant to be in charge of making sure that the programming of the project is efficient and oriented on ensuring results.

Figure 5.2. Students are able to do their work on the computer using the help of the internet for research. This makes all the work much easier.

Source: http://thinkonline.smarttutor.com/3-types-of-web-based-instructional-activities-wexamples/.

Researchers are able to collect data using the internet through online research methods. This is also referred to as internet science or web-based methods. Most of these methods that are used to research have a relation to other methods that are already existing but these methods have undergone re-invention and re-imagination in different ways using the developed technology and states that have associations with the internet. These methods of research are still undergoing development and evolutions. There has been the creation of a whole new level of opportunities that is complex, due to the development of social media. Being able to utilize social media to research can help in providing insights that are important when it comes to opinions given by the consumers and the society, as well as being able to gain opinions, that are emotional, from the population (Blake, 2009).

Some of the methods commonly used on the internet include: questionnaires, online focus groups, online interviews, qualitative research conducted online, analysis of content that is found online, interviews online, online clinical trials, etc. There are many new and different types of research methods that are used these days due to the development of social media, for example, being able to mine for data from large datasets that are found on these forms of media, or, experiments that are conducted on the web within the different social platforms, of which are conducted by researchers. These methods can help in making research work much easier, as almost everyone these days uses social media.

5.3.7. Student-Created Media like Podcasts, Videos, or Slide-shows

Media that is created by students helps increase the level of engagement. It helps promote individualistic learning, interaction among students socially, and immersion. It is also very easy to customize and collaborate with. It helps provide alternatives or complements to the normal methods of research used by students. Student-created media helps promote communication and personal reflection (Blake, 2009).

Podcasts have shown a huge impact on education. There are very many schools that have stopped using textbooks due to the introduction of technology in education. Institutions have chosen to invest on technology as it has proven to be a more efficient method of learning. Podcasts these days have been incorporated in the education sector, and are one of the newest emergences, as they are very mainstream.

Podcasts provide opportunities for teachers to broadcast their content in an easy manner, allowing students to listen to these audios from anywhere and at any time, no matter where they are. Students are only required to have subscriptions to these channels and feeds so that they are able to receive notifications immediately they are released. This is much more efficient for the students who prefer not to wait for lessons in class. These help in engaging students in all levels of education, and helps in improving the learning experience (Donohue, 2014).

Many positive results have been reported in many different schools that have been able to incorporate podcasts into their education system. This has been seen due to the fact that it is easy to create and listen to podcasts, as well as being able to improve the learning experience of the students. There are many different advantages to the incorporation of podcasts in the education system. One of them is how portable and convenient they are. It is very easy for one to download a podcast on their phone, laptop, etc. allowing students to access the information required to learn, at any time and any place they are, with the least effort put in. Another major advantage of podcasts is that it helps in attracting masses. It is a bit difficult to ask students to read an article or book for 30 min. It is also quite hard to have them watch the video of a lecturer teaching. Texts and videos can only be helpful if the student pays full attention to them. This requires the student to be patient and do one thing at the time, which is watching or reading. This can be a bit distracting.

Podcasts can be done in what the students consider time wasted or as they are doing a different routine activity. It is much more likely for a student to listen to a podcast while riding the bus, walking, working out, driving, etc. This is because they are able to pay attention to it despite their distractions. Podcasts can run for over one hour while still being able to do your routine activities, in comparison to texts or videos that may have the student struggling even 2 minutes in (Donohue, 2014).

Figure 5.3. Podcasts are a very easy way to keep students engaged with school work.

Source: https://techcrunch.com/2019/09/27/cracking-the-code-on-podcast-advertising-for-customer-acquisition/amp/.

Videos are also beneficial to students in the educational system. They are very convenient and versatile, and this makes them a major tool to students, instructors, and even the institutions. Videos are able to create an experience that is much more engaging due to the engagement of the sensory organs, in comparison to using just print materials. The students get the opportunity to see and hear the aspects and facts that are being taught, allowing them to process this information in a similar manner to how they do it on a daily basis in their interactions every single day.

They help in providing a resource that students are able to access and watch from any part of the world as long as one has an internet connection, as they can be accessed from many different computer devices such as a mobile phone, laptops, and tablets. These computer devices help the students access information wherever they are and at their own convenience. They also help in improving content retention for the students, because it is possible to stop, pause and replay as many times as the student sees fit. It is also possible for one to review the videos way after the lesson was taught. They help students learn many different subjects, especially those that may require a higher visual understanding such as explaining step by step procedures in math, science, etc. They also allow students to improve their levels of digital literacy as well as communication. These are very important skills in the 21st century (Donohue, 2014).

Another student created media through the use of PowerPoint. Students are able to use PowerPoint in the classroom for many different purposes. These skills need to be learnt, but once they are, it is possible for them to apply this knowledge in many different ways. Learning how to use PowerPoint also allows the students to improve their tech skills. Some of the ways that students are able to use PowerPoint in the classroom include: creation of graphs, creation of games, presentation of work to the classmates and teacher, providing visual representations, creation of instructions, displaying of their work, being able to present a slideshow of certain school or class events or activities, writing of poetry, etc.

Teachers are also able to use PowerPoint in many different ways in the class. They are also able to decide how much or how little they choose to incorporate it. Some of the ways include: writing agendas for meetings, creating routines for each day, presentation of notes and lessons, displaying images, creating and displaying graphs and charts, presentation of multimedia content, etc (Donohue, 2014).

5.3.8. Collaborative Online Tools like Wikis or Google Docs

Collaborative online tools refer to those applications that are based on the web and help in offering services that are considered basic, such as collaborative search engines, file sharing mechanisms, and being able to have instant messaging within groups, so as to access information that has undergone distribution within a system that may involve a team, community or an organization.

In addition, it is possible for its functionality to be provided with further expansion for example, calendars that have been integrated online, shared whiteboards that can also be found online and help in the organization of tasks and ideas or even integrations that allow for peoples to have teleconferencing properties. These online collaboration tools have many different ranges, some may be easy to use and others complicated, some may be cheap and others quite expensive, etc.

Wikis are some of these online collaborative tools. They have a couple of advantages:

- It is possible for anyone to edit them.
- They are very easy to learn and use.
- They are normally immediate, and one doesn't have to wait for a certain person to publish them so as to have new editions or for the updating of information.
- It is possible for different people from different parts of the world to work on the same document.
- The software used is able to keep track of every single edit that is done, and it is also easy to find a previous edition of the same article.
- It helps to widen the accessibility of the importance of web publishing to those who do not use technology.
- They don't have any structure that is predetermined. This means that they have a high flexibility and can be used for many different applications.
- Licensing costs are not considered a barrier because they use a wide variety of open source software, allowing for them to be installed easily in any institution.

Figure 5.4. Google docs have made work easier for many different students and companies.

Source: https://blackgirlnerds.com/can-google-docs-replace-the-need-for-microsoft-word/.

Despite the fact that Wikis have many advantages, they also have a couple of disadvantages. These include:

- The fact that they can be edited by anyone makes them too open for some applications, e.g. documentation of confidential material. This however, can be avoided by regulating the access to user.
- They are susceptible to SPAMs and vandalization if they are not managed in a proper manner. This however, can be fixed by restoring the page which there are many ways to do. On Wiki Educator, one needs to be logged in so as to make changes on the articles, and this helps in reducing the level of vandalism by the usage of spam bots that are automated.
- They can only collaborate with internet connection, however, there is development of technology that makes it possible for one to produce print versions of articles.
- It is possible for the information to be disorganized due to how flexible the structure of wiki is. As the wiki develops, the community has the task to plan and administer the structure in a collaborative manner.

Google Docs is also another online collaborative tool. Businesses are now using this tool as a means to improve effectiveness and efficiency, as well as making it easier to use the information. It is not proven that there are companies that use Google Docs daily, but there are many advantages that have been seen. There are advantages and disadvantages of Google Docs that can be considered before implementing the use of Google Docs.

Some of the advantages include:

- They are very accessible. Employees are able to have an access to the database at any time they see fit, as long as they have a connection to the internet. This level of flexibility is very beneficial, especially for those workers who travel and work a lot from their portable computers. This can help in improving productivity.
- Being able to collaborate in the workplace and classroom is very important. It helps in allowing teachers and employers to control the version of whatever document that the student or the employee is working on. This is very beneficial. Google Docs allows one to include or remove someone who they are collaborating with, using the tab with the specific instructions, when on is working

on a specific document. This allows for the user to control the exact person able to have access to and also be able to change aspects on a certain document.

- It is easy to learn. It is quite straight forward and also easy to understand. Especially if one has already had experience using Word and the other Google apps.
- It is free. It does not require for one to buy it. It comes together with the computer software.
- It is very flexible when it comes to importing and exporting documents. If one requires to import or export a certain document, one will not encounter different messages on errors, and also compatibility issues. This app allows for the import and export of many different types of files. This gives one a high level of flexibility when sending and receiving documents.

5.3.9. Using Social Media to Engage Students

Technology, especially social media, has proven to be very important in everyone's daily life. Being able to integrate its use into the education sector is very important, seeing as students have already made social media a part of their daily lives. It is only natural. Each social media platform offers a different advantage. Some of the examples include being able to share announcements in a class group on lectures or meetings, etc.

Social media helps in providing a communication tool that is smooth as well as more direct, between the parents, teachers, and students, all who are able to communicate on different queries. It also helps in promoting opportunities for e-learning. This is important seeing as online classes and remote jobs are used much more today than before. Social media can be important in training students to do work from far away from the classroom as well, and this is a very important skill (König, 2012).

All in all, it is important for teachers to understand how social media can impact education before incorporating it into the classroom; however, there are many benefits that have been seen from the incorporation of social media.

Figure 5.5. There are many different ways in which Facebook can be incorporated into the classroom. These can help in improving student engagement.

Source: https://neilpatel.com/blog/Facebook-traffic-messenger/.

There are many different social media platforms, and each of them can have a specific use in the classroom. It is important to choose wisely on what one should want to use each platform for. One of the uses includes using Facebook to communicate updates and alerts. Facebook is considered the easiest social media platform to incorporate into the classroom. It is easier to deal with something that everyone is already familiar with, instead of using new learning curves when using a classroom dashboard that is used online traditionally. Students can follow the class's page and the teacher is then able to post any new information on updates, homework and even discussions in a more efficient manner. It is also much easier for the students to keep up to date using this platform. These pages can also be accessed by students who are not active in Facebook. They can be found even when one has signed out. Students and teachers need to be aware that Facebook pages are open and it is possible for anyone to see the posts and also comment.

It is also possible for teachers to create groups for every different class they teach in. These could be either private or public. In addition, the teachers can stream lectures live on Facebook, post questions for the students to discuss on, homework assignments, and also making class assignments for them to do in groups.

Teachers can also use Facebook to keep the students engaged during their holidays by posting reminders and assignments so as to have the students go through some work that can be avoided at the beginning of the semester (König, 2012).

All these should be done while still maintaining a professional boundary. This is maintained because when the teachers create groups, they do not have to send friend requests to their own students.

5.4. WAYS TO INTEGRATE TECHNOLOGY INTO YOUR CLASSROOM

Despite the fact that many technology-based methods and resources that are used for teaching help in building student engagement and improving the skills of the students, there are many teachers who are still not well aware of how to efficiently utilize the different sets of technology in the classroom, so as to achieve these results.

This may be due to the fact that it might be difficult to introduce new platforms, or even having difficulties running these platforms on their devices. Regardless pf these challenges, it is important for them to note that education technology has a lot to offer in the classroom. There are many ways that technology can be incorporated into the classroom:

5.4.1. Having a Virtual Trip in the Classroom

If there is an out of reach location, or one that may have many difficulties to reach, that the teachers would like to show to their students, it is possible to use a simulation to achieve this. This can be achieved by purchasing a Google Cardboard which normally costs less than fifteen dollars. There are applications that can be used in the classroom to allow student to observe buildings that are well known such as the Empire State Building, and even structures such as the Great wall of China. This can help teachers promote learning by using mock conversations in the foreign landmark, that are done in the language spoken in the specific country. It is also possible to use this tool to study certain areas from a geographical perspective (Willmann, 2017).

5.4.2. Being Able to See Previews of a Field Trip Virtually

Google earth is an application that allows educators to see certain locations before they actually go to the destination. The teachers can find out the specific areas of a certain location, such as a zoo or museum, that the students are most interested in. This can be achieved using the street view in the app. This application can also help the students discuss the parts of the trip that they are more excited for, which can help in increasing the level of excitement for the trip. Certain popular destinations that are mostly visited by schools are normally also found on the website, in the form of visual media. This can allow one to complement the preview. The one component that will be needed to achieve this is a projector or a large screen.

Figure 5.6. Virtual trips can allow the students to experience experiences that they would not have been able to go through due to different circumstances.

Source: https://thejournal.com/articles/2017/03/27/3-tips-to-successfully-create-virtual-field-trips-in-your-classroom.aspx.

5.4.3. To Make a Noisy Classroom Quiet

There are tools that help track classroom noise, which can make lessons easier to manage. There is an accurate noise meter called Too Noisy which promotes silence in a classroom when there is a spike in the meter. This allows in reducing the level of disruption when the teacher is giving a lesson or when running a work activity that is independent. It even allows the students to remain accountable to each other. This allows the teacher to feel comfortable when presenting content.

5.4.4. Using Videos to Create Mini-lessons

Teachers are able to create lesson plans by utilizing videos as standalone overviews for certain topics. Video content that is created by teachers can be hosted by many different websites which are available as previews and reviews of skill. An example is the education version of YouTube called Teacher Tube that helps teachers cover major school subjects.

This platform makes it easy for one to search for a certain topic or also in browsing by categories, which helps one to find specific videos that are relevant. A student can be able to search for "middle school geography" and the search engine will provide a page of results that contain study guides, reviews of exams, and even in specific lessons. This method of integrating technology in the classroom is easy and also includes an element of multimedia to the teaching plan. This can help in effective resonance with learners who prefer to use a visual aid. There is also a study that has shown that using videos that are animated in the classroom can help in impacting the development of a child positively, in areas such as creativity, memory, problem-solving, etc (Willmann, 2017).

5.4.5. Coordination of Live Videos

Teachers do not have to pre-record videos to teach their students, because there is the availability of video conferencing that allows for teachers to deliver lessons using videos, live. This can be done even by teachers that are found in other schools or teachers that too far to teach the class in person. Being able to bring in experts as well through conference calls can help in exposing the students to newer ideas and also make the workload lighter.

Figure 5.7. Live streaming in the classroom can help engage students that depend on an audiovisual aid to learn.

Source: https://www.educationworld.com/live-streaming-education-sharing-learning-experiences-world.

This person can be added as a contact either through skype or google hangouts, allowing them to give the lesson using the program. Skype also provides a list of guests that speak on topics they are experts in voluntarily.

You can make this more interesting for the students by asking them to prepare questions that they can ask during the video conference call. This also promotes student participation.

5.4.6. Playing Podcasts

Being able to play podcasts that are relevant does not only help in the supplementation of lessons, but also in engaging learners who prefer audio learning and thus allowing it to act as a station for learning. There are many podcasts that can be found online. They are made by both media specialists and even just the ordinary person who is passionate on a specific topic. Some of the topics that can be found are:

- Lessons on the techniques and strategies of learning.
- Lectures from popular professors.
- Recorded interview with authors of books that the students might be reading at the time.
- Exploring of topics that are related to the curriculum.

It is also beneficial to allow students to make and presentation their own podcasts, which can be achieved by designing projects within the school course. Podcasts have been confirmed to be one of the easiest ways to integrate technology into the class. All one needs are effective speakers.

5.4.7. Addition on Multimedia Aspects to Presentations

Students are easily disengaged by slideshow presentations that are only made up of texts. Using aspects of multimedia can help in holding the student's attention due to the variety of content delivery.

Some of the things that can be included are:

- Graphs
- Videos
- Images
- Podcast clips
- Sound effects
- Pictographs
- Clips from movies, tv shows, etc

Figure 5.8. Using videos and pictures in the classroom can help the students understand certain concepts faster, as well as retain the information easier.

Source: http://ictpost.com/multimedia-in-our-classrooms-engage-and-empower/.

Teachers do not have to struggle with finding graphs and pictographs that are relevant on the internet. It is possible for them to create these themselves. There are many tools that are found online and are free, that can guide one on the steps to input the data, modification of data and adjusting if labels. Most teachers already teach using slideshows. Adding this aspect can help in making the lesson much more engaging.

5.4.8. Sending of Content that is Adaptive

It is possible for teachers to use smartphones in the classroom to their advantage, seeing as students are always on their phones. They can deliver learning content through phones. There are learning programs that can be accesses by students through their tablets and phones.

For example, it is possible to have grammar lessons using ClassK12. Thus, system involves different applications that the students can download on their phones and tablets. Teachers are able to create classrooms that are virtual, so as to deliver homework and also for running reports. Being able to deliver content that is appropriate through these programs may look complicated but it is normally an automated process that is intuitive.

5.4.9. Sharing Class Calendars Online

This can help in ensuring that students are well informed on the content that they will be dealing with. Teachers can create and share the class calendars has details on the lessons they will have, as well as highlights of the important dates. This can be done using Google Calendar. One can email the link to the calendars to either the students or their parents (Willmann, 2017).

This does not only help in informing the students, but also in ensuring organization – teachers are able to see situations in which they have set too many due dates. Keeping the students well informed on their schedules can also allow then to come to the class prepared.

5.4.10. Using Virtual Manipulatives

During the teaching and reinforcement of certain mathematical concepts, students are able to use virtual manipulatives in ways that are not only physical. For example, Geo-boards can be used in 6th grade geometry activities, from the National Library of Virtual Manipulatives, to help in the illustration or areas, perimeters and concepts that are rational.

Despite the fact that there are not many websites that can provide these manipulatives, the most versatile and engaging website that is used by most teachers is the National Library of Virtual Manipulatives.

It includes different tasks that target students from the stages before kindergarten, all the way to the 11th grade. It is an appealing method to most hands-on learners (Willmann, 2017).

5.4.11. Running of Learning Stations

It is possible to deliver a wide range of content as well as allowing the students to have different ways of processing the information provided using learning stations. It is possible to provide videos, slideshows, podcasts, etc. using these devices at each station.

Some of the aspects that can be involved include:

- The use of virtual manipulatives.
- Using computer games to solve relevant problems.

- Allowing them to record their opinions and responding to podcasts.
- Contribution of notes to a wiki page.

This approach is efficient as it allows students to work in groups at their working stations.

5.4.12. Provisions of Online Activities for Those Students that are Able to Complete Their Work Early

There are also stations that can be set up for the students that are able to finish their work early, allowing them to engage further in the processing of content. This can be done by setting up certain devices that have educational games and videos. It is important for the teacher to make sure that this content involves the learning materials in the lesson at the time. This allows them to remain engaged and enjoy relevant topics. Doing this encourages the students to use every single minute in the class involved in the lesson content.

5.4.13. Saving Time for Exit Tickets

Being able to save a few minutes after a class for exit tickets helps in opening the door for the easy use of technology. Exit tickets can be seen in different forms, including:

- *Journal entries done online* – using notepads that are found online can allow students to summarize what they were able to learn in the lesson as a journal entry.
- *Comments in a slideshow* – being able to share copies of the slideshow from the lesson of the day can allow students to make comments to review and allow for the expansion of points that were important. This can be done using Google slides and PowerPoint.
- *Tweets on Twitter* – Students are able to summarize the main points that they learned during the lesson using less than 140 characters. It is possible to see what they have written by asking them to use a classroom hashtag.

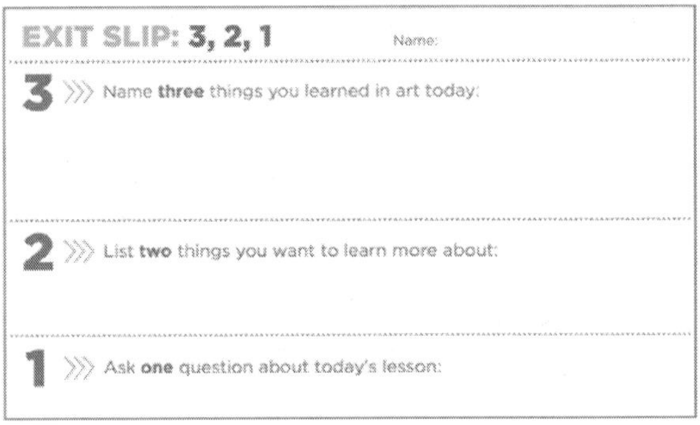
EXIT SLIP: 3, 2, 1 Name:

3 >>> Name **three** things you learned in art today:

2 >>> List **two** things you want to learn more about:

1 >>> Ask **one** question about today's lesson:

Figure 5.9. Above is an example of an exit ticket that can be integrated online.

Source: https://theartofeducation.edu/2017/01/27/use-exit-tickets/.

These are easy to introduce into the classroom.

5.4.14. Using Twitter to Receive Questions Using Hashtags

It is possible for teachers to use hashtags to receive and answer questions outside the classroom throughout the day. Searching for the hashtag can display the questions during the class on a screen for the teacher to respond to the questions, and also on the phone. It makes it possible for all the questions to be answered at once, or as they pop up. All in all, it will be hard to find a feed that is empty. Students should be encouraged to ask questions on issues they did not understand or need further explanation on. This can be very beneficial for introverts who are not comfortable with asking these questions in the classroom.

5.4.15. Studying, Reviewing and Critiquing Content on Web Page

This involves finding a web page that involves content that is related to the lesson being taught and asking the students to make notes from that specific page. This can be achieved programs such as Bounce which help in the creation of screenshots that are interactive by putting in the URL required to access it. When the students access the screenshot, they will be able to see the instructions they need to create notes, edits, etc. (Donohue, 2014).

Students are able to do this individually in classrooms that have a one to one device use. In the classrooms that do not have this activity can be done as a group. The groups can be asked to write notes and feedback that aims at the improvement of the content on the web page.

Once each group has completed this task, they can do a comparison to see who did the job better. This makes writing notes engaging.

5.4.16. Using Mind Maps That Are Found Online for Brainstorming in the Classroom

There are websites that can be used for the creation of clear and detailed mind maps in a faster manner in comparison to the ones that are written. This is considered digital brainstorming.

Mind-Meister is a program that is used by many teachers and students. It works by displaying the program on a screen that can be seen by everyone, where the teachers work with the students to brainstorm on ideas. This helps in keeping students engaged in the classroom as well as in the launching of problem-based learning exercises. This technology can be set up in a few minutes.

5.5. FRAMEWORKS FOR TECHNOLOGY INTEGRATION

5.5.1. SAMR (Substitution, Augmentation, Modification, Redefinition) Model

This framework was created by Dr. Ruben Puentedura. It deals with the categorization of the integration of classroom technology. There are four different degrees: Substitution, Augmentation, Modification, and Redefinition.

The first letters of each make up the word SAMR. This mode was invented so as to help in sharing a language that is common across the different disciplines, as the educators work to provide easy visualization of complex concepts by the students.

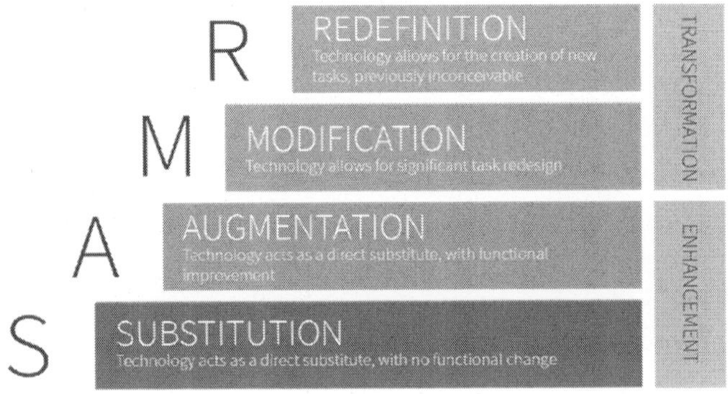

Figure 5.10. Above is a visual representation of the SAMR model.

Source: https://www.schoology.com/blog/samr-model-practical-guide-ed-tech-integration.

Substitution and Augmentation are referred to as the steps of enhancement, and modification and redefinition are referred to as the steps of transformation. Enhancement refers to making the old methods much more efficient and effective, white transformation is the creation of methods that are entirely new and original (Blake, 2009).

Substitution: This stage involves directly substituting technology for those that are much more traditional. It is seen as a direct replacement. For example, teachers can use versions of information that are either electronic or based on the web, instead of using hard copies, to teach a lesson on the constitution during a history class. Another example includes students using Microsoft Word to answer questions on the same topics, instead of writing them down on a paper. Substitution also involves the use of slides, PowerPoint, Keynote, etc. for the presentation of information on a certain topic to the class. Teachers need to ask themselves what that will gain from the use of this step which involves replacing traditional methods with technology. There are some situations that may still require the use of pen and paper (Blake, 2009).

Augmentation: This also involves the direct substitution of technology for traditional methods, however, with student experiences that are enhanced. It ensures that the productivity and potential of the student has been increased or augmented in any way. Using the same example of the constitution, it is possible for the student to augment the experience by using a video clip to explain a segment of the constitution. The student can also use links that are interactive and relevant to the decisions that are made by the courts on the constitution.

Modification: This stage moves from enhancements to transformations. Instead of replacing or enhancing, this involves including a change to the specific way the lesson is conducted, as well are the outcome of the lesson. The main question a teacher needs to consider is whether the technological change will alter the task significantly.

Using the same example on the constitution, the student presenting is able to perform the creation of his or her own graphic organizer, that is unique, for the class. It will not only have the normal resources of multimedia that are normally used, but also be able to represent new products or synthesis of materials that are already existing. It is also possible for a group of students to work in collaboration in a workspace that is based on the cloud to make propositions on modern definitions on certain aspects of the constitution and be able to receive feedback on the propositions from the classmates (Blake, 2009).

Redefinition: This is the last stage of the model and it represents the main point in how technology can promote the transformation of the experiences of students. The main question to ask yourself in this stage is whether the tools provided in the technology allow for the teachers to find a whole new definition of the traditional method that was used, in a way that is impossible without technology, helping in the creation of an experience that is novel. For example, students can be able to use technology to communicate with students in different states from the ones they are in, so as to see how the regional differences impact how they understand the constitution. This can be done after they have finished they group work. Students can also be able to communicate live with other students in other countries so as to see and learn the differences that are found in the two constitutions of the two countries.

5.5.2. TPACK (Technological Pedagogical Content Knowledge) Framework

The TPACK framework is a framework for integration of technology that includes three aspects of instructors of knowledge that are needed to be combines for the successful integration of educational technology. These are technological, pedagogical, and content knowledge. This is what makes up TPACK. There are many times that this framework is compared to the SAMR model, but these two are very different (Willmann, 2017).

This framework was invented by Punya Mishra together with Matthew J. Koehler in 2006. They were able to identify three primary forms of knowledge with this framework: Technological knowledge, content knowledge, and pedagogical knowledge.

This framework helps in allowing us to understand how to achieve teaching using technology. This is normally not the same as being able to attain all the information of each specific concept individually. It however, involves being able to understand how one can teach using technology, in a manner that helps to enhance the learning experience of the student.

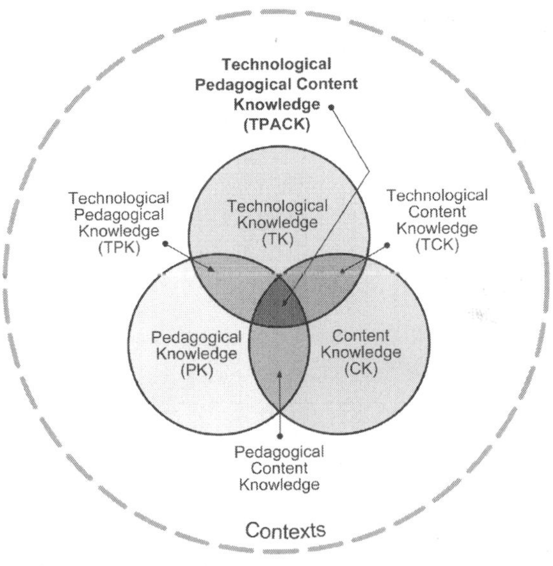

Figure 5.11. This shows how all the aspects of the model have to be integrated for it to work.

Source: https://educationaltechnology.net/technological-pedagogical-content-knowledge-tpack-framework/.

For example, when the teacher delivers content to the students using the learning management system, they will still be required to subject the student to the full course that is found online using PDFs that are based in texts, despite the fact that the teacher has sufficient knowledge on the content that is being taught (Willmann, 2017).

Despite the fact that this can show that the teacher has knowledge on both the content and the technology used, it is possible to argue out that it does not enhance the learning experience of the student. However, being able to recognize that the content can be provided to the students using digital mediums that are much more interactive and engaging (videos, games, etc.) together with being able to make it happen using the learning management system, shows that the teacher is also equipped with technical content language.The SAME framework is different from the TPACK. It is important to know the difference and how they each affect the instructional strategy. There are many educators are aware of all the benefits that technology can bring into the classroom. Whether it refers to being able to prepare the students for a world that is driven by technology, or being able to make the course and school easier. Many of them see technology as the answer to all their problems. They assume that it will help in the improvement of education.This is why the TPACK model is very important. It shows is that adding the best learning management system in the classroom is not the only step to enhancing student learning and performance. It shows us that there is a relationship that needs to be well understood for technology to be efficient and effective in the classroom, and thus includes knowledge on technology, content, and pedagogy. Being able to use them all together is the key to effective technology use in the classroom (Willmann, 2017).

This framework allows the teachers to take a step back and make sure that the full strategy is bound to work using all the aspects of the model. There was a study that was conducted by the Australasian Society for Computers in learning in the tertiary education that showed that this model was able to enhance the ability of the educators to utilize technology in their learning and professions.

5.6. FACTORS INFLUENCING INTEGRATION OF COMPUTER-BASED TECHNOLOGIES IN EARLY CHILDHOOD

5.6.1. Teacher's Attitude towards the Integration of Computer-Based Technologies

Teachers' attitudes are known to be among the major factors that affect the successful integration of computer-based technologies in teaching. With the modernization of the world today, technology is being used in various aspects of human life even education. The use of computer technology has been incorporated in the higher learning education systems where it has been beneficial for students as it enables them to carry out research. This has led to the idea of incorporating the use of computer-based technology in the early childhood education (Blake, 2009).

The teachers' attitudes generally refer to their feeling and belief toward computer-based technologies. With the introduction of the computer-based technologies in the learning process, it has stirred up mixed feedback which may be positive or negative. Some teachers feel that the use of such technologies will have a positive impact on the students improving their performance while some feel that it is not necessary to incorporate the use of these technologies in education. They therefore do not embrace it.

It is important to note that for such technologies to be initiated and implemented in the education system, it greatly depends on the teacher' attitude towards the technologies being used. In the definition of attitude, it is said to be a response to an object which may be positive or negative. The response of the teachers towards the computer technologies is what the government used in order to determine whether the technologies will be implemented or not. This will affect the usage of computers in the education system as per the response of the teachers (Blake, 2009).

The government personnel are able to get the feedback on the use of computer technologies by carrying out surveys in the various schools. The teachers are usually the respondents in this case. The survey may be through questionnaires or through interviews. But first they technology is tested in selected schools. After a given period of time, the government officials come for the feedback form the selected schools. There the teachers are questioned why the government officers and they get to relay their experiences when using the technology. The gathered data is then analyzed so that the ministry of education can decide whether to implement the computer technologies or not.The teachers' attitudes affect the integration of computer-based technologies in that if the teachers feel that the technology is not beneficial for them or the students, it is more likely that the technology will not be implemented into the education system. This is because if it will not be beneficial, then there will be no need to set aside funds to purchase the computers that would have been used by the students to avoid wastage of the resources which can be used to improve other sectors in the education system. The negative attitude towards the technology may be as a result of past experiences with such technologies.

This may lead to the teachers refusing to use the technology even though adjustments were made to solve the previously experienced challenges in the computer-based technology. This may negatively affect the learning of the students which may have been improved if the computer-based technologies would have been incorporated to the learning process. This may be the reason why teachers are encouraged to be open minded when being introduced to the computer-based technologies. This will remove barriers such as teachers having a perception of the technology even before they are introduced to it (Blake, 2009).

There are teachers who have a positive attitude towards the use of computer-based technology in the learning process. If a good number of teachers have such a mentality, then it is most likely that the computer-based technology will be incorporated into the education system. As attitudes are formed due to experiences and situations, these teachers may have had an easy time interaction with the technology. They therefore view it to beneficial to themselves and the students as it will make the learning process more efficient and effective. This may end up boosting the child's performance and create more interest for learning.

The positive attitude helps with the integration of computer-based technologies into the education system as the teachers will provide insight on what can be successfully adopted and integrated into the learning process. This may lead to the smooth running and integration of the technologies when used in learning. Support is also crucial for the technologies to be integrated into the learning process. If the teachers have a positive attitude towards the computer-based technology, then they will support its incorporation into the learning process. This may speed up the process of incorporating the technologies.

Therefore, teachers' attitudes play a key role in the effective use of technology in the classroom and generally in education as a whole. It will determine the initiation, adoption and implementation of the technology in the classroom. Having a positive attitude will make the use of the technology to be much easier (Blake, 2009).

5.6.2. Teachers' Prior Knowledge in Computer-Based Technologies

In the learning process for teaching to be effective, the teacher should have knowledge on teaching methodologies that will produce good results at the end of the learning process. According to the type of students the teacher has, he or she is able to choose the most effective methodology to use that will greatly benefit the students. For instance, if the students are fast learners the teacher will be able to choose a learning methodology that suits them and if they are slow learners, the methodology will have to use frequent revision of the previous lesson. They also choose the methodology depending on the level of competence they have to the given methodology (König, 2012).

For the teacher to use computer in the learning process, he or she should be knowledgeable on the various learning methodologies that revolve around use of computers. The more the computer learning methodologies the better as it will keep the teacher at an advantage. For effective learning, the term computer competence is brought about. This refers to the ability of being able to handle a wide range of different computer applications for various purposes with the aim of meeting the users need.

Figure 5.12. For computer-based technologies to be successfully integrated, it requires the teachers to have the required knowledge and skills.

Source: https://www.welt.de/wirtschaft/webwelt/article130509428/Wie-das-iPad-die-Tafel-ueberfluessig-macht.html.

When teachers have the required knowledge and skills, they will be able to effectively teach the students. This will make the incorporation of the computer-based programs useful and beneficial as the teachers will have the ability to use the technology in the learning process making it advantageous for the students and the teacher. For teachers that have the skills and knowledge, they attribute that it is much easier using computer-based technologies in the learning process rather than using the previous learning methods (König, 2012).

It has been attributed that teachers having high knowledge and skills on computer-based technologies has led to production of high-level technologies being integrated into the learning process. For the schools that have been used to experiment this theory, the results were reflected on the students' performance whereby most of them were able to score high grades and some even attaining grades that previously seemed impossible for them. Such results have led to the push for implementation of the computer-based technologies in the learning process which has been championed by both teachers and students.

The lack of knowledge and skills among the teachers has been a major factor that caused the slow rates of computer-based technologies being incorporated in the education system. As majority of the teachers lack skills, it renders them unable to use the technologies in the learning process. It is now termed as the second most inhibiting hindrance to the use of computers. It is the second after teachers' attitudes towards the use of computers in education. This has led to the production of low level of technology integration that will later on reflect on the students' achievement negatively (König, 2012).

As there is a correlation between attitude and interest, the lack of knowledge and skills among the teachers has been attributed to the negative attitude of the teachers towards the use of computers in education. This makes lots of sense because it is natural human behavior that once an individual develops negative attitude towards something a subject, for instance, that individual will lack interest in the subject and will end up ignoring the subject so that he or she can pick up what interests them. The lack of knowledge and skills may have contributed to them being unable to make informed decisions.

As they lack knowledge on computers, they cannot easily use them in their interactions causing them to have bad attitudes towards the use of computers in education. If they had the required knowledge and skills, they would have tried to advocate for the integration of computer-based technology in teaching and learning. With an aim of trying to eradicate the lack of knowledge and skills, various ministries of education such as the one for Kenya, have tried to come up with possible solutions. One of them being introduction of vocational training of teachers. This involves teachers being trained on the latest tools used in education which includes the use of computers (König, 2012).

With such training, teachers are equipped with knowledge and skills that will help them able to handle the various programs used in computers. Not only teachers, students also require such training. Therefore, various schools have allocated a given time in the day for the students to receive training on computers. This may not be the scenario in the schools in urban areas as majority of the children are exposed to computers even before they join school. They are capable of handling basic programs but may require training on complex programs.

For the teachers who regularly use the computer-based technology, they have confidence in it and say that it is very useful in their teaching. Several of the teachers plan to use computers as they continue to teach as it is more enjoyable compared to the previous methods of teaching (König, 2012).

5.6.3. Teachers' Access to Computer-Based Technologies Tools

For the computer-based technologies to be fully integrated into the childhood education system, the teacher needs to have unlimited access to the computers. This is very crucial that the computers being there because if the schools lack computers, what is the use of the government incorporating something to the education system that will not be used by the teachers or the students. Access to the computer-based technologies is important. This is because studies have shown that there is an existing relationship between access of the tools and the using of the computer-based technology (Sharma, 2002).

The relationship has been used to measure the rate at which the computer-based technology is being used. For instance, if the computers are available for both the students and the teachers then the technology will be frequently used and will be employed by the other subjects to enhance the learning process. The vice versa is also applicable. If there is a limited number of computers, the students and teachers will have limited access to the computer-based technologies. This will affect the integration of computer-based technologies in education in that not much progress will be made in using the technology in the learning progress.

Figure 5.13. In the recent studies, it has shown that most math teachers opt to use computers in the learning process.

Source: https://www.edutopia.org/blog/math-education-roots-computer-science-lincoln-sedlacek.

With the recent advancements in technology, computer scientists have been able to come up with programs that suit the learning progress. Most of the programs are usually for math and science subjects as they both involve solving of problems and the skills are then passed on to the students. The use of such programs has been proven to be effective in the long run and is therefore preferred by most math and science teachers (Sharma, 2002).

However, most schools have computers. This may be attributed to the positive impact that computers have had on teachers and students. For instance, the use of computers has enabled easy access to the internet which has been useful in research. Also, the use of computers has enabled both teachers and students to access to computer-based technology equipment as well as materials that will make the integration much easier enabling the learners to directly access the relevant learning resources. For schools that use more of the internet and e-learning resources, they have made the largest records of implementation of computer-based technologies compared to other schools (Sharma, 2002).

For such schools, the students usually attain good grades which is attributed to the access unlimited access to learning material. With the much need of computers in order for the computer-based technologies to be integrated, the government and other stakeholders have come up with strategies so that several schools can access computers. It has involved the building of computer laboratories for the schools. Some individuals take it upon themselves to donate computers for the students and the teachers. For schools that are not given such support, they come up with events such as fundraisers or clubs that will earn the school money so that they can purchase the computers.

Figure 5.14. Depending on the type of subjects taught in the school curriculum, with the access to computers they will be able to access e-content that is relevant to the curriculum.

Source: https://atulhost.com/advantages-of-students-having-access-to-computers.

For the schools that have integrated the computer-based technology, they have been encouraged to have internet connection. This will enable them to access the e-resources that will be relevant for the given curriculum. This has led to schools embracing the use of Wi-Fi networks within the school premises. To boost the integration of the technologies into education, the government has taken up exposing various schools to e-learning centers within the given education location (Sharma, 2002).

Even though there is access to a computer laboratory, if the subject is allocated one hour, it limits the exposure time for the student. This means that the students may not have regular or reliable access to a computer which may contribute to the slow integration of computers in education. This may limit the frequent use of the education technology as the teachers may have a hard time incorporating the technology into the already existing lesson plans. This has led to some schools taking up initiatives such as BYOD (Bring Your Own Device) in which the students are allowed to carry their own devices to schools.

This is beneficial as the school will cut costs on buying the computers and instead use the resources to improve the school's network so that the network can be able to accommodate several users. This will positively impact the integration of computer-based technologies in education as the student computer ratio will facilitate the use of technology. These are among the initiates that the government and schools are taking up so that the students have unlimited access to computers (Willmann, 2017).

In general, if the access to computers for the students and the teachers is increased, it will enable the fast integration of computer-based and the level of technology integrated to the system will also be high.

Chapter 6

Computer Science in the Elementary School

CONTENTS

6.1. Interactive Computing 146
6.2. The Main Categories of Educational Use of Computers 148
6.3. Impacts of Computers on The Current Curriculum System 150
6.4. Computers As An Aid To Instruction 153
6.5. The Benefit of Computer Studies In Elementary Schools 156
6.6. Role of Calculators In Elementary School Education 157
6.7. What Preparatory School Teachers Should Understand About Computers? 159
6.8. Primary School Computer-Based Activities 162
6.9. The Cognitive Obstacle 163

6.1. INTERACTIVE COMPUTING

Previous versions of personal computers are nothing similar to the computers found in the present world though it has evolved over the years with important modifications being incorporated to the latest model that we currently have which has very nice features and functionality. In the early years, computers were only usable by a single individual at once, plus there was minor or lack of complete interaction with the parties involved that is the user and the computer if the computer was being operated on with difficulty. The advancement of technology has enabled the use of computers by many users at the same time and communicate with the computer as it solved their issues. During the mid-1970s a new development of the machine known as the microcomputer was created. It is modified to be used in a reciprocal mode though by only a single person at a go. The original general-purpose electrical digital machine became functional in December of 1945. It had 18,000 vacuum tubes, occupied a very big space, consumed too much electricity and needed a vast air cooling system. For one to adjust the computer to operate on a specific type of issue might take more than seven days this limited the number of users who will use the computer in solving their difficulties.

Figure 6.1. Personal computers initially entered the market in 1951 and transistorized computers got well-known from 1958.

Source:-https://www.pinterest.com/pin/AaOf1WrP0IV4_p3-LPOYY-wpR0t7R8XD873T-zv0GJQAktHISN2p3sLA/?lp=true.

Computers started reducing in size, got more reliant and reduced electricity consumption and air conditioning though only one user could use the machine at ago and the configuration time between tasks was also an issue. There was a minor or no chance at all for a user to communicate with the computer while it was in the middle of solving an issue. In the 1960's achievements in the computer world brought a significant effect. At first, there came an ideology of using a computer's resources amongst many users at the same time. The computer is modified to operate a couple of outputs and inputs and to communicate with a group of simultaneous users. This is known as interactive computing (Khine, 2018).

A time-shared network system may also serve as a communication system. Another development that followed was the integrated circuit a similar concept used to make one transistor could make a circuit consisting of numerous transistors and other components. These are made on a small piece of silicon known as a chip. Advancements in the manufacture of chips led to the know-how of developing cryptic circuits from a number of chips plus the required connectors and electricity. Also, as Chips became affordable to produce the cost of machine tremendously reduced. Entering the 1970 we had two types of machine systems the interactive computing system was made so as to enable a number of concurrent collective users and shared its central memory and its components amongst users. On the other hand, there was batch processing system. The configuration between users was decreased to very few seconds in most situations.

Before 1975, there was the introduction of more affordable, small machines known as many minicomputers and they were commonly used in high school and became a fundamental tool in higher academics. Chip technology continued to be modified and the microcomputers electrical circuit system used a very small number of chips. These computers are so affordable that they can be used in a mixture of both processing interactive computer mode thus one user has maximum control of the computer over a vast time period and communicates with it the same way as interacting with interactive computing system. The user has some merit of both an interactive computing system and batch processing system though also various demerits. The interaction between concurrent users of an interactive computing system is missing the numerous storage capacity and flexibility of larger machines which is available in time shared and batch system is unavailable. In spite of this, microcomputers are highly elevating the scope of computers in high school education. Its cost is relatively lower which enables institutions to afford the computers. The interactive capabilities of the machines have shown to be an important tool in educating students. It is known that feedback is vital to help learners study the response can be given by a tutor or other students. It can also help with answering booklets. This interactive computer system is a magnificent response mechanism which can input and output complicated student reaction and then give appropriate responses to a given input situation. The interactive component of machines provide the power of cycle growth in instruction (Khine, 2018).

6.2. THE MAIN CATEGORIES OF EDUCATIONAL USE OF COMPUTERS

Computer usage can be categorized into managerial, commanding and investigative uses. Universities in the United States of America uses approximately three percent to four percent of the whole financial plan on computer science plus the finances being evenly supplied among the users. A common High School academic system uses one percent to two percent of its financial plan for computer science. In management, use of computers completely overtakes the other two categories that is commanding and research since there is minimal investigative use of computers in education system. Minor tutor states in the United States of America presently using about one percent of their financial plan for commanding so there has been a rising use of instructional use in institutions. It is thought that a user is particularly intrigued with commanding purposes of computer machine, thus, the next sections of this chapter is meant to discuss about commanding features of computers presently we are talking about managerial and investigative use of computers in school. About ninety percent or there about of learning institutions in the United States of America design managerial consumption of computers. Well elaborated records and findings must be written down and the statement must also be written down by the state administration. Tutors must be given income and Levy reports must be clearly listed by the state administration. The information on learners should be kept well and performance report should be availed to a parent or guardian. Inventory from procurement of supplies, reading materials and command materials should be well kept and preserved. All these assignments can be achieved by use of 'by hand' technique. Eventually, computer usage clears a job at an affordable rate, more precise and quicker. Managers from schools require quick availability to precise knowledge and information to assist in making rational decisions (König, 2012).

The concept of an administrative computer information system is prevalent in commerce and in the industry and steadily oozing into the education sector. Information needed to decide is gathered and preserved in a computer system for data retrieval. An operating system is designed to enable the processing of information. With a proper computer system for data retrieval a manager can access feedback to "what if" questions" like "what if csr #8 does not move because of heavy rainfall?" Or "what if chef salary be increased by 9%?" This is due to the fact that computer is vital to academic managers (König, 2012). We can predict that usage will greatly increase in the future. A computer is a vital component in investigation in universities. Statistics show that about one third of universities computing financial plan is aligned with this purpose. Little investigation happens in pre-college academic system thus little financing is designated for usage in this section, though this usage type is developing examples will be cited. The United States of America administration sponsors a handful of an investigative intelligence Centre known as ERIC centers which coincides with plenty of academic diary and tries to find out literature on academic investigation. The department employees note down a synopsis of the findings and indicate the essay. All the data is fed into a computerized information retrieval system therefore making it readily available to investigators (Chao, 2012).

For instance, you were drawn to bilingual, bicultural forms of learning in the early forms of learning. It is estimated that a computerized search of the subject using the Eric data bank approximately cost fifteen dollars. In a short period of time like a few minutes you can easily retrieve and find heading and a summarized abstract of a couple of trending writing around the geographical area. In addition, the system that the computer is using can also perform other tasks lake booking and order for copies of microfilms of the reports. Studies have shown that there are more than 100 of computerized data banks of bibliographic information. Furthermore, libraries around the world especially the big libraries like the library of congress found in the United States of America have shifted to a computerized switch up of the card catalog system. Another common study of the usage of machines that is being done involves statistics. That is the statistical analysis of academic information (Yadav, 2014).

An educational institution to incorporate specialized program that gives out orders and commands in a number of its school and institution. Exams are set and given out to students wanting to enter the special program similarly as well as to our control group of similar students who will not be a part of the specialized program. After some period of time, the participants are examined again so as to try and make a comparison to observe and note down what type of changes have taken place. Computer machines have revolutionized and they are able to work with large set of data by collecting and observing them then performing statistical analysis both management in investigative (administrative and research) use of computers in academy portrays a vital statement. Computers have advanced and they are vital as it is useful in attacking specific issues.

In most times these difficulties are also being tried to be handled by other problem-solving techniques.

If the user has decided to use a computer, then she should have already analyzed the merits and demerits that the computer has when executing the command, it has been assigned.

Though most times computers are able to solve numerous problems it does not mean it should solve this specific problem. Hold that concept in mind and revisited when you're learning about different aspects of computerized machines (Yadav, 2014).

6.3. IMPACTS OF COMPUTERS ON THE CURRENT CURRICULUM SYSTEM

The main objective of education is providing the participants with the appropriate skills, vital tools and vast knowledge to handle the different difficulties experienced by people and institutions in our community. A lot of people from different walks of life agree that being able to write and read and do mathematics is a very important skill when it comes to comprehending, representing and solving difficulties experienced by people and institutions in their day-to-day life (Guzdial, 2015).

For years and years, humans have always tried to improvise and improve ways of trying to solve issues they face in real-life. Currently, machines like calculators and computers have been modified in design to help solve problems that are mainly faced by adults and grownups.

Elementary school academics have a task of deciding which job this machine will perform, which user will be given the job of studying it mentally, what they will learn to execute using basic tools like a piece of paper and finally what they will learn to do using books, computers and calculators (Guzdial, 2015).

Figure 6.2. In business, computer and calculator are the most basic and used tools in working and solving problems.

Source: https://www.canva.com/photos/MAA3v-pfCpg-hands-working-on-the-calculator/.

The government and industry use these tools every day and this clearly shows how the current world is reliant to these components. The world of academics is yet to understand the effects of this fact. The current curriculum system needs to be amended for it to suit the system even though calculators and computers are not readily available to school. Education has many objectives but the most important one is to provide the student with the necessary skills to help themselves solve issues they are facing in the society. It is, in this case, we stress on the three R's and wanting to learn. Being able to solve difficulties and practicing to handle different issues is what the education system mainly focuses on. Steps involved in solving problems involve:

- Comprehending the problem, studying about essential skills, general education and common is vital
- Finding ways of solving an issue and elaborating a plot: Your background knowledge is important as it will guide you. A computer program is a way of representing a plan
- Executing the plan: This includes a routine, speed, accuracy, determination and persistence that are desirable while solving the task
- Comprehending the meaning of the findings: Check whether they make sense and if the results can be applied.

Among the 4 steps, the easiest one to teach and the easiest to examine is number 3. However, at the same time it's the most essential step. This is why in schools they stress on developing skills that will enable one in carrying out routine tasks. Computers and calculators do this best. We have a rough idea of the effect of calculators and computers in the education system especially in middle school. It takes a few years to master arithmetical skills by students. There is some difference in comprehending concepts of these operations versus understanding paper and pencil arithmetic. Calculators are better alternatives though it might be a disadvantage as it might hinder students from getting their skills and knowledge that is needed to improve mental knowledge and bring about experience in solving issues (Willmann, 2017).

Another example is the digital watch which it can be well read and students can easily tell time but it does not teach the concept behind time and how it is calculated so it is an essential tool but it does not help or add value to the curriculum because it does not help student understand time and also problems related with time but a digital watch just like the calculator is a valuable tool and it should be included in the curriculum to some extent. The availability of such technology has expanded the scope of revision in the education system (Willmann, 2017). An example is word processing which currently comprises of the keyboard and display screen a typewriter and external storage tool like a hard disc. It enables for easy correction, checking of errors and printing out of the typed work out on a paper.

This increases productivity in workplaces and school. A music synthesizer is also a good example as it helps develop talent of children by the use of an interactive computer system incorporating this is the education system will have a huge impact is the music education sector. In our current world we have a lot of machines like vehicles, smartphones, medical related machines and printers. Our curriculum only teaches us on how to use them but not how to complete with them. The education system needs to change so as to teach more about high-level skills of understanding how to solve problems, recreating plant in a digital from and interpreting the findings.

There are points to notice. First, basic tools such as paper, pens and pencils are important in the education sector. It is mostly the continuous routine paper and pencil manipulation that is reducing in importance. Also, there is a much-needed increase in accuracy and fast mental skills like understanding mathematics and learning how to spell. We need to make students learn how to execute task using computer and not competing with them (Sharma, 2002).

6.4. COMPUTERS AS AN AID TO INSTRUCTION

Researchers have been on the search on how the computer is used as an aid to instruction for close to twenty years now. It has been discovered that computers for this year have been an important tool in sending out instructions. It is noted that when students learn using the computer, they tend to perform better than the students who learn traditionally without the use of the computer. How the student performs however, highly depends on the availability of the appropriate software and hardware. Most students and schools however, use the microcomputers since most computer hardware and software are very expensive (Chao, 2012).

A field was invented that deals with students teaching and learning of students using computers which is called the computer-assisted learning abbreviated as CAL. It was founded as early as the late 1950's with institutions such as rhea university of Illinoisan 1959. The project was named PLATO and with time it started being sold at a fee by an institution called controlled data corporation. This project has been funded largely federally and other mini projects on computer-assisted learning developed. Another project that was developed was Pat Suppers that was discovered by the Sanford University and distributed by the United States. It should be noted that a lot of projects have been developed but not all of them have proved to work appropriately but those that worked appropriately have enabled studies to be faster and have brought about growth in performance.

Initially, computer-assisted learning was very expensive. IT could not be incorporated in public schools because it was too expensive for them to be implemented. This saw the manufacturing of microcomputers that closed this gap (Chao, 2012). Initially, the CAL was incorporated in armed schools, medical schools and remedial education where studying traditionally was expensive. The development of microcomputers has been of great help since it is cheaper than CAL it has enabled many people to obtain it hence it has enabled educational materials to be accessible easily by a large group of students.

There are three types of Computer-assisted learning but two are adapted in elementary school setting. They include:

- Computer augmented learning
- Computer managed instruction
- Computer-assisted instruction

These parts have been discussed below:

Computer-assisted learning is the use of computers to support education. Augmented learning is a type of learning that is currently very high on demand. It is where the environment adapts to the environment. According to research findings, augmented learning is the cheapest and can be found easily. In this type of learning students write programs to solve the problems that arise in their learning. It is implemented in various forms such as e-learning, it ensures that students focus on embracing the studies rather than using memorization which is proved to be more beneficial. There is software that enables students to form the programs to assist to their learning. Most students teach themselves how to utilize this software but, in some cases, there is little teacher's assistance. It is used in university and collages and in some high schools too though in next few years it will be greatly incorporated in high schools. In primary or elementary schools, they are not experienced a lot of problems therefore they are not greatly familiar with them therefore the use of computer admitted learning may not be very appropriate (Beauchamp, 2016).

Computer managed instruction is where there is the use of computers in classroom by the teachers to enable them to manage the class and perform some functions that are associated with the classroom (Beauchamp, 2016). The teacher manages the process hence the computer knowledge of the student does not count. This assisted teachers to face an easier time to manage a classroom unlike in the olden days. The computer can perform several functions for the teachers such as grading results for them after a test or exam, it also assists teachers to mark tests that have ABCD answer, analyses the students results in a way that can help them to grade the students and it can print the students' results. Also, a teacher can use a computer to make tests for the students and give the students to do.

The main disadvantage of computer-managed instruction is that it requires very expensive software that disadvantages most teachers in public institutions that they prefer to use the traditional method. Another disadvantage is that the required software for elementary schools has not yet been invented and hence it is not applicable in primary institutions or elementary institutions. The computer-managed institution is highly being introduced in the forming of online textbooks such that instead of one buying a textbook from a bookshop they can access it through the computer. Most textbook manufacturing companies are therefore making their textbooks present in computerized supplements (Beauchamp, 2016).

Figure 6.3. Computer-assisted instruction abbreviated as CAI is the use of computers to give students instructions.

Source: https://www.britannica.com/topic/computer-assisted-instruction.

Students can use the computer to improve on their studies by accessing materials important in their study from the computer. This material can help students gain new knowledge or add to the knowledge that they had before. It can also correct on some misconceptions that the student has. The students access the materials directly from the computer. This material may have been initially installed in the computer. How a student is able to understand this material depends on how they progress. At a higher level, the students and the computer may engage in a dialogue in order to find a solution of a certain problem at hand. It makes learning interesting and results in substantial learning (Kadijevich, Angeli, &Schulte, 2013).

Computer-assisted instruction is slowly replacing teachers in the education sector since the computer replaces the teacher's role. The computer gives information to the students that they could be given by the students. This hence pose danger to the teachers since they can easily lose their jobs. Students can have their own personal studies at the comfort of their homes or public libraries and still perform as well as they could if they were being taught by the teachers. According to AI Bork who supports CIA, he says that by the year of 2000 more than half of the institutions will give half of the instructions through the computers.

Although the computers may replace the teachers in the education sector, the love and care for students by the teachers will still be required therefore teachers cannot be eliminated completely. The progress of integration computer-assisted learning is slow and gradual and it will most definitely interact the current traditional system of education (Hazzan, Lapidot, & Ragonis, 2011).

6.5. THE BENEFIT OF COMPUTER STUDIES IN ELEMENTARY SCHOOLS

According to research, the leaders stated that it is of great importance for all students to know about the computer. They should understand what a computer is, how to operate a computer, the advantages and disadvantages of a computer, the computer limitations and the benefits of the computer. They say that it is of great importance for not only the college students to know about the computer but also the pre-college students.

In elementary school, there are two levels of education one being awareness level and functional level. Awareness level is the creating of awareness of a new thing. It can be integrated in the studies by being introduced as a subject or integrated into each subject. Functional level requires instruction in the use of a computer. One can train to be a professional in the field of computer later in university or college in some courses such as computer science though some high schools also offer professional computer studies (Willmann, 2017).

What a student should know about a computer has been discussed by many professionals over time. It is not disputed that all students should have an understanding on computers but what they should learn about it is still being discussed. In the past computer literacy referred to the ability of a student to understand a computer or the awareness of the student about a computer. Students would basically know what a computer, it advantages and disadvantages, its limitations and how it affects the worlds around them. Many students could not access the computer since it was very expensive therefore, they could not gain first hand workability of the computer by using it.

Later it was discovered that computer was much more than that. It was necessary that students at all educational levels can learn computers from the problem-solving basis. This has been enabled by the decrease in price of computer hardware and the development practical application of microcomputers. This has assisted many educational institutions to have access to computers for their studies hence making computer studies more of practical than theoretical. The goal of computer studies therefore graduated to a functional level of knowledge about using a computer. This can begin as early as elementary schools (Strickland & Alvermann, 2004).

The use of technology in elementary schools may be shared among the students and the person in charge of them must be keen to ensure the repairs are performed at the required time that is immediately a malfunction occurs. The sharing of microcomputers should be regulated to ensure that all the students benefit to promote computer literacy. This way certain goals may be achieved as stated below;

The students will be able to learn how to use a computer both theoretically and practically. The student will be able to know the practical application of a computer and the student will get to enjoy the whole process. Several activities can be done using the computer to improve the understanding and these activities will be discussed later. In case a student can access the computer in school at home during lunch and supper breaks and the teacher has perfect understanding of the computer then the school may begin computer lessons and computer clubs.

With time the understanding of teachers and students will increase if they follow the plan. If a school decides to integrate computer studies in the school, then they should ensure that they have high access to computers all the time so that they ensure the students gain understanding of the computer studies (Strickland & Alvermann, 2004).

6.6. ROLE OF CALCULATORS IN ELEMENTARY SCHOOL EDUCATION

Calculators are tools that aid one to perform mathematical calculations effectively. They are a type of a computer only that they deal with mathematical calculations only. This therefore means that there is little distinction between computers and calculators. The national council of teachers strongly support the use of calculators because they enable students to perform their calculations fast and accurately (Beauchamp, 2016).

Students become familiar with the use of calculators at the elementary levels so that they can build their skills from an early age. Limited use of the calculator can free up some time to think about important levels of activities needed to solve a mathematical problem.

The calculator is similar to the computer as it has several features that are present in the computer therefore it can help students gain understanding of the computer. A good example is the memory present in a calculator is very similar to the memory present in a computer. The calculator has a 4 key memory which is the exact same memory that the computer has. Also, the computers number system is the same as the computer number system.

Calculators are commonly used today by adults because life revolves around calculations. Close to 30 million calculators are being sold in the United States of America. Calculators come in different styles shapes and models. Some are very small, some are big, some are used to carry out complicated calculations, some are used to carry out simple calculations, some models are more superior than the others, some are cheap and some are expensive depending on their functions and models (Beauchamp, 2016).

Some issues that arise in the use of calculators and education include why should students learn abbot calculators, when should they learn it and when are students allowed to use calculators. Most people fear that when students use the calculators, they will be dependent on the calculator to an extent that they cannot perform simple calculations without the pretense of the calculator. They fear that the calculator will decrease the use of paper and pen or mental arithmetic skills. This has led to the use of calculators being studied so as to eliminate this fear. It is noticed that the use of calculators judiciously does not damage the curriculum but improves it instead.

At the lower grades such as grade one to grade three, the use of calculators has only modest value such that they are used for simple addition math manipulative and as a tool for exploration. The use of calculators at this level may aid learning topics being taught at their level.

For primary grade students, using the calculator is fun and they use it as a play tool. They enjoy pressing the computer and as they press it the not only have fun but they can learn a thing or two from it. During this level, student develop a deep understanding of the major four basic mathematical operations which include addition, subtraction, division, and multiplication. If the understanding they obtain is associated with the solving of real-life problems, then the students may understand but fail to solve therefore the use of the calculator may be integrated to solve the problems (Beauchamp, 2016).

At intermediate level that is grades four to six it is of benefit to have classroom set of calculators. Students can receive instructions on how to use the calculator and they can use it to develop the necessary skills. At this level performing arithmetic calculations mentally may not be emphasized very much and hence the use of paper and pencil may not be emphasized very much. This is as a result of the increased emphasize on geometry, logic and statistics.By the end of grade school most students have the required skills for the using of the calculator to perform the four basic arithmetical functions. They can also have the knowledge of the use of the memory features of the four key memory system. Hence, they can solve calculations involving fractions and more complex calculations. To achieve this, it requires some classroom time to be educated on how to perform them and a lot of the student's effort to do practice on their own. It requires high knowledge of the calculator that the teachers should process (Beauchamp, 2016).

It has been discovered that maximum usage of the calculator will influence the curriculum positively in the intermediate and higher grades. However, parents discourage the use of calculators basing their argument on no one knows he long term effects of using those calculators and hence they may cause more damage than good. Calculators are very easy and simple to use though they require one's effort to learn how to operate them and the features and use of the memory. The teacher and students should have understanding on the calculator because some features may differ from what we know an example being the calculators numbering system is different from the normal numbering system. It is therefore neccssary to understand the calculator in depth (Beauchamp, 2016).

6.7. WHAT PREPARATORY SCHOOL TEACHERS SHOULD UNDERSTAND ABOUT COMPUTERS?

Figure 6.4. Students performing class activities through modern computers.

Source: https://www.theatlantic.com/education/archive/2016/10/a-plan-to-teach-every-child-computer-science/504587/.

Preparatory school teachers must be literate in using computers and calculators, plus realize the anticipated outcomes of introducing this equipment in schools. Some degree of awareness on computer literacy may come from going through this booklet. The literacy ratio can be increased through practical computing experience, as well as by using computers and calculators with pupils. For educators who are truly impressed by computers, nevertheless, a significant course of study at university or college level is probably necessary.

Many people realize that one may start studying a field like mathematics, writing, science or literature in preparatory school and remain study it all through a university degree or up to Ph.D. Assuming you had never learnt mathematics (arithmetic) previously, and then somebody approached you and claimed that you should be math literate. It's apparent that going through a small pamphlet on mathematics won't provide you the amount of math literacy sufficient to becoming an elementary school instructor.

Also known as Information Science, Computing or Computer Science is a new field. The preliminary university degree courses in this field were launched during the early 60's. However, this subject already has an impact and scope similar to the other key academic areas of study. Presently, there are multiple research papers in computer science. Plus, many learners are pursuing bachelor's qualifications in computing subjects, such as math or statistics (Blake, 2009).

This brief pamphlet is intended to help students begin to gain a minimum amount of computer literacy. A few hours of practical computing experience plus the reading of this brochure can have a significant impact on your overall understanding of computers, particularly as it relates to education. Though you should notice that you've just perused the surface. You might spend considerable time studying computing and computers in school, though still not grasp all that's presently known in these subjects. Below are a few ways to enhance your awareness of computer science (CS) and computing education.

- Get cognizant of computing trends in your daily reading, and TV watching. Other materials like magazines, newspapers, news broadcasts and education journals also have content about computers. Because you now have foundational knowledge concerning computers, it won't be difficult to grasp more advanced computer concepts. Be particularly aware of adverts for computer-based products. They provide a clear sign of the present trends in firmware and software.

- Discuss more on processors and calculators together with your buddies and fellow teachers, plus with your pupils. Go through the next part of this pamphlet, which features a number of class-based activities, then start to try a few of these alongside your pupils. Learn by performance, and allow other individuals to assist you in the learning process. A few of your pupils may understand more about processors than you do. While you and your class may learn from these scholars as well.
- Register for an official computer science program. Most probably you may find a computing course at a local college or university. Perhaps you can have your school administration organize a workshop or some in-school program. If you're concerned about knowing more about processors, then ultimately you'll require this formal instruction.
- Subscribe for and read multiple computer-based journals. A catalog of some publications is provided in the Short Guide to Journal Literature segment of this pamphlet. By all means, sign up with the Computing Tutor, since it's designed for educators.

Various elements of computer science have been highlighted just shortly in this pamphlet. Among the subsectors where one may focus their studies include corporate data processing, artificial intelligence, information retrieval, computer graphics, numerical analysis, coding languages, simulation, and model of computation. Individuals can also view the field of computing from a mechanical engineering standpoint. The makeup of chips plus of computer circuitry, including interfacing computers together with other machines, are of key concern to mechanical engineers (Blake, 2009).

While thinking about pursuing a formal program in computing, you might contemplate if you have sufficient math background. The average college-level preparatory computer science program uses various materials from 2nd-year secondary school algebra. In case your math background isn't up to this ability you may require to do some additional work on mathematics to comprehensively go through the program. However, math and computing are two separate fields. You don't have to be some mathematical genius to understand computers. Every tutor is capable of gaining a practical knowledge of computing in education.

6.8. PRIMARY SCHOOL COMPUTER-BASED ACTIVITIES

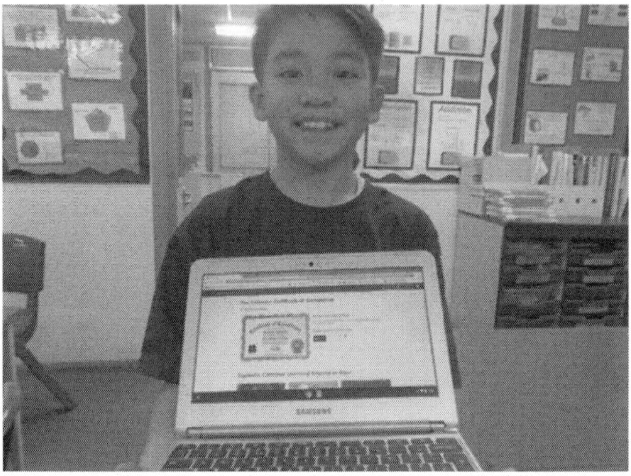

Figure 6.5. A student proudly shows his elementary coding skills in class.

Source: https://Twitter.com/bedeprimschool/status/1071092417040912384.

This segment consists of a variety of computer-based activities which can be applied in a primary school or even in a teacher preparation setting. Among the activities are those particularly modeled for teacher preparation, whereas others are intended to help students understand more about processors and calculators. A few of the arithmetical and computing activities can be performed without access to modern machines, and need very minimal teacher knowledge.

Nevertheless, others need some handling of calculators and computer equipment, including an equivalent expansion in knowledge on the teachers' part. Computers are impacting the elementary school class setup in three key ways:

- They lay the foundation for an impressive new field, computer science. A computer is a flexible and useful facilitator to problem-solving in nearly every scholarly area. Ultimately, its usage will be regarded among the "elements" of a relevant present-era education; training in computer science shall start in the elementary level.
- Computers are a recent and versatile teaching medium. Computer-based learning will ultimately be widespread at both learning centers and home.

- Computers determine what's learnt and what is meant to "understand" something. This can be witnessed even with basic computational instruments like a pocket calculator. Pupils can learn to divide numerical square roots by using a calculator, plus the learner can study the significance and uses of square root. It's a great substitute to spending limited time learning how to find a square root manually through pencil and paper, or developing knowledge in practically applying that algorithm.

6.9. THE COGNITIVE OBSTACLE

Most tutors have at least a basic understanding of computers. Considering that you're reading this content, it's a great sign that you possess a considerable interest in learning more about computers (König, 2012).

In case you're ina similar situation as most primary school tutors, then workstations have had minimal effect on your classroom. You might determine right now that computers shall have an impact in your classroom the next time students meet.

Still, this resolution could be difficult for some teachers. The Thinking Actions (TAs) provided in this segment are aimed at helping you become conscious of your anxieties and fears. These actions may be role-played within an educator training setup. Otherwise, you may also work with them personally, as is recommended in the succeeding paragraph (König, 2012).

Make yourself relaxed in a comfortable chair, couch, or even some cushions. Choose a suitable TA from those available and carefully read it. Next, shut your eyes and reflect about the action. Tap into your bodily responses and your feelings. Take a few minutes to mentally expound on these feelings. Finally, open your eyes, unwind, take some few long breaths, and meditate on the experience. Did you learn anything about yourself?

TA1. Envision yourself at a seminar with school parents and staff. A parent to one of the children asks the headmaster this particular question: "I handle computers regularly, and I need my kids to learn about them. What steps are you taking to assist pupils in this institution to gain knowledge on computers?"

You're pleased that the query hasn't been focused at you, however, your school principal comes back to you then says, "Could you assist us on this matter?" Now you've been put on the spotlight again!

TA2. Consider yourself at a skilled education conference during an educator in-service day. An individual is showcasing a micro-computer to a couple of teachers. They are showing how simple it is to utilize a program that's been stored in the device's memory.

You apparently are at the frontbench of the crowd when the demonstration forerunner requests for a willing volunteer. The goal is for an individual to test the project which has just been showcased. You contemplate on volunteering.

TA3. Visualize yourself at the fore of your classroom tomorrow. A curious pupil asks: "My parent mentioned that they received a new workstation at the workplace. She mentions that it's a rather smart device. Are computers sharper than people?" Exactly how do you address this question?

TA4. Imagine you're at a faculty gathering next week. A guest speaker from a college is talking about calculators, including how pupils who're permitted to utilize calculators make considerable achievements on problem-solving aspects of nationally regulated tests. Then, your principal specifies that each instructor who feels confidents enough can get a classroom ready of calculators for activity during the rest of the school year. The headteacher focuses on you and mentions, "Do you want to get a classroom set?" What's your response?

6.10. COMPUTER-BASED ACTIONS

Figure 6.6. Computer-based activities can help students increase their understanding of key concepts.

Source:http://my.ilstu.edu/~hpparet/Foundations_Technology_Integration/Foundations_Technology_Integration_print.html.

You have already decided, you now want to go, the next day you'll do something associated to workstations in your classroom; however, what will be your say?

It's not a must to be a computing professional in order to assist your learners to understand computers. Certainly, it's not even essential that you must be more knowledgeable than your pupils, even though it's more likely that you are. What's required is a readiness to attempt and a disposition to learn.

The few Computer-Related Actions (CRA) listed in this segment are intended to improve pupil awareness and knowledge concerning computers. Others are computer preparation activities, equivalent to reading readiness. Whereas some are intended to impart particular knowledge on the abilities and limits of computers.

CRA I. What do your pupils understand about computers? Pose this question to them! Have each pupil write a few sentences or multiple paragraphs showing something interesting they know about computers. Let several pupils read their write-up to the classroom. You might be surprised and pleased at the outcomes. Pupils gain knowledge about processors from their caregivers and peers, from TV and movies, plus from comic books. Therefore, most of what these youngsters "know" may actually be fiction.

CRA II. How do computers help students, plus what issues do they cause? Develop a module around this question. Learners can collect photos of different kinds of machines. For every device, show the problem it's intended to help resolve. Moreover, the pupils must try to deliberate about problems in the modern society which have been triggered or instigated by the machine.

CRA III. Who are the people who use computers? Let each pupil discuss with their caregiver about this. Roughly a half of all individuals now have professions which pertain to computer usage plus/or in areas where processors are a daily tool. Preferably, have each learner write a short report on their discoveries. Another method is having students prepare a list of professions, and then explore how computers are impacting on these professions.

CRA IV. One principle aspect of a computer's abilities is how many practical instructions per second the device can perform. An average computer, presently costing around a few thousands of dollars can be ranked at one MIPS. Meanwhile, the quickest computers presently available, costing roughly $10 million each, can be graded at between 50-to-100 MIPS. A command may entail adding or multiplying a pair of decimal numbers, matching two quantities to check if they're equal, or other similar matters.

There are various things you can perform to help your pupils understand MIPS. Some are listed here.

- Pick an arithmetic knowledge drill sheet suitable to the pupils you teach. Time them while they tackle these drill questions. Assist each pupil to decide the amount of questions that they can answer every minute. Depending on this information, assist each pupil to decide how long it shall take to answer certain amounts of questions.
- A device ranked at one MIPS is capable of examining and performing various processing tasks on characters like letters, punctuation marks and digits within a second. Also determine how long it takes students to read certain characters? What are the necessary books? This question entails timing learners while reading a number of pages, determining the amount of characters found on these pages, approximating the amount of characters present in a book, and so on. As for younger students, the instructor will require that you provide detailed guidelines and perform most of the additions. Remember that a calculator may be a valuable tool in solving some of these problems. A long adult novel, probably 500 pages or so, is capable of containing around a million characters. Get such a manuscript and present it to your classroom.
- What duration of time does it take for one to count up to a million through 1's? A processor rated at 1 MIPS is capable of doing it in one second. While pupils struggle with this inquiry, you can highlight matters like: "You may count 1 up to 4, rather quicker than 100001, 100002 or 100003 and so on."

CRA V. Computer scientists explain the term procedure as follows: It's a step-by-step number of instructions that can be technically deduced and performed by some agent. It's developed to solve a particular kind of problem. Computing experts are especially interested in techniques whereby the intermediary is a workstation or individual operating a computer. Most of the things that we teach learners are simply situations where the main agent is a pupil, probably aided by pencils, paper and a publication. Algorithms from arithmetic, including how to locate a word within a dictionary, are some good examples. The actions listed below are developed to familiarize pupils with the idea of a procedure.

- Get each pupil to draw a map displaying how to go from the class to lunchroom (or any other venue that you decide). This map should give clear directions, effortlessly followed by the students.
- Subdivide the class into distinct teams of two then provide each side with a dictionary. Provide each team with a unique word to check up. A member of the group holds and utilizes the dictionary. Another member of the same group provides guidelines to the dictionary user, though isn't permitted to view any specific sections of the dictionary. The handler is only permitted to follow the guidelines being provided, and to answer any queries on request. Once a word is detected, change roles and consider a different word. A similar activity may be applied with checking up a name or phone number within a directory.
- Pick a few pencils or paper arithmetic activities suitable for your students. Group students into pairs. Carry on with the same concepts highlighted in (b) above. One pupil is to complete an algorithm that's being identified by the second pupil. The learner with a paper and pencil must instinctively, in a non-thinking way, specifically follow the guidelines being given.
- Arrange a set of between 25 and 50 cards, each having a unique digit on one side, with a different phrase (or individual's name) on the opposite side. If resources allow, it's recommendable to have a certain number of cards for every pupil. First, have each pupil arrange their cards in numerical manner, with the lowest digit first. Next, have the pupils jot down (or describe to an associate) how to arithmetically order a group of cards. Proceed to repeat by alphabetically arranging the cards this time. The activity is especially interesting since it shows that people can perform a task, like numerically organizing a group of cards, however, they might not be in a capacity to articulate or put in writing the particulars of what they're carrying out. For a workstation to complete such functions, it must detail every stage of the process which should be explicitly mentioned.
- Group students into pairs. Assign one pupil in every pair to act as the ROBOT. Meanwhile, the other pupil directs the ROBOT with guidelines like TURN RIGHT, LEFT, MOVE FORWARDS, STOP and so forth. At first, pupils can practice with transferring their robots to diverse points within the room.

Once each pupil has developed the necessary skills in commanding and acting as the robot you can magnify the task's difficulty levels. A possible way is requiring that the guidelines be jotted down in advance. Another approach is to provide the ROBOT additional capabilities. For instance, STRETCH RIGHT ARM FORWARD. ONCE YOU REACH THE WALL, THEN HALT, ELSE… That is, given that the MACHINE the capacity to test if a particular condition is contented, the task is to arrive at a given decision depending on the outcomes. A ROBOT having decision-making abilities can copying a suitable program, finish very complex chores.

Pupils know many procedures, like checking out a book upon visiting a library, looking up a digit in the phone book, using a phone, getting from one location to another through bus or subway, tying a shoe, and the like. As a teacher, have each pupil prepare a list of the procedures they know, meanwhile in each example showing what problem has been solved.

There are also different methods to represent procedures. For instance, a musical mark signifies a procedure for producing music. Meanwhile, a carpenter's plans might be a procedure for building a house. A flowchart might be applied to symbolize a mathematical procedure, while a recipe works as the cook's procedure. Generally, have pupils recommend as many methods as imaginable for demonstrating procedures.

Chapter 7

Technology Acceptance of Cloud Computing in Schools

CONTENTS

7.1. Introduction 170

7.2. Cloud Computing 171

7.3. History of Cloud Computing 172

7.4. Technology Adoption Frameworks 174

7.5. Clouding Computing 191

7.6. Cloud Computing Challenges 193

7.7. Cloud Risks 196

7.8. Cloud Migration 198

7.1. INTRODUCTION

Technology acceptance is an information system theory that shows how users accept and use technology. This theory suggests that when a new technology is introduced, some factors determine how they will use and when they will use it. This includes,

- The technologies usefulness where one checks to see if the technology will improve on his work and performance.
- The technologies ease of use where most people prefer a technology that is easy to use to escape some barriers brought about by complicated technology like the need for qualified personnel.
- External variables where a person may have an attitude towards a certain technology that is why technology must aim in bringing out a positive attitude to people's mind. How it is perceived may also change depending on age and gender.

All these are stated according to Davis's technology acceptance model.

There is increasing demand in educational applications of information technology.

Teachers spend most of their time examining the anatomy of the technology to determine how it will be incorporated in teaching and learning practices though they are guided strictly with the national and local policies on the technology used in classrooms.

The benefits of technology acceptance in education include,

- It makes teaching easy
- It helps teachers track their student's performance
- It saves on the environment because the most paper that would be used can be reduced by working with technology
- It makes studies fun
- It helps make distant learning more accessible
- It makes collaboration more effective.

In this chapter, we will aim to explain the technology acceptance of cloud computing in schools.

7.2. CLOUD COMPUTING

Figure 7.1. Cloud computing is the largest generation technology that provides means by which we can utilize the applications and utilities via the internet.

Source: http://redlaser.net/cloud-computering/.

Cloud computing provides several services called cloud services. Therefore, cloud computing is the using of a network of remote servers hosted on the internet to store, manage and process data rather than a local server or personal computer.

There are several ways in which cloud computing affects human lives today. This application is very affordable and hence very easy to use. It is also can be done anywhere and anytime. It provides new social services through social media and it lessens the usage of propriety operating systems in computing (WANG, 2017).

Storing in the cloud also has its advantages. It reduces one the pressure of carrying many devices around like the thumb drives and compact disks. It also easy to access, stable and secure such that your content is secured with a password. Also sharing information stored in the drive is very easy and one does not require a hard disk or CD.

In schools as children prepare to fit in this generation, then cloud computing needs to be introduced to them. Cloud computing has transformed education systems in ways like instead of the teacher being the provider of information, they act as the facilitator of helping students find information from the internet.

It should, therefore, be noted that the introduction of cloud computing in schools has brought growth in the education era.

7.3. HISTORY OF CLOUD COMPUTING

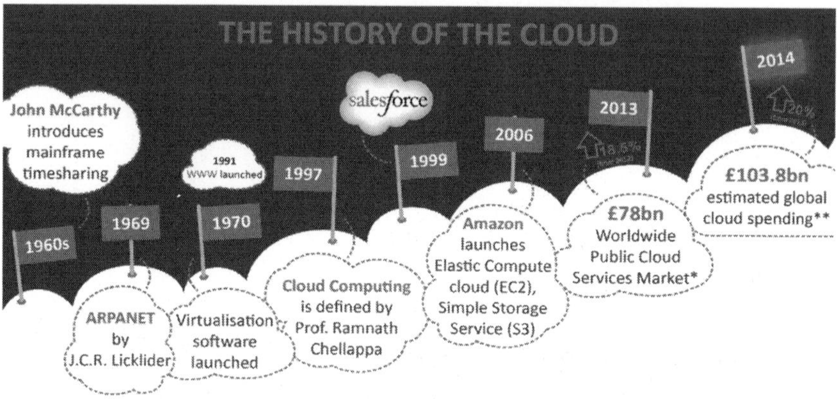

Figure 7.2. Cloud computing has evolved through several phases that include grid and utility computing.

Source: https://cloudcomputing521.wordpress.com/2017/05/01/history-of-cloud-computing/.

Cloud computing was invented by Joseph Carl Robert Lick liter in the year 1960s with his work on ARPANET to connect all people and data from anywhere at any time.

In 1963, DAPRA which is Defense Advanced Research Projects Agency gave two million to MIT for project MAC. MIT was to develop a technology that enabled two individual or more than two individuals to use one computer at the same time. Therefore, a computer that was gigantic and archaic that used reels of magnetic tape for memory was the precursor to cloud computing.

In the 1970s, the virtual machine that acted as the real computer was invented. This machine had a fully functional system that was operating effectively. In 1900 the use of these virtual computers became very popular which brought about the birth of development of modern cloud computing infrastructure.

In the early stages, the use of the cloud was to express the end space between the user and the provider. In 1997, Professor Ramnath Chalupa of Emory University brought a new definition of cloud computing. He defined cloud computing as a new computing paradigm where the computing boundaries will be defined by educational rationale rather than technical limits only. With time companies gained a better understanding of the cloud and this brought about the popularity of cloud increasing gradually.

In 1999 Salesforce used cloud computing to deliver computer software to the end-users. This made them popular. The software that was delivered could be downloaded from the internet by anyone with internet access.

In 2002 cloud computing services gave Amazon the capability to use the capacity of their computers to develop and introduce its web-based retail services.

In 2006 Amazon launched Amazon Web Services (AWS) which provided consumers with a wide array of cloud services. Among the cloud options offered included; AWS and Amazon elastic compute cloud, Amazon simple storage service, Amazon virtual private cloud, Amazon Simple DB and Amazon workspaces. This allowed individuals to rent virtual computers and still use their programmers and applications.

At the same time Google launched the Google docs services. Its a word processor included as a part of a free, web-based software office suite offered by Google within its Google drive services. It was based originally on two separate products; Whitely and Google spreadsheets. Whitely offers the ability for one to edit documents, save them and transfer them to the blogging systems while Google spreadsheets allow users to edit, update and save spreadsheets and share the data online. It is internet-based and was acquired from web technologies in the year 2005.

In 2007 Google, IBM, and various universes joined hands to develop a sever research farm for researching projects. The universities included the University of Washington, Carnegie Mellon University, MIT, Stanford University, the University of Maryland, and the University of California at Berkeley. According to this university research and computer experiments, they discovered that research could be done faster and cheaper.

Netflix video streaming services was launched in 2007 that offered to stream videos to their subscribers. It cost them about 40 million to acquire a license and build out its data. It streamed the videos using cloud and provided support binge-watching.

IBM developed the IBM smart cloud framework in 2011, which is a line of enterprise-class computing technologies and services for building and using private, public and hybrid clouds. Smart Cloud offerings can be purchased as self-service or managed services.

In 2011 Apple also launched iCloud which stored more personal information ranging from photos, music, videos, and documents. Microsoft began advertising cloud on television, radio and other social networks making people aware that they can save their documents, pictures, and videos to avoid losing them and to create space in their devices.

Oracle Cloud was introduced in 2012. Oracle Cloud is a cloud computing service offered by Oracle Corporation providing servers, storage, network, applications and services through a global network of Oracle Corporation managed data centers. The company allows these services to be provisioned on-demand over the Internet.

Security from accidental deletion, theft and data leakage has become the primary focus of cloud computing.

Private clouds can now be invented by businesses for different needs. Also, a combination of private cloud and public cloud called a hybrid cloud can be invented. This cloud store sensitive and important data for the organizations.

7.4. TECHNOLOGY ADOPTION FRAMEWORKS

7.4.1. Depone and McLean IS Success Model

Depone and McLean IS Success Model is also known as DeLeon & McLean Information Systems Success Model or D&M IS Success Model or the information systems success, model.

It is a theory that seeks to provide a comprehensive understanding of information system success by identifying, describing, and explaining the relationships among six of the most critical dimensions of success along which information systems are commonly evaluated. Information systems are formal, sociotechnical, organizational systems designed to collect, process, store and distribute information. The purpose of an information system is to turn some raw data into useful information that can be used to make decisions (WANG, 2017).

Therefore, the Depone and McLean IS Success Model is a model that measures the information system complex-dependency.

Dimensions of the Depone and McLean IS Success Model include: the system quality, the quality of the service, the quality of the information, the usage intentions, the satisfaction of the user and the net system beliefs.

The system quality is one common dimension. It denotes how well the hardware and the software can do their work together. The system quality is among the most studied dimensions of the Depone and McLean IS Success Model. System quality refers to the weight of the information processing system (WANG, 2017).

The quality of the service uses various research approaches to capture service quality information. It ensures service improvement planning and resource allocation. Information systems are evaluated with the quality of service they offer.

The quality of the information needs to be of very high quality for it to be used usefully. The quality of information can be rated by how accurate it is, how complete it is, if it is unique, its consistency and if it arrives at the right time. Information quality refers to the quality of the information that the information system can deliver.

The usage intentions are majorly influenced by the information system and service quality. It is also referred to as the system use (Islam et al, 2017).

The satisfaction of the user is the opinion or what the user thinks about a computer application that determines how they regard it. It is the subjective measure of success of a system.

The net system beliefs is an ideology that helps interpret the reality of the system. It is the overall value of the system to its users. It is affected by the satisfaction of the user and system use. How the user views the system depends on how satisfied they are. If they are quite satisfied then they have a positive net system belief.

Technology adoption lifecycle is a sociological model that describes the adoption of a new product or innovation. A new system must be adopted before it is used.

The advantages of the information system success model include, communication where it enables the passing of information with the help of information technologies. The information being passed include messages, emails, voice, and video calls become faster to be passed and hence more efficient. It also enables businesses to be open most of the time hence more available. Making purchases from other countries also becomes easier and the process becomes faster (Islam et al, 2017).

It has also brought about the creation of new jobs such as hardware developers, software developers, web designers, and many other new employment opportunities. Lastly, it has led to cost-effectiveness and productivity. It promotes efficiency in the operation of the company.

The disadvantages of Depone and McLean IS Success Model include, unemployment where people lack jobs because most paperwork can be processed and financial transactions carried out automatically and faster rather than when involving manpower. using technology is cheaper and way faster than when human beings do the job.

Despite information technology making the world a global village, it has also brought about one culture dominating others. For example, in today's world, most of the influence comes from the USA. The system has also brought about security issues such as hacking and theft of important information. Most of the hackers in today's world can easily access information by hacking into the company's computers and stealing the information, therefore, putting a company's secret at risk of getting stolen. Lastly, it has brought about expenses especially in implementing. To integrate a new information system, it requires a lot of money in the cause of software, hardware and the people involved in introducing the information system (Islam et al, 2017).

7.4.2. Diffusion of Innovations (DOI) Theory

It originated in communication to show how a piece of information diffuses between individuals and reaches a lot of people. It developed in 1962 from E.M. Rogers. It is therefore among the oldest theories. When a piece of information is developed, it gains momentum and is spread over a specific population over a specific period. Adopting means an individual begins to do things differently from how it was being done before. When the new idea is communicated, the individuals who receive the information are required to adapt to what the information states so that it can ensure the process of diffusion is complete (Yadav, 2014).

Characteristics of the target population are focused on five major areas which include, innovators, early adopters, early majority, late majority, and laggards.

- Innovators are the people who try out the idea of being the first. They are very creative, innovative, curious and they love trying out new things. They are willing to take risks and they are go-getters.
- Early adopters are the leader's they have leadership skills and they are hard to change their opinion on something.
- The early majority are neither leaders nor do they fall in the average person sector. They do not need the information to convince them to change.
- The late majority do not accept change easily. They are very hard to adopt new information and hence adapt very slowly to change.
- Laggards do not accept change and they are very skeptical. They fear change and pressure from other people.

Diffusion research focused on five major areas which include, innovation characteristics which may influence innovation, decision-making process that occurs when a specific individual wants to adopt a new idea, characteristics of an individual adopting the innovation, the outcomes and consequences of adopting the new idea or innovation and the channels used for the communication process.

Some elements are involved in diffusing information and according to Rodgers, there are 4 major elements:

Human capital: This is one element for diffusion because for an information to be transferred from one place to another there is a cost that is incurred. If the capital of the individual is enough then a media for communication that is fast enough can be used and hence diffusion of information becomes faster. Technology and its modes can be used in the diffusing of information since it is faster than other modes.

Leaders opinions: This is also an element for diffusion since what the leaders say and think influences the others because they depend on their leaders for information. This will determine how the mass that receives the information adopt to it. Leaders may influence either positively or negatively.

The nature of the network: This is also a key element for diffusion. Some networks are fast while others are slow. Fast networks diffuse information very fast and hence are more likely to be preferred. Slow networks are a disadvantage because they cause lagging of information. It is also important to note that fast networks are more often more expensive than slow networks.

The decision-making process of diffusion occurs in five steps which include: awareness, evaluation, trial, interest, and adoption.

- Awareness is making a new thing known to people who have no information about it.
- Evaluation is analyzing to check if the information or invention meets the required standard.
- The trial is trying the good for the first time to check if it is working correctly.
- interest is wanting to know more about the information or invention.
- The decision-making process, therefore, helps one to adapt easily.

Adoption is getting used to a new thing, information or invention and being able to incorporate it appropriately to everyday living. In the adoption process, there are five major steps which include Knowledge, persuasion, decision, implementation, and confirmation.

- Knowledge is when the individual is given information about an innovation introduced to him.
- Persuasion is when the person is being encouraged to adapt to the innovation by being cited for the advantages of this innovation.
- The decision is the point where the individual decides to adapt to the innovation introduced.
- Implementation is when the individual uses the innovation itself.
- Confirmation is when the individual confirms and ascertains the workability of the innovation.

7.4.3. Task Technology Fit (TTF)

Task technology fit is how a specific technology is suitable for a certain task at hand. When one is working and the technology, he is using does not interrupt his workflow then this technology may be used but in case it interrupts the workflow then this technology does not fit hence should be avoided. If the technology matches the work and does not interrupt the user workflow, then it will impact positively.

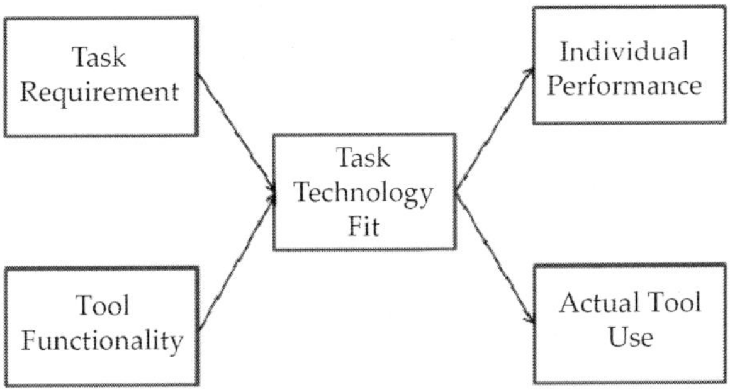

Figure 7.3. Task Technology Fit can be used to measure the effectiveness of an information system.

Source: https://www.researchgate.net/figure/The-task-technology-fit-model-Goodhue-Thompson-1995-p220_fig2_284920968.

Goodhue and Thomson in the year 1995 stated that task technology fit existed in eight factors which include, the quality, the accessibility, the authorization, the compatibility, the ease of use, the production timelines, the system reliability and the relationship with users.

- The quality describes how excellent technology is when performing its duty.
- The compatibility is how suitable or how the technology suits the task.
- The system reliability is if the technology is reliable and can be trusted to perform a certain task.
- Its relationship to its users is the technology is easy to understand and operate with.
- Production timeliness is the technology is produced when it's in need.
- The authorization refers to when the technology is accepted legally to be used.
- The accessibility describes if the technology is accessible for use at its location.
- The ease of use describes if the technology is not complicated and is easily understood.
- Task technology fit links the characteristics of the task and those of the technology. It evaluates if the information system and services that are given in an organization meet user's needs.

This model has been improved in several ways since 1995. Gebauer and Ginsburg in the year 2006 suggested that to increase the user's performance it is important to understand the linkage between the information systems and the individual user to ensure that the task is done appropriately. How users evaluate a task technology fit is used to examine it (Yadav, 2014).

Task technology fit exists in two main models. These models link the technology to its performance. The models include: 1) utilization model and 2) task technology fit model.

Utilization model is trying to explain that the more a person utilizes a technology than the more they adopt and hence improvement in performance impact. It is mainly based on users' beliefs, attitudes and behaviors.

Task technology fit model states that if the technology suits a certain task then the performance results will be positive (Yadav, 2014).

Technology task fit model and utilization model are used together to rate and evaluate the information system. In case one is used and the other left out, it may result in some disadvantages, for instance, utilization model may not necessarily be voluntary. At a certain level, utilization model is not voluntary for example if it exists alone and the user has no other option than to use it. In such a case, the impact of performance will depend mostly on the technology fit model than utilization model. On the other using task technology fit model alone may ignore the fact that technology must be used first hence utilization precedes task fit.

The combination of the task technology fit model and utilization model according to Goodhue and Thompson brought the rise of technology to performance chain that states that for a technology to meet the required performance it must be utilized and the technology must fit the task appropriately.

Other integrated models were invented with time including, technology acceptance model fused with task technology fit model by Dishaw and Strong in the late 90s. The Technology acceptance model reasons that the behavior of the technology is determined by its willingness to perform the behavior. The disadvantage of using it alone is it does not focus on the task that is why it is integrated with the task technology fit model to eliminate this disadvantage.

Several ways are used to evaluate the performance of the task technology fit which include, evaluating the user where the user gives his opinion on the technology and identifying explicit user evaluation construct which works better than the user's opinion (Chao, 2012).

The community has its thoughts concerning task technology fit. Different communities have differences in their beliefs. According to an article written by Massey et al in the year 2001, it suggested that research was conducted between two global organizations and different cultural beliefs were found out between different communities. Therefore, technology can bring about different reactions to individuals of different communities. These cultural perceptions are useful when it comes to using task technology fit to evaluate a certain technology.

7.4.4. Technology Organization Environment Framework (TOE)

This refers to organization, technology and environment frameworks. The model was created by Tornatzky and Fleisher in the year 1990 to state the factors that influence the adoption of a certain technology in a firm.

How a certain technology adapts to the organization depends on the context of the technology, environment and that of the organization according to DE Pietro, Wierda and Fleischer in the year 1990.

By technology, we mean the internal and external technology that is present in an organization. Specifically, by internal and external technology, we mean the technology that is already present in the firm and those not yet bought though they are in the market but can be used or needed in the firm at a certain time. According to Collins 1988, the technology in the business can influence how adoption process because they determine how technology will evolve in the firm. Innovations are created to improve the technology and therefore new evolution of technology and hence the firms adapt to them. There are three types of innovation which include, incremental which only introduce versions of an existing model, synthetic or discontinuous changes.

The organizational context is how an organization is arranged and its resources. It includes the size of the firm, how its management is organized, the relationship of employees to each other and the degree of formalization. It also refers to the characteristics and resources of the firm. How the communication process is in an organization can determine the innovation (Cartelli & Antonio, 2013). If there is good and appropriate passing of information in an organization, then its innovation is increased. How employees relate with each other also affects adoption of technology because the promotion of teamwork enables growth. Formalization is the degree to which rules and procedures are followed in an organization. It enables technological adoption since some rules are set aside to dictate how a certain technology is adopted in an organization.Lastly, the environmental context is the situation of the firm, its size, structure, presence or absence of service providers and regulatory environment. Where the firm is situated may affect the adoption of new technology because different technologies are designed for different situations. For instance, a machine that needs electricity cannot be used in areas where there is no electricity. The size of the firm also influences the technology because it will depend on the size of the technology they will use. If the firm is large then a large machine can be used and if it is small, the firm is limited to small machines.

The presence or absence of service providers dictates the kind of technology being used because if there are people in the organization who can work and understand the technology to provide service then it may be adopted into the company's business but in case there is no one who understands the technology then it is not adopted. Firms in industries that are growing fast are also likely to grow and develop quickly in the sector of technology. This is due to competition from other firms in the industry therefore the firm needs to up its game by improving its technology skills (Cartelli & Antonio, 2013).

These three elements state how an organization decides the appropriate technology to use and the need for it to adopt it into their system.

Technology, organization and environment framework has not evolved since it was first discovered because it was described as a generic theory by Zhu and Kraemer in the year 2005 this has enabled the theory to become easily adaptable as it is used as a framework. This makes the scholars and scientists find very little need to vary the theory.

The theory also blends with explanations for the adoption of technologies and does not counteract the explanation therefore there are very minimal tension between the technological, organizational and environmental theory and other technology adoption theories.

With the continued invention of new technologies, the technological, organizational and environmental framework is being used for empirical research. Empirical research is the research using empirical knowledge that is gaining knowledge employing direct or indirect observation or experience. The technological, organizational and environmental framework, therefore, digs deep to provide deep insights to the scholars about the adoption of the technology (Cartelli & Antonio, 2013).

It also shows the adoption of technology in inter-organizational systems.

It is therefore evident that technological, organizational and environmental context influences how technology is adopted in an organization.

7.4.5. Theory of Reasoned Action

The theory of reasoned action was stated in 1980 to predict the intentions of an individual. This theory aims to explain the relationship between attitudes and the intentions of an individual within the human action.

The theory of reasoned action was developed by Martin Fishbein in the year 1967 with the help of Icek Aizen. The theory suggests that when a person wants to perform a certain behavior then how they perform the behavior is determined by the attitude of the person. If a person has positive attitude towards the behavior, then they perform the behavior better.

There are key concepts and conditions that explain this theory which include, behavior, attitudes, behavioral beliefs, evaluation, subjective norms and normative beliefs, motivation to comply, behavioral intention and conditions.

The theory of reasoned action aims to explain if one intends to do a certain behavior. Behavior can be defined in the terms of action, context, time and target. The action stands for the process of getting the behavior, the context is where the behavior is acquired, the time is the specific duration taken to acquire the behavior and the target is what the behavior is intended for (Chao, 2012).

The theory of reasoned action shows that attitudes determines how individuals adopt to a certain behavior. How an individual feel and the opinion of an individual determines how they adopt to the behavior. How a person perceives a behavior is highly determined by what they originally perceive a certain behavior that is their beliefs about it. It is also determinant on the possible predictable outcomes of the behavior. If the individual perceives the outcome as positive, then they will easily adopt to the behavior but if they perceive as negative then they may fail to adopt to the behavior.

Behavioral beliefs are the beliefs that people hold to a certain behavior. For instance, if a person has a belief that something will happen only under a certain condition then it may fail if this condition is not present. Behavioral beliefs are important in explaining how one adopts to a certain behavior because the person will adopt only when the conditions required are present (Chao, 2012).

Evaluation is mainly how people predict the outcome of a certain behavior. If people perceive the behavior to bring positive outcomes then they will adopt very easily to the behavior but if they see it bringing negative outcomes, they will not adopt to it.

Subjective norms are how one's family, relatives, friends and society perceive a certain behavior. Ones family may affect how one adopts to a certain behavior because they may discourage the individual and hence causing the person to quit. On the other hand, they may encourage the person hence making them to adopt very fast and well to the technology.

Normative beliefs are how the relative group approves of an action. It may affect the adoption of an individual to a behavior since the more likely the relevant groups approve of an action the better its probability to be adopted appropriately and the less likely the relevant groups adopt to a certain behavior the less likely it is adopted (Chao, 2012).

Motivation to comply is the motivation received to enable one to adopt to a certain technology. How a person adheres to the social pressures depend on how they will adopt to a certain behavior. If the person easily gets swayed by the social pressures then how they adopt to the technology is determined.

Behavioral intentions are inclusive on both attitude and subjective norms towards a certain behavior. The attitude is how one feels about a certain behavior or how he perceives the behavior while subjective norms is how the family, friends, relatives and society perceives the behavior based on the social norms. If the person's attitude is positive and the social norms are also positive towards a certain behavior then the adoption of the behavior is easier and faster.

It should be noted that there are certain conditions that can affect the behavioral intentions and the behavior. One condition is that there must be stability between the behavior and behavioral intentions. The intention must also not change with time. The intention of the behavior must also be very specific. The condition is highly dependent on an individual such that he determines whether to perform the condition or not.

In technology adoption framework in respect to the theory of reasoned action, the behavior being adopted is the technology or information system. Therefore, how and information system is adopted is dependent on an individual's attitude towards the technology (Chao, 2012).

7.4.6. Theory of Planned Behavior

This is a theory that provides a link between what one's belief and his behavior. Icek Aizen came up with this theory as an improvement from the theory of reasoned action since this one offered or was inclusive of the behavioral control.

According to this theory, what one believes will determine how they behave. When one perceives the behavior as positive, then the likelihood of an individual adopting this behavior is high. The main difference between the theory of planned behavior and the theory of reasoned action is that Icek Aizen introduced perceived behavioral control which is the belief that one can control a certain behavior. This means that individuals can decide what they want to have or the kind of behavior they want to portray as compared to the theory of reasoned action that one did not have control over the behavior and hence their behaviors was determined by social norms and their beliefs. This theory has continued to be improved with time giving rise to reasoned action approach by Icek Aizen and Martin Fishbein.

The concepts and key variables include: normative beliefs, subjective norms, controlled beliefs, perceived behavioral control, behavioral intention and behavior. Each is discussed further below.

Normative beliefs are how one belief and take on a certain behavior. If one perceives a certain behavior as positive, then they are likely to adopt to it but if they perceive it as negative then they are likely to adopt very slowly to it or not adopt at all (WANG, 2017).

Subjective norm is what family, friends, society and the people around the individual take on a certain behavior. It influences how a person thinks and how they react towards certain behavior. If the society perceives a certain behavior positively them the person could adopt to the behavior.

Behavioral intention is the attitude one has towards a certain behavior. If one has a positive attitude towards the behavior, then they perform the behavior better than when they have a negative attitude towards it. It is also determined by how ready one is to perform ascertain behavior.

Behavior is how an individual respond to a certain thing or how they react to it. It will determine how they react towards adoption of a certain behavior.

The human behavior is guided by the behavioral beliefs, normative beliefs and control beliefs.

The behavioral beliefs are the attitude towards the behavior. What one belief are towards a certain behavior. It produces the attitude towards the behavior being either positive or negative (WANG, 2017).

Normative beliefs are what one belief being dependent on an individual's environment that is how people who surround the individual believe. They result in a subjective norm.

Control belief is when an individual believes that they have control over a certain behavior hence is brings about perceived behavioral control. If one belief to have control over a certain behavior then they can control whether to adopt to the behavior or not.

It should be noted that both the theory of reasoned action and the theory of planned behavior, social norm is the major variable. How one reacts to a behavior is highly dependent on what others think.

The limitations of this theory include, it does not take into consideration that a person should first perform the behavior you determine if they will adopt to it. One may have a positive attitude towards a certain behavior but when they actually engage in this behavior, they discover that they cannot adopt to it. On the other hand, one can have a negative attitude towards a certain behavior but when they perform the behavior, they adopt to it very well.

Technology adoption framework in respect to the theory of planned behavior the behavior being adopted to is new technology. How one adopts to a new technology or information system is highly dependent on all the variables discussed above. It is therefore essential that one gains understanding of this theory to be able to effectively explain how individuals adopt to a certain technology or information system (WANG, 2017).

7.4.7. Technology Acceptance Model

Technology Acceptance Model (TAM) is a theoretical model that is commonly used as the grass roots in studies relating to technology adoption frameworks involving certain types of contextual situations. Technology acceptance model (TAM) is a broadly used theoretical tool when it comes to the analyzing and assessing how decision making is executed by individuals on matters pertaining the endorsement of up to date mechanization. Technology acceptance model is more often than being put into use in intelligence systems and also in other scopes of studies. Thus, TAM is mostly helpful when a research study is mostly keen on the possible endorsement of technology that is coming out (Islam et al, 2017).

Technology acceptance model is commonly used by developers to foresee how potential users have accepted a certain technological design and puts to attention supposed manufacture difficulties prior to participants of the new technology mingle with the structure. Technology acceptance model was designed with the help and resources of North Americas IBM and it is mostly driven by the concept of fundamental theory which is psychological called the psychological reasoned action.

Development of Technological Acceptance Model: A number of investigators and researchers have proven the impact the technological acceptance model tool has in various scenarios.

According to a meta-analysis research performed a while back by computer scientists, the three main drivers that have led to the expansive endorsement and usage of the Technological acceptance model is the vigorous non-practical foundation and a powerful estimation scale, robust observed aid of the general detailed explanation power given by the framework, plus its vast applicability in an expansive horizon of frameworks and mechanization. In the meta-analysis that spanned over 15 years, it has shown that there is a very high relation when it comes to 'field setting' in PU and PEOU and their ideas to use different types of mechanization (Islam et al, 2017).

The corc use of the technology acceptance model is the actual user that is the end point and how they can communicate and interact with the technology so as to achieve a form of behavioral intention, and it is an important element which drive people to utilize the computer. Attitude is the at the forefront of influencing the overall sense of the technology and this also influences the behavioral intention (BI) is influenced by the attitude (A).

The framework implies that when the potential end users are exposed to this new technology, there are a number of elements that particularly have a significant effect on the criteria of decision making that the users will consider and apply when users are presented with a new technology. These factors are perceived usefulness (PU) and Perceived ease of use (PEOU).

Perceived usefulness (PU) – Fred Davies had a definition where he stated that "the degree to which a person believes that using a particular system would enhance his or her job performance." It measures how the new technology has influenced the jobs of users

Perceived ease-of-use (PEOU) – According to Fred Davies, PEOU was defined as "the degree to which a person believes that using a particular system would be free from effort." If the technology is easy to use, then the barriers conquered. If it is not easy to use and the interface is complicated, no one has a positive attitude towards it. When the new technology has a lot simple and easy-to-use features, this means that the faults and difficulties have been solved previously. Therefore, this is predominantly a positive attitude. However if the endorsed mechanization has numerous complications in its interface, this implies that work has not been made easy, which in turn implies a negative attitude (Islam et al, 2017).

Other factors including social influence are vital elements for determining the kind of attitude that a technology holds. When technology acceptance model has passed the standards of the two factors it can be incorporated into the real world since users have the intention and attitude of the technology. Though, factors such as gender and age will still linger around to influence it (Islam et al, 2017).

There has been a continuous broadening in the research of technology acceptance model and the two known modifications is TAM 2 and the Unified Theory of Acceptance and Use of Technology (UTAUT). There has been a proposal of the design of TAM 3 to be applied to e-commerce.

In this article, some disadvantages and limitations of the technology acceptance model were outlined. Some of the disadvantages reported among the few limitations reported in the literature and the most common one is the self-reported usage. Not only that but also researchers argue that since the technology acceptance model foresees the behavior of people when it comes to endorsing technology, there is limited exposure and usage of the endorsed technology before the investigation for one to make an appropriate analysis. Furthermore, the initial framework of technology acceptance model did not adequately stress on social influence. Though the investigation was undertaken by an individual and there is not much proof of the study (Islam et al, 2017).

7.4.8. The UTAUT Model

The UTAUT a framework that is an upgrade of technology acceptance network which was designed by Vankatesh and his colleagues in" User acceptance of information technology" It aims to achieve the explanation behind user intention to utilize an intelligence system and the following usage habit. The hypothesis indicates that there are four main establishments which include: effort expectancy, performance expectancy, social influence and facilitating conditions.

Factors one, two and three are the straight indicators of usage purpose and behavior, and the last one is the straight indicator of the behavior of the user. Gender, age, experience, and voluntariness of use are employed to control the effect of the four main constructs on utilization intention and behavior. The hypothesis was constructed through talks and discussion and the consolidation of the construction of eight frameworks that had previously been used to elaborate the usage of information systems behavior (theory of reasoned action, TAM, motivational model, theory of planned behavior, a combined theory of planned behavior/mechanization endorsement framework, framework of PC use, diffusion of innovations hypothesis, and social cognitive hypothesis). Subsequent validation by Venkatesh et al. (2003) of UTAUT in a longitudinal study found it to account for 70% of the variance in Behavioral Intention to Use (BI) and about 50% in actual use.

Application: UTAUT was applied in the research of the perceptions which had two hundred and forty-three participants by Koivumäki et al in North Finland regarding mobile services and mechanization. From the study, he was able to discover that the amount of duration used by participants in using the technology did not influence their perception of consumers though, the skills of the user and how familiar you are to the device had an influence on perception.

A research was conducted on social influence in workplaces on a specific group that is the superiors by Eckhard by applying UTAUT on intention to endorse technology in one hundred and fifty-two German companies and found out that there was a huge effect of social influence in adoption of technology (WANG, 2017).

UTAUT model was also used to investigate the adoption of social media by and he used four hundred and nine nonprofit organizations. In the past, UTAUT has not been used in testing the usage of social media in public relations. It was known that institutions that have an organized public relations department have a higher chance of endorsing social media related technology which eventually leads to their goals being achieved. Females found the use of social media to be more helpful and men were also drawn to social media usage.

The frequency of computer use was also studied using UTAUT by Verhoeven in seven hundred and fourteen college freshmen in Belgium and found out that UTAUT was helpful in elaborating the difference in frequencies of usage. Also, et al. applied UTAUT to study computer use frequency in 714 university freshmen in Belgium and found that UTAUT was also useful in explaining varying frequencies of computer use.

Extension of the theory: Two computer scientists Lin and Apol predicted an add-on framework of the unified theory of acceptance and use of technology involving the impact of internet on online help on socialization of internet intelligence technology utilization. A study was performed on tree hundred and seventeen university students in Taiwan on matters dealing with their individual online social help in the usage of short service messages and discovered that social effect heavily influences online social help.

Sykes suggested a framework of endorsement with peer aid (MAPS), consolidating previous studies on single endorsement with investigation on social networks in institutions. They partook in a 12 weeks long research of eighty-seven workers in the same institution and discovered that learning about social network concepts can help in comprehending recent intelligence system usage.

The set-up that discerned playfulness and self-handling of studying was extended by Wu, Wang and Wang. In their UTAUT in the studies they discovered that these are vital components of behavioral purposes in order to apply the use of mobile learning with all the participants (WANG, 2017).

The UTAUT was a further added-on with Wang in their investigation of three hundred and forty-three people in Taiwan to investigate the parity in internet acceptance based on sex. From the study they included three setups They added three constructs: discerned sport fullness, discerned worth, and palm-sized computer self-effectiveness. Experience, behavioral use and facilitating terms and conditions we removed. Age and participations were also removed because the tools were used in an optional circumstance and the adopters were aged between twenty to thirty-five years. Perceived value had a huge effect on endorsement purpose palm-sized computer self-effectiveness was vital in foreseeing mobile net endorsement. There was little effect when it came to Perceived playfulness regarding behavioral purpose though this might have been brought about by service quality difficulties when the research was taking place (WANG, 2017).

Criticism: A computer scientist named Bagozzi judged the framework its and following add on, quoting that "UTAUT is a well-meaning and thoughtful presentation," though it outlays a framework with forty-one free moving factors for foreseeing objectives and not less than eight free moving factors for foreseeing behavior," and that it heavily impacted and brought contributions to the research of mechanization and its endorsement "reaching a stage of chaos."

Van Raaij and Schepers judged the UTAUT saying that it cheaper as compared to the earlier technology acceptance model and technology acceptance model two since the high R2 is solely achievable if you moderate the main relations of up to four factors. There was also an introduction of collecting and tagging of objects They also called the grouping and labeling of item designs difficulties due to the fact that a number of contrasting objects were mixed to portray a sole psychometric construct.

7.5. CLOUDING COMPUTING

Cloud computing provides numerous chances to interaction designers and also shifting the components they use.

7.5.1. Innovation has Become Affordable

Cloud computing technology has made it affordable for users since it provides software in the form of services rather than getting very costly operating.

Innovation has been democratized in that it has enabled availability of high-end software to all software developer as it has made them affordable to most of them. Cloud computing has significantly brought down the price of purchasing software's as it has made them accessible in the form of software as a service (SaaS). Software Developers can utilize these services mostly with minimal modification struggles in product development. Take for example, artificial intelligence growth, language of machines, chatbot other mechanizations can be accessed in the cloud. Nowadays, small institutions utilize APIs that are able to perform computer translation and image recognition in an affordable and efficient manner (Yadav, 2014).

Because cloud computing has made the design of many software's easy, features that were being given little or no priority are now able to be developed in a cheaper and more efficient way making them achievable. For example, the AWS Elastic Transcoder service has made it easy for the conversion of numerous media files to different formats enabling information to be transferred to varying devices.

With such opportunities and capabilities, interaction designers have realized that they have a powerful tool. In an article called "Applications of Machine Learning for Designers," there were points namely:

- Detection: All cloud enabled software's can be of value to the owner since they can trace automatically, for instance, in the case of identifying spam.
- Prediction: They have been tailored for you in that they can predict what you are interested in e.g., hotels and clubs.
- Invention: In the days to come, smart software applications and creative developers will work together to design user interfaces and other features. Such capabilities are vital mostly because they will minimize manual work.

7.5.2. Tailored Experience

A big advantage that cloud has offered is the ability to have a tailored experience when using devices in different locations

A major opportunity of the cloud is enabling seamless experiences because the main function of the service is not on the device but on the cloud across locations and devices. Because the main reason of a service experience is not on the device, but in the cloud, a tailored service can be able to personalize someone's internet usage and it can be able to trace the users search history enabling the user to access their favorite searches even on different devices (Chao, 2012).

Deezer music application is a perfect example of an application that has such capabilities. The application has many ways of making the user experience seamless since it is tailored to your own liking and one can enjoy the application from different devices without feeling any change.

Designing a tailored experience needs a proper software design and the required infrastructure that will support it. In different scenarios such features is barely applicable due to the unavailability of cloud technology.

Tailoring of user experience is increasingly trending in our current world and it's done by mixing personal information and learning of machines. The cloud makes this possible by reducing the default technical barriers that are often faced when trying to personalize an application, for example, to create tailored recommendations. Deezer has crested tailored music playlists and this enables a user's personal experience to remain the same even when accessing the same application on different device (Chao, 2012).

7.5.3. Native Collaboration

Cloud related software's allows their users to stay in touch and communicate.

In the online world, you are most of the times not alone since cloud technology lets users to collaborate and interact. Unlike old computer software's which their data used to be stored within the device, Cloud-based applications enable other users to easily access your information by sharing with them.

Twitter is a good example of how cloud technology gives you an increased access into your followers' lives is given permission. Twitter gives you a feel of a person's feeling and it gives you their general awareness.

7.5.4. Robust User Experiences

For a user to say that they have a good user experience the online digital services must be able to operate easily and function according to its specification. The software should be able to be quick, dependent and consistently work. Barriers like delays, shutting down and errors normally makes users to get frustrated with the application. Functionality is the most vital factor when designing applications and it surpasses usability though they are both are necessary to ensure a great user experience has been achieved.

The design of cloud technology enables digital services to have high levels of stability and give room for updating the application and this reduces errors.

7.6. CLOUD COMPUTING CHALLENGES

7.6.1. Security

In a survey undertaken, seventy-seven percent of users say that security is the most common problem ever since the designing of the public cloud while the other twenty-nine percent say it's a significant threat. Companies have the worry of a possible cyber-attack since the risks are prone and the situation is not about to change.

Cybersecurity experts specifically fear the possibility of loss of data and leakage of information. Data privacy and confidentiality breach is also a concern but to a lower scale as compared to others.

On the other hand, companies that have used cloud technology longer seem to have less concerns about their data security as compared to users who have recently started using the technology. The challenge gradually shifts but cost of maintenance generally increases.

7.6.2. Managing Cloud Spending

According to research, cloud spending has overtaken cyber insecurity as the leading challenge in cloud technology. It is estimated that companies are wasting about 30% of their finances on cloud spending.

Organizations have plenty of errors that lead to such wastage like when developers spin up cloud instance that is meant to be of a short horizon and they fail to turn it off. make a number of mistakes that can help drive up their costs. Often, developers or other IT workers spin up a cloud instance meant to be used for a short period of time and forget to turn it back off (Chao, 2012).

Services offered by vendors can be used to curb this problem. Such offers involve; Cloud cost management solutions, automation, containers, server less services and auto scaling features. Centralizing cloud management to monitor usage can also help reduce wastage. Tools offered by the cloud vendors can be used to solve this issue.

7.6.3. Lack of Resources/Expertise

This is the third most challenging issue in cloud management. Inadequate resources have been placed third after a survey was conducted and about 75% of participants stated that the problem is significant. Efforts to boost knowledge and skills in cloud computing has been at the forefront but there is still a shortage of skilled experts on the market. Hiring more experts and training employees about cloud technology can help in strengthening cloud technology.

7.6.4. Governance

Management and control of cloud technology has become a challenge in most companies. Although there has been a quick and easy way of implementing cloud technology, it has become a challenge since there is substandard control and governance of the cloud technology. This makes hybrid cloud and multi-cloud environments hard to be controlled. Enforcement and establishment of standards can help curb this cloud challenge and vendors normally sell software's that can do the job.

7.6.5. Compliance

There has been a disturbance off late with the General Data Protection Regulation (GDPR) whereby they have made laws that companies are required to comply with. The law requires that organizations should hire an officer who will be in charge of data protection and will ensure there is privacy and security of data. In the case that the officers pass the test and they comprehend the needs of their companies, centralizing the task for compliance will help them avoid being sued by the law.

7.6.6. Managing Multi-Cloud Environments

Recently, companies are using multiple clouds as they get well versed with it. This is according to a survey which showed that 81% of companies are undertaking multi-cloud techniques while 51% already have a hybrid cloud mechanization. This means that public and private clouds have been consolidated. Such environments are complicated and experts suggest that practices, like partaking in research, training employees and creating a close relationship with vendors, will help curb the challenge.

7.6.7. Migration

Initiating a new software in the cloud is simple but shifting the same software in a cloud environment gets difficult. Surveys show that moving an application in a cloud environment is time-consuming and costly. Other difficulties faced include trouble-shooting, difficulties in configuring security, slow data shifting, trouble getting migration tools to work properly, difficulty in synchronizing data before cutover and downtime during shifting.

7.6.8. Immature Technology

Cloud technology are currently making use of high-end technology like artificial intelligence, virtual reality, and advanced big data analytics but the problem comes in when these kind of mechanization does not properly integrate with cloud technology which eventually leads to low performance, unreliability and usability challenges (Koutsopoulos et al, 2017).

In a survey 91% said that the workload of analytics was not moving into the cloud as fast as expected. Unfortunately, there is no way to deal with this situation but to only wait for future prospects on the cures of the challenge. Companies are advised to adjust their expectations and try to design their own cures. One can also wait for vendors to find a solution though no one knows how long this will take.

7.7. CLOUD RISKS

The following are cloud risks

- Control: When moving assets to the cloud, some companies misplace some level of visibility and command over those operations. The CSP gains takes up the roles of some regulations when one used external cloud services. The cloud service framework used will influence the actual shift, which leads to a major change for institutions with regard to security checking and logging. It is vital for companies to monitor and analyze data regarding services, data, applications and users without the use of network-based monitoring and logging which if easily accessible for on premises IT.
- Internet-Accessible Management APIs can be compromised: A group of software programming coherence are normally put at risk which are used by clients to control and communicate with cloud service which is also called the management plan. Companies utilizes the APIs to provide, overlook and take care of their users and assets. Application dangers can be found in these APIs like that of an operating system, etc. CSP of APIs can be accessed by the internet but with administration APIs for local computing and this heightens the risk of potential exploitation. Risk players are always considered to be vulnerabilities in administration APIs. If detected, they can be converted into achievable attackers and the companies stored assets in the cloud can be under threat and hackers can continue to cause harm to clients using the company's assets.
- Separation among multiple tenants fails: This is caused when hackers take advantage of the system and application threats within a CSPs platform that can house multi-tenancy. A hacker can take advantage of this situation and gain access to data of different companies and manipulate them which might cause harm. In the

event separation control breaks down, there will be more leakage of data since multi-tenancy heightens the vulnerability area. Once the hacker has taken advantage of the vulnerabilities in the CSPs software's or hardware, the attack is considered accomplished. Cases of hacking of a CSPs SaaS platform have not been reported anywhere in the world up to this date though, proof that one can take advantage of the concepts have been elaborated.

- Data deletion is incomplete: Since data has been virtually stored in the cloud, one can fail to locate the data because their visibility has been minimized unlike when they were being physically stored. A user is normally not sure if they erased data. This data is just within the CSPs infrastructure in a multi-tenancy surrounding at it has been scattered in different storage Furthermore, the process of erasing data usually varies from one service provider to another and this makes companies unable to verify with certainty that there are remains of any information which can be accessed by hackers.
- Stealing of credentials: If a hacker is able to access a user's credential in the cloud, the hacker will also have entry to the CSPs services to provisioning added resources in the case the credentials allow for provisioning access and will also claim to attack a company's property. The hacker can take advantage of this situation and manipulate a company's management team and other companies that are interconnected in the same cloud. In addition, the hacker is able to use that information to gain access to systems. Management tasks differ from CSP and an institution. The CSP manager has authorization to enter the CSP network and applications depending on the service of its infrastructure. But with administrators that are consumers, they only have entry to the implementation of the cloud. This implies that CSP administrators have more administration rights and supports
- Vendor Lock-In complicates moving to other CSPs: In the event a company want to migrate its assets from one CSP to another, vendor lock in becomes a challenge. It gets costly, a lot of effort is involved and time becomes scheduling for the moves rises that what was originally estimated. This is due to non-standardized data formats, non-standardized APIs, and relying on ones CSP's proprietary tools and unique APIs. This problem is deeply faced in service frameworks where the CSP has more tasks. The exposure

heightens even further when a company utilizes more application, services and APIs. A shift is needed when the capabilities are migrated to another CSP. In the event a CSP runs out of function, information can disappear or data will not be moved to another CSP on time.

Other risks include increased complexity strains on IT Staff, abuse by insiders when it comes to access. This is an operational risk, the loss of stored data and resources and insufficient due diligence which increases cybersecurity risk.

7.8. CLOUD MIGRATION

Cloud migration is the procedure of shifting information, software's and various commerce components to a cloud computing area. Cloud migration comes in many forms and the most notable framework is the migration of information and software from a local on-premise information centre to a public cloud (Chao, 2012).

Most companies are putting into use the advantages of cloud computing. The department sector is heavily performing the migration practice. Migration has solved numerous issues that would have been a nightmare to IT experts in the past. Such problems are data availability and scaling, expenses involved in hosting a database infrastructure locally and disaster management plans.

Some of the cloud computing platforms are Oracle, Open Stack, Microsoft Azure, IBM cloud, Amazon Web Services, Heroku, Google Cloud Platform and Cloud Foundry. Services provided by these platforms include storage, security, database, application, integration management, testing-as-service and information.

Most of the times, cloud services are framed around storage, platform, software or infrastructure and this makes them the four main types of cloud computing.

In the event you are migrating to another database a change of schema is appropriate so as to house the new one when shifting into different but similar databases, the migration process can be less complex because they contain the same features which make the transition smooth. Data dictionaries are also available in the market so as to help in choosing a compatible with other vending lenders, e.g., EDB Postgres and oracle practice this (Chao, 2012).

However, other databases have no relation and this is more difficult to migrate and will need a full application to rewrite, e.g., NoSQL.

In the event you are using a standard SQL, a full-blown schema migration is not tool is not necessary. For example, a text editor is enough to substitute oracle databases with Postgres SQL equivalents.

Furthermore, the EDB migration portal is now easily accessible in a quicker manner to compatibility and align the necessary steps of obtaining a fruitful migration. Its function involves analyzing converting meanings, indices charts, preserved articles, etc. (Chao, 2012).

When the schema is ready mapped, data will be able to be changed and distributed into another data storage. If you want to save more time, you can get hold of automatic tools like HVR Data Replication, Attunity Replicate, Oracle Golden Gate. In the event you are using massive data sets, which will need some batch mode systems, you can use Talend or Informatica. The Amazon Database Migration Service (DMS) is more specific to AWS for streaming information into an AWS-based information storage, and also offline components like snowball for pet byte data sets.

The migration of application logic is most often than not being overshadowed and this is due to the fact that its database is different and this makes it difficult to migrate it as compared to relational databases as it uses a standard SQL system to enter and alter information. Though, if software is designed to make use of complex proprietary elements in SQL, there will be several hindrances or obstacles in the implementation process.

Compatibility can be achieved in a database using EnterpriseDB for oracle which includes PL execution pro c compatible connectors and OCI and other elements. Compatibility from The EDB Postgres Platform is given to PL/SQL which is the programming language used by oracle databases and automatic shifting tools are used so as to enhance accuracy and save on time. Codes of databases rewrites have been running without errors for quite some time and it is due to automatic migrating tools.

As EDB Postgres eradicates almost every change to native oracle pl or SQL, also the EDB postgress migration tool comprehends PL/SQL Oracle specific packages such AQ and others and ways of managing any conversion that may be vital to migrate it to EDB Postgres.

A complete rewrite of the code will be required in moving to a NoSQL database that interacts with the database which is closely the same situation to the schema.

A serious test is performed so as to check whether the migration was successful and the migration involved the schema, data, and application, this helps to check if the application has the same behavior it has before the migration. To achieve the expectations of the users, thorough tests of performance, availability, scalability, network speed, along with security is undertaken (Chao, 2012).

Migrating database work to a cloud is worthy process of advancing your architectural workload and getting ready for future changes. A perfect example is EnterpriseDB because it can spot the software and database that are prospects and migrate them to the cloud. This enables them to perform inspections and adjust workloads to achieve optimum conditions.

To ensure a successful database migration, we check for the following:

- Assess database size: this will enable us to see what storage size is needed and at what point will it be vital after moving it and this can be performed by their experts.
- Test applications before migration: The applications the service provider uses to connect to the database have to be fine-tuned to the applications that will use the database. Applications running on the cloud database should also be compatible with cloud infrastructure, and provide better performance than in-house set-up. The cloud data centers may not be in the vicinity, and there may be high latency issues. Applications should be able to perform in such situations. Raise the issue with your service provider, and make sure you're both on the same page.
- Data confidentiality: One needs to move data and applications that are not sensitive if the environment that it is migrating to is not secure.
- Design the service level agreement (SLA) document carefully: There are applications which will require 99.99% up-time. Make sure scheduled down-times don't interfere with your business needs.
- Ensure scalability: the major objective of database migration is the immediate scalability. This will obviously have to be discussed with the giver. Keep the service vendor on the know regarding your business development plot.

- Mind your OS: One should find the operating system that perfectly fits with your database. Finding the operating system (OS) e.g. Oracle is compatible with Linux and also windows. Even though they serve the same function. You should always check for the operating system on the cloud.
- Removing trash will reduce costs: cleaning data is vital as financing of the migration relies on the size of data. Size and costs are directly proportional therefore before you migrate a database ensure you have removed trash so as to make the migration process economical.

Chapter 8 Role of ICT in 21st Century's Teacher

CONTENTS

8.1. Introduction 204
8.2. ICT Helps Teachers Interact With Students 204
8.3. ICT Helps In Improving Teaching Skills, Helps In Innovative Teaching 206
8.4. ICT Helps In The Effectiveness oOf The Classroom 209
8.5. ICT Helps In Improving Professional Development and Education 211
8.6. It Helps Teachers In Preparation For Teaching 212
8.7. ICT Prepares Teachers For The Use Of Their Skills In The Real Classroom Situation 214
8.8. ICT Is A Tool For Teaching And Learning Itself 216
8.9. ICT As A Popular Tool For Organization And Management In Institutions 218
8.10. ICT Plays An Important Role In Student Evaluation 220
8.11. ICT Helps Teachers To Communicate Properly With Their Students 222
8.12. ICT Helps Teachers Pass Information To Students In A Short Time Frame 224
8.13. ICT Helps Teachers To Design Educational Environment 226
8.14. ICT Helps Teacher To Identify Creative Child In Educational Institution 228
8.15. ICT Helps Teacher To Motivate Students And Grow Interest In Learning 230
8.16. ICT Helps Teacher For Organizational Preconditions (Vision, Policy, And Culture) 231
8.17. ICT Is Helpful For Technical Preconditions (Infrastructure) 233
8.18. ICT Is Helpful For Both Vocational Education And Training Of Future Teachers (In The Teachers Training Institutes) ... 235

8.1. INTRODUCTION

Currently, technology is present everywhere we go. Technology has been incorporated into the various aspects that evolve around man's day to day activities such as communication, work, and education among others. This has been beneficial for the man leading to the recent advancements being made to technology to make it more suitable for use in the long run. In education when the subject of technology is raised, it focuses more on the use of technology in the classroom to improve the learning process for the students. As technology is being incorporated into the education system, it enables the interaction between teachers and students.

The use of ICT in the learning process is still being integrated by schools as it has proven to be beneficial for both the teachers and the students. The role of ICT in learning in most cases tends to revolves around the students but it is important to note that it plays a key role for the teachers. For instance, it has been proven to improve the interaction between teachers and students, it has been a useful resource for teachers as they are preparing for their lessons, they are also able to access e-resources and the can easily and effectively use the computer hardware and software among other roles. This is beneficial in making the learning process much easier and smoother for the teacher in the long run.

8.2. ICT HELPS TEACHERS INTERACT WITH STUDENTS

Since the world has been modernized, there have been advances in technology so as to improve the ways in which people communicate. This is the reason why ICT has been integrated into the education sector so as to improve the effectiveness of the learning process. The use of ICT has led to the creation of social media platforms such as Facebook, Twitter, Instagram and Telegram among others. These social media platforms have been successfully integrated into the learning programs such that the learning process is made more effective. For instance, telegram has been used in majority of the schools to create a platform where teachers and students are able to freely interact. This is through the creation of groups that may be based on the subject or the grade that the students are in. this gives a great platform for the teachers to be able to share more knowledge with the students (Kumar & Turner, 2006).

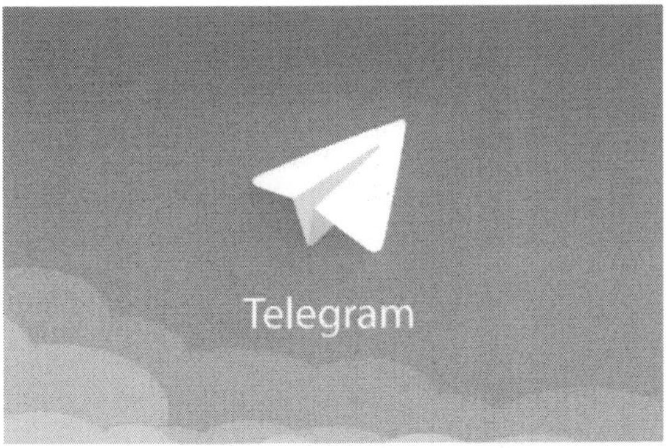

Figure 8.1. An image of telegram which is used to facilitate interaction in the classroom.

Source: https://techweez.com/2018/02/01/apples-app-store-shows-popular-messaging-app-telegram-the-door/.

ICT has helped teachers improve the interaction with students by improving the teacher's teaching techniques. The teacher will employ the use of equipment such as projectors during class presentations. This has been known to increase the students' concentration rates as they study making them more alert as the lesson progresses. For instance, if a teacher is giving a presentation on the Second World War, most of the students will pay attention and ask questions, leading to creating interactions between the teacher and student.

The use of ICT has helped teachers prepare for their lessons. If the teacher was to give notes on a given topic, the teacher is able to use a printer to print several copies of his or her notes for all the students. This is beneficial as the time that the teacher would have used in dictating notes, he or she will use that time to elaborate more and also engage the students in class activities as the lesson progresses. ICT has also brought about the interaction between teachers and students in terms of research. Though there is plenty of information on the internet, some of the information may be false and some cites may have information that may not be suitable for the students' level of education (Kumar & Turner, 2006).

This will require the students to always refer to their teachers on what cites to use, which knowledge they should take up and which on they should ignore among others. Though it may make the students to be quite dependent on the internet for research, it will facilitate the interaction between them and their teachers as they discuss on their findings. For teachers who are highly knowledgeable on ICT skills, the use this to their advantage by coming up with several ways to enable them easily approach their students. This they use with their students by encouraging them to use high levels of thinking and creative ways in which they can use the technology in the classroom and also in their homes to effectively help them express how they are understanding what they are being taught. This enables the teacher to get feedback which he or she will use in improving the classroom interaction.

The use of ICT in education has been used to create advancements in the teaching environment. This include flipping of classrooms whereby the students can learn several topics and carry out several practices while at home. This may fall under e-learning as the lecturer will be able to demonstrate all that is being taught. With the topics being covered at home, when the students get to class they cover the learning activities. The learning activities are usually facilitated by the teachers who will take part in the entire process, therefore, creating more interaction time with the teachers (Kumar & Turner, 2006).

In the previous learning methodologies, the learning process was majorly teacher oriented. This had its negative impact more so on the students whereby they lost interest in learning as they were not given time or the chance to contribute. This is different in the current day as technology has been incorporated and the learning process has become student-oriented. This means that in an ongoing class session, the teacher will be present to facilitate the class and the students are allowed to contribute in the learning process thereby creating interaction between the teacher and the students.

8.3. ICT HELPS IN IMPROVING TEACHING SKILLS, HELPS IN INNOVATIVE TEACHING

The use of ICT has greatly impacted teachers' teaching skills in a positive way. The fact that ICT has been integrated into the education sector means that the teachers are required to have knowledge and skills to be used in the learning process. This has required the majority of them to acquire knowledge and skills on such and since it deals with technology, the teachers after the training process will be more innovative and have high thinking as well as analyzing abilities which they will incorporate in the learning process. The use of ICT has improved teaching skills by bringing about collaborative work.

The use of ICT champions for collaborative work. This is employed by the teachers in the learning process whereby the learning process is no longer teacher-oriented but student-oriented. For the learning process to be successful, both the teachers and the students will have to take part in making it a success. This is through the employment of activities such as group work among the students and also encouraging teacher-student interaction (Unesco, 2011). This has been effective more so for the shy and quiet students in class.

As teachers have knowledge on the various principles in ICT such as networking, software and programming, they are able to use this to their advantage. This is referred to innovative teaching. They use the knowledge to come up and create programs for their students that are essentially weak in a specific subject or in various chapters. The students are able to use those programs as they study either at home or in schools. They have proven to be effective for most students as the teachers understand their students better and they know the type of content or presentation that will boost the students learning abilities.

The teachers have also been able to come up with programs that will aid the learning of students with disabilities. The programs may help such students to understand better keeping them at the same academic level with the other students. They can also use the programs to identify students that are struggling academically. For instance, students with a disability in understanding a specific subject like math. The teacher will then have to employ new teaching tactics so that such students may get to improve on the given subjects (Unesco, 2011).

The use of ICT helps teachers to innovate their teaching practices. This may involve them comping up with new teaching strategies so as to improve the students' motivation and interest. For instance, some teachers have taken up use of academic clips. As they teach, the teacher takes brakes so that he or she can show the students a clip concerning the topic they were studying. This has been effective for most teachers as it has increased the students' interest rates in the subject and also motivate them to contribute to the topic by asking questions or giving feedback. As the videos are motion pictures, they have improved the ability of the student to recall what they had learnt (Unesco, 2011).

Figure 8.2. An image of a teacher using a computer during class time.

Source:https://dissolve.com/stock-photo/Pretty-teacher-using-laptop-computer-class-elementary-royalty-free-image/131–446391.

The use of ICT has improved teachers teaching skills by changing the methods of teaching. Initially, teachers applied the lecture method which was not completely effective. By using technology, the teachers are able to learn new ways of teaching the students, for instance, using methods such as allowing the students to teach simple topics so as to engage them. It also makes the student to learn and retain more knowledge. Also, the teachers are able to incorporate the use of ICT tools in the learning process making it more attractive for the students.

The use of ICT has enabled teachers to improve their professional development in that they are able to get experiences of various classroom scenarios in a virtual sense. This enables the teacher to handle various cases that may occur in the classroom ensuring that the learning process is not altered with. It has also contributed to the improved lesson planning ability of the teacher. The teachers are able to use e-resources to learn how to plan their lessons so that the allocated time scheduled in the timetable is effectively used. For instance, if the allocated time is forty minutes, the teacher may decide to use the first five minutes to review the previous lesson, use twenty-five minutes to teach a new concept and the remaining ten minutes to carryout various classroom activities. Depending on the allocated time the teacher will be able to make a lesson plan that will be effective (Unesco, 2011).

8.4. ICT HELPS IN THE EFFECTIVENESS OF THE CLASSROOM

The use of ICT by teacher in the classrooms has been used to improve the effectiveness of the classroom in various ways. They incorporate the use of ICT tools such as smart boards among others. The use of such tools has improved various teaching techniques. Rather than using chalkboards, the teachers use the smart boards that will enhance the learning experience. For instance, in a chemistry class, the teacher can be able to easily illustrate effervesces by use of the smartboard whereby the teacher may draw a container with bubbles coming from it and the smart board will put the action into play. It will come in the form of a motion picture. This will make the class effective as the students will find it easy to recall what effervesces is by relating it to the lesson (Cartelli & Antonio, 2013).

Figure 8.3. An images of students using a smartboard.

Source: http://www.makerstudiosf.com/.

The teachers have used ICT to make learning effective by coming up with forums for projects where the students are allowed to take part. The projects are usually related to the topics that were taught in class. The teachers allow the students to use the technological resources that are available in the classroom to come up with the projects and actualize them. The teachers also take part in the projects together with the students. This makes the learning process effective as it will improve the students' critical thinking as well as problem-solving abilities.

By engaging in such projects, there will be an improvement in the students' collaboration in class. As the projects will require the students to work together in order complete the projects. This will enhance teamwork among the students which is a good attribute for the students to have. The aspect of teamwork will come in handy when the teacher creates classes for group discussions. As the students will have had guidance on what to do in the group discussions, they will be able to use the knowledge to make the discussion effective thereby making the class session effective and the students will get more knowledge (Cartelli & Antonio, 2013).

The use of ICT will make the classroom effective by removing boredom. Previously teachers used the lecture method in the learning process which the students would have ended up being bored and it reduced the concentration span of the students. With the use of technology in learning, the students will not get bored because technological tools will be applied in learning. The use of gadgets such as computers will fascinate them so that they will want to contribute to the lesson. This will also increase their concentration span therefore making the class to be effective.

The use of ICT is also effective in class as it has been used to make the class livelier. Take the scenario of two cases of classrooms. In one, the teacher only dictates the notes as the students write and as the lesson progresses, the teacher may explain a few concepts and continue with dictating the notes. In the other classroom, the students have their notes printed and the teacher explains the concepts as the students are able to contribute and also ask questions. In the second scenario the class is effective as it involves both the teacher and the students contributing to the lesson and it is a clear indication of how ICT has facilitated the class being livelier (Cartelli & Antonio, 2013).

ICT has made the class more effective by allowing the teacher to have an easy time teaching. This is made possible through the use of the ICT tools such as computers so that if the teacher was to give a presentation to the class, the can easily make such with the help of computer programs such as powerpoint that will require less time and effort. Also as the presentation will involve the use of flashy pictures, it will captivate the students making them to listen and be attentive as the lesson progresses.

It has also made it effective by making the teaching aspect to be fun and if it is made fun for the teacher, it will reflect on the students. Some ICT programs have educational games that are used by the teacher during the lessons. Though playing the games is fun and interactive for the students, it will enable them to recall several things. The teachers may also use it as a chance for feedback. As the students answer the questions, they will be able the gauge whether the learning was effective (Cartelli & Antonio, 2013).

8.5. ICT HELPS IN IMPROVING PROFESSIONAL DEVELOPMENT AND EDUCATION

ICT has enabled teachers to improve their professional development and education in various ways. For instance, the use of ICT has enabled teachers to gain up to date knowledge that is being used in various learning institutions. As research continues to be done, there is more knowledge being incorporated into the education system and the information that is not relevant is omitted. For the teachers to have this information, they use ICT tools such as Google to search for information on the various subject that he or she teaches.

For a teacher to improve his or her professional development, he or she requires feedback on the effectiveness of the classroom. This is made possible through the use of ICT tools that include the self-evaluation programs that have been created for the teachers use. The programs work by testing the students' knowledge on the taught topic after the end of the class session. The programs then compile the data and relay it to the teacher who at the end of the day will use the data to analyze whether the class was effective or there are areas that the teacher needs to work on (Cartelli & Antonio, 2013).

It also improves the professional development of the teacher by helping the teacher improve their teaching skills. Through the use of e-resources, the teachers are able to gain information on the latest teaching techniques that are effective in the classroom. The teachers are then able to apply the learnt techniques in the classroom and end up using the techniques that prove to be effective for them. Not only the teaching techniques, also the teaching practices that are beneficial in the learning process. This will enable the teacher to be equipped to handle various classroom scenarios.

Professional development can also be improved by gaining insight from teachers who are succeeding in the education sector. ICT has been used to facilitate this. Through the use of communication platforms such as LinkedIn and telegram among others, it has created a community of teachers where they are able to interact and share ideas on various issues. The younger teachers can get insight on how to handle various class scenarios and get possible solutions to the problems they face as teachers. Through these forums teachers get to be equipped with more skills and know other teaching methodologies (Unesco, 2011).

ICT has come in handy for teachers in terms of storage of information. For instance, in countries like Kenya teachers are required to have written their schemes of work. Most teachers end up rewriting such schemes at the beginning of every year because the previous once may be lost or destroyed and it may be a tiring and time-consuming process. With the use of ICT tools such as computers, this problem is sorted as computers can safely store such information and if lost there are options of retiring them from backup storage areas such as the cloud.Teachers also use the ICT tools in other areas such as administering of tests, computation, and recording of marks. Some teachers prefer to give online tests to the students for them to evaluate themselves while they are at home so that most of the hours in class is spent on teaching and carrying out learning activities. The same case in computation of marks. Rather than spending many hours with a calculator adding the marks of individual students, the teachers prefer to use computer programs such excel to carry out the calculations. In the long run it is efficient and will save on time giving the teacher more time to interact with the students (Unesco, 2011).

Teacher education comes with gaining of knowledge and skills. ICT has made this an easier process for the teachers by availing the required resources to them through the use of tools such as the internet. The use of the internet gives teachers opportunities to further their knowledge through the use of online classes. This enables them to further their education and enable them to be more competent for the teaching industry. It equips them with skills such as lesson planning that will enable them to effectively use the time allocated for the given subject. They will also learn on the most competent teaching methodologies as well as teaching strategies to use to make the learning process more effective in the classroom. This will improve the professional development of the teacher. By improving the professional development of the teacher, he or she will be able to handle various classroom scenarios making learning effective (Unesco, 2011).

8.6. IT HELPS TEACHERS IN PREPARATION FOR TEACHING

Preparation is a key element for effective teaching. This has tremendously affected the students' performance positively which is the goal of the teacher. Preparation involves organizing the teachers' approach and lesson planning among others. Though some teachers may view it as a waste of time, it is actually the opposite of it. The teacher will be able to set goals for the lesson and afterwards identify if the goals have been met. Though lesson planning may take up time, it is actually a positive approach towards effective teaching.

The use of ICT has made the preparation process much easier. This is because several tools are availed to the teachers for easy access. The use of ICT helps the teachers store content that may be required for preparation. For instance, teachers are required to have schemes of work. Rather than writing them over and over again, the teachers store them in computers so that when the year starts they are able to retrieve the information. As the computer has good organization modes, the teacher will be able to access the content he or she needs for the given lesson (Unesco, 2011).

Preparation involves the teachers obtaining the content knowledge for the given subject. They require different approaches to the given content so that students that tend to be inquisitive as questions that are not within the syllabus context, the teacher will be capable of answering the given questions. ICT has greatly helped teachers in obtaining further knowledge to their benefit. They can use the internet to research more about the topic. ICT also avails e-resources to them. The use of e-books will be useful in referencing and also helps the teachers gain more knowledge as they prepare for the lesson.

For a teacher to be prepared for a lesson, he or she needs to have acquired various instructional strategies so as to make the class effective. Choosing the instructional strategy to use while in the classroom is part and parcel of preparation for teaching. It will be useful in helping the teacher to manage the class in various events in the class. ICT has been used by teachers to help them gain more strategies that they can use while instructing students in the classroom. It also challenges the teachers to come up with their own strategies in event that the strategies given do not work for them.

For some teachers the classroom management tactic requires some experimentation and luck for it to work. This is the reason it has been incorporated into the preparation for teaching. The teacher needs to know the kind of management tactic that he or she will be using in class to make it effective. The use of ICT has enabled the teachers get to know a variety of classroom management tactics. This is made possible through, for instance, YouTube videos that some teachers uploaded showing the kind of strategies that they use as the lesson progresses (Cartelli & Antonio, 2013).

Lesson planning is a major part of the preparation process. Here the teacher is able to outline what will be done during the lesson be it a revision or various classroom activities. ICT has come in handy for lesson planning as it enables the teachers to research on the various lesson plans that may be effective in the classroom. They may end up adding some activities in their lesson plans. For instance, according to the allocated time, the teacher may plan to start with reviewing the previous lesson, teach for a specific duration and later on involve the students in some classroom activities.

Preparation involves the teacher identifying the type of practices and materials that will be used during the learning process. According to the subject being taught the teacher should identify the type of materials to use, for instance, when elaborating something. ICT has been useful in that it has enabled teachers to learn of new learning materials that can be used in the classroom. This is through research in the internet or e-books that are written for teachers. It also helps them to know the kind of classroom practices to employ while teaching. This will help them to be effective in their teaching (Cartelli & Antonio, 2013).

Figure 8.4. ICT has also enabled teachers to identify the type of teaching methodologies that would work for them in the classroom.

Source: https://palonhscradle.wordpress.com/2015/08/27/in-the-news-technology-integration-workshop-in-leyte-schools-intensified/.

8.7. ICT PREPARES TEACHERS FOR THE USE OF THEIR SKILLS IN THE REAL CLASSROOM SITUATION

For the teachers' skills to be effective in the classroom, the teacher should be able to apply their skills so that the students can understand what is being taught. Along the process of learning to be a teacher one learns of various skills that are required by the teacher in a classroom but if the teacher is unable to apply such skills then there is no use of acquiring the skills in the first place. ICT has been useful in helping the teachers know how to use their skills in the classroom.

For a teacher to manage the classroom, he or she requires to have management skills. ICT has enabled teachers know how to apply this skill through online videos that give simulations of various classroom scenarios. In such videos, the teachers in the given class is faced with a particular challenge and uses the management skills taught to teachers to solve the problem. The teacher is then able to learn how to apply the skill and for a test run he or she is given a virtual simulation of the class and will be required to apply a management skill.

For a teacher who uses e-books to know more about what is expected of the teacher in a classroom, that teacher will get to know that the teacher will be expected to use some of the skills they acquired. For instance, collaboration is a skill that the teacher will be required to implement on the students. This will require the teacher to create groups where the students will carry out projects and also conduct group discussions. This will enhance teamwork among the students hence create the habit of collaboration among the students (Cartelli & Antonio, 2013).

The teacher is required to apply the skill of critical thinking in the classroom. This is in case a student may ask a question that may require the teacher to have the skill of critical thinking. ICT helps the teacher prepare to use the skill of critical thinking through the use of E-books that usually outline the various scenario in which a question may be posed by a student and the various ways in which the teacher can apply the skill of critical thinking in different point of reference in order to answer the given question. This will enable the teacher apply the skill in a real classroom scenario.

Among the skills that the teachers have, problem-solving is one of them. This may not be in terms of solving issues among students, though this skill is required. Problem-solving is mostly in the sense of solving either mathematical or word problems. Though the syllabus outlines methods in which math problems can be solved, the give method may not always apply for all questions. This is why some teachers tend to use e-resources to research on other methods that can be used in solving various sums giving them a variety of options to choose from. It will also teach them on how they can apply their problem-solving skills. This will prepare them for the real class scenario (Cartelli & Antonio, 2013).

Presentation is one among the practical skills that a teacher is required to have. Be it presentation of a topic or content, for the teacher to successfully introduce a topic as something interesting for the students. Through the use of internet searching tools such as Google, teachers learn the different ways of presenting knowledge to students such that the impact will be high retention of the given knowledge. They are also given demonstrations on such so that they know how to apply the skill while in the classroom.

Teachers use ICT programs in their day to day living. They use it for communication which will involve them interacting with different people. Good communication skills is also required of teachers. They are required to effectively relay information to the students. As they use the communication platforms, it enables them practice using this skill as they communicate with others. This will help prepare them for a real classroom situation as they will be able to easily apply the skills while interacting with their students. Teachers are also required to have listening skills which will enable them know the challenges that the students have. ICT enables them know how to apply this skill by the use of virtual simulation whereby the teacher will be required to apply listening skills. This will contribute in helping teachers apply the skill in a real classroom situation (Cartelli & Antonio, 2013).

8.8. ICT IS A TOOL FOR TEACHING AND LEARNING ITSELF

The integration of ICT into the education system involves using it as a key resource for teaching and learning and it has proven to be beneficial for both parties (Willmann, 2017). Its use in education has enabled the support, enhancement and optimization of the delivery of information so that teachers both teachers and students achieve their goals. The teacher effectively relays content to the student and the student is able to understand and apply the given knowledge. In the long run it has brought about the improvement in the quality of education.Presence of platforms such as YouTube and telegram have also improved learning. For instance, YouTube has been a key resource for students. In such platforms there are educational tutorials on various subjects such as math and science. This enables the students to get a different approach in terms of method to apply when solving a certain problem if they cannot easily use the one taught to them. Telegram has enabled the students to have groups where they are able to discuss on various topics and it has come in handy when they have projects (Willmann, 2017).

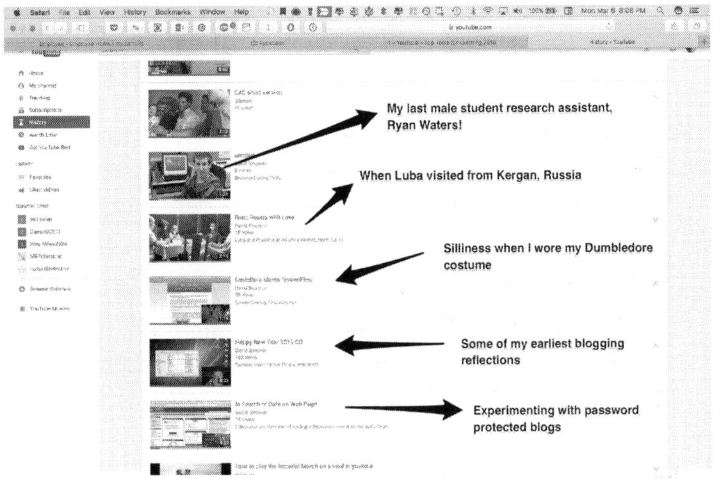

Figure 8.5. YouTube has been used as a teaching and learning tool.

Source:https://david-in-carroll-land.com/2017/03/06/re-discovering-you-tube-as-a-teachinglearning-tool/.

In learning, ICT involves the use of tools such as e-learning which presents itself in various ways such as mobile learning (Unesco, 2011). This is an upcoming trend in the education sector that has enabled students to access the classroom virtually; physical presence is not a requirement. This learning tool has been beneficial because students can attend classes whenever and wherever they want. If they did not understand a particular lesson, they can also replay the class session so that they can acquire some information that they may have missed out on. This makes learning to be very efficient for students.

ICT has been used as a tool for learning in the sense of computer programs that are specially made for students. They include virtual laboratory programs that enable students to carry out practices at the comfort of home and at their free time. For students that have problems with various subjects, there are programs that are specially made for such students so that they can work on their weakness. There are also educational games that are incorporated in the given programs. This is a great resource for students that will enable them gauge how much they have understood the topic.

ICT is a key learning resource more so for students in high school and those in the university. For one the internet has been useful for conducting research on various topics. Also, it avails resources such as e-books which enables the students to get vast knowledge from different authors. Such books have been useful for the students when they want to get in depth knowledge on a given topic or when they want to investigate how various theories came to be. These resources have assisted in bringing up students who are more of research-oriented making the learning process to be effective (Unesco, 2011).

Not only is ICT a tool for learning, it is also a key tool for teaching. For instance, initially teachers used to use chalkboards as a teaching resource but in the current classroom scenario, teachers use ICT tools such as smart boards to teach students. Not only does it not put the health of the teacher at risk unlike using chalks, but it is also more efficient in delivering of information. This is because it makes the presentation of the content more appealing to the students making them interested in what is being taught. It has also helped students in the retaining of content.

ICT tools such as printers have recently become trending. The teachers are able to print notes for their students for use during the lesson. This saves on time as time that would have been used by teachers in dictating notes is now used to further explaining concepts and giving more time for learning. In terms of presentation, teachers have used applications such as PowerPoint to create presentations and the fact that it makes the content interesting for the learners. They also project notes or content for the students so that the learning process may go smoothly (Unesco, 2011).ICT has been used as a reference material for teachers to get in depth knowledge on the given topic. E-books have been a major resource for teaching as it equips the teacher with the content to use in the classroom. In general, from the illustrated examples, ICT is a major tool for the teaching and learning process.

8.9. ICT AS A POPULAR TOOL FOR ORGANIZATION AND MANAGEMENT IN INSTITUTIONS

ICT has been incorporated into various institutions so that the management may run smoothly. It has proven to be a more efficient tool as it has made several processes in the institution to run with ease saving time and also resources. In the learning institution, down the chain has been used to carry out various tasks. This implies that from the school management down to the teachers, ICT has been used to facilitate easy organization and management of tasks so that the institution does not face much challenges in the long run (Kumar & Turner, 2006).

School administrations have used ICT for strategic management. Strategic management is important to an institution as it plays a crucial role in determining whether an institution will exist after a period of time. ICT has been useful for example computers have been used to store financial records of the institution. These records are important to the management of the institution when they are planning to purchase more resources such books or desks. It is also important in identifying the financial status of the institution so that if it were to take up more workers, they would know how many workers to employ.

Such records play a key role in establishing whether the funds the institution is receiving is being properly used or if it is being managed. The records will show the funds received and the equipment that were bought using the funds. They are them able to establish the remaining amount of money that should be within the institution and if some is lacking then a problem would have been found in the administration and drastic measures should be taken to solve the problem. This will in turn improve the management of the leaning institution.

ICT has played a key role in improving the management institutions. This has been made possible by equipping the management of the institutions with key management concepts. This is through the use of the internet and also e-book on organization and management. This equips them with skills that will enable them make decisions and actions that will benefit the learning institution. This is also made possible by use of the social media platforms such as telegram where they will be able to interact with other managers of other learning institutions. Through the interactions they will be able to get insight that will influence their decision making skills (Kumar & Turner, 2006).

ICT has facilitated organization and management of learning institutions by facilitating more communication channels. Communication is a key tool in ensuring that an institution runs successful. By creating communication mediums such as the use of electronic mails and social media platforms among others, it has enabled even the lowest employee in an institution to communicate to the managers. This is important in a case where there is a problem within the institution and it needs to be urgently sent to the managers, the information will the relayed to the managers of the institution and the problem will be solved as soon as possible.

ICT has been used to create an organization in learning institutions through several ways. For instance, it has been used in the creation of timetables for the entire school. It has made the process of making such timetables easier as there are programs that can be used to draft them. The use of the timetables will enable both the teachers and students to know when they have a lesson and which teacher will be facilitating the lesson. This will ensure that the learning process goes smoothly and the advantage is that it will be in an organized manner (Kumar & Turner, 2006).

For some learning institutions, the major problem they have faced is time management. This is attributed to the cases where students have reported late for classes or some teachers attending their classes later than what is expected. This has created a sense of lack of organization within the school. ICT has been used to solve this problem with the use of technology that include the electric bell. For this bell to work a computer is linked to the bell and the computer is programmed in a way that when a set time reaches, the bell will ring indicating the start or end of a lesson. This has been used to make the learning process more organized and time will be well utilized. These are among some of the ways in which ICT has been used to improve organization and management of learning institutions.

8.10. ICT PLAYS AN IMPORTANT ROLE IN STUDENT EVALUATION

Student evaluation refers to the assessment that is carried out by learners of the quality of services given by the teachers. It may be based on the classroom or learning experience. In most cases, the evaluation is restricted to the performance of the teacher while they are teaching in the classroom. This information is very crucial in making decision that will help improve the quality of education provided to the students as the challenges they encounter will be worked on ensuring that learning is effective. It is a form in which teachers get feedback from the students.

One way in which ICT has been used in student evaluation, is by monitoring their understanding. There are programs that have been generated that are used in carrying out such activities. An example is the diagnoser that was developed in the US. The program works by asking the student questions related to the topic that they had studied. It aims at knowing how the student understood what the teacher taught. The teacher is then able to get the students' answers which will be used in analyzing how well the understood the topic (Kumar & Turner, 2006).

Also, ICT has come in handy by creating online platforms in which the teacher and students get to interact. During the process of interaction, the student may share information as well as concerns on a given subject for instance. This on its own is a way in which student evaluation is being carried out. As the student interacts with the teacher, the teacher is able to identify the student's strengths and weaknesses. The teacher may also be able to identify teaching methods that may be effective when teaching the particular student. This satisfies the objective of student evaluation.

One of the ways in which teachers carry out student evaluation is through administering of tests. As there may not be enough time in the class schedule to give tests frequently, ICT has assisted by creating ways in which the students can take the exams at any time or place. This is through the use of cloud-based learning which gives complete access to online tests for the students. The students are then able to take the tests and after some time get the results. Their teachers are also able to access the results and are able to use them to evaluate the student (Donohue, 2014).

Student evaluation can be carried out by the use of the students' performance. Based on how the student performs for a given period of time, the teacher is able to evaluate whether he or she understands what they are taught in the classroom. ICT has been incorporated to this method of student evaluation though the use of programs that are design to monitor the performance of the student. Depending on the results from the analysis of the given program, the teacher is given an upper hand in evaluating whether the student understands what they were taught in class.

ICT has been used in student evaluation by giving them opportunities such as creating educational evaluations with the use of tools such as podcasts. This is only made possible with the use of technology that is used in ICT. With the use of podcasts, the students are able to talk about the things they have learnt. They state what they remember during the lesson and also they elaborate the concepts in the manner in which they had understood it. This the use of such the teacher is able to evaluate the student and know how they understand various concepts (Donohue, 2014).

Figure 8.6. An image of students carrying out a podcast which is one of the methods of carrying out student evaluation.

Source: https://www.kqed.org/mindshift/40841/inspired-by-serial-teens-create-podcasts-as-a-final-exam.

ICT has been used in carrying out student evaluation through the use of audio visuals. This involves the students making animations related to the given subject. In may also involve them making videos on them dramatizing what they learnt or the videos may be of them explaining various that they have already interacted with. It has been advantageous for the student in increasing knowledge retention ability and the teachers as well. The teachers are able to use these videos as a basis for student evaluation by analyzing how they are able to explain various concepts and how they relate them to others.

There are advances being made to the technologies used in education so that the teachers are able to accurately evaluate the students through the improvement of programs that are being used in evaluating students. This information will then help the teachers know the type methodologies and tactics to employ for effective teaching (Donohue, 2014).

8.11. ICT HELPS TEACHERS TO COMMUNICATE PROPERLY WITH THEIR STUDENTS

For the teacher and students to attain their goals it is important for the teacher to be able to communicate properly with the students and also their colleagues. This brings about the importance of teachers having communication skills and being able to apply them in the classroom. Not only are good communication skills important for the students' learning but they are necessary for teachers in order to advance their career. Lack of proper communication form the teacher will stall the learning process and their careers.

In order to help teachers to communicate properly to the students, ICT has been a useful resource that has been used by teachers to communicate to the students. For instance, for a teacher to communicate on certain topic effectively to the students they are required to know quite a number of terminologies. This is for a class scenario where a teacher says a statement but the students seem not to understand what the teacher has said. For instance, the statement,' it is mandatory for you to do chemistry.' Therefore, ICT has become a major resource where the teachers can learn a variety of words that they can use to make communication effective (Blake, 2009).

Like in the initial statement the teacher may end up replacing the word mandatory with compulsory to make the students understand what he or she was implying initially. This will be useful in facilitating proper communication from the teacher to the students. For students with disabilities such as hearing and speech difficulties, it may pose a great challenge for the teachers to communicate properly to them. Also, the fact that there are not as many sign language teachers makes it even harder to communicate to such students.ICT has played a major role in eradicating this barrier in communication. With the presence of e-resources such as e-books, teachers have been able to learn of the various sign languages. They can also take up online classes on sign language. This will equip them to be able to properly communicate with such students. Also, with advances in technology, there have been creation of devices such as hearing aids among others that can be used by both physically impaired teachers and students. This will enable the classroom communication process to be effective as the physically impaired student will be able to understand what the teacher is saying (Blake, 2009).

For the teacher to be able to ensure that all the students will be able to hear what he or she is saying. This is referenced to the seating arrangements in the classroom. If the seating arrangement is improper with some students seating at the very back of the class, then the communication process will not be effective. ICT has been useful in improving proper communication whereby if the teacher is handling a larger class, equipment such as microphones can be used to ensure that every student in the room will hear what the teacher is saying. Use of microphones come in handy more so in lecture halls.

For proper communication to occur, the communication process will not entirely be based on verbal communication. Usually both verbal and nonverbal communication work together to ensure that the communication process is effective. Therefore, if the teacher says something and the nonverbal communication says otherwise then proper communication will not occur and the students will end up being confused. ICT has helped in that the teacher has been able to use the internet to learn of the various nonverbal communication skills. This will enable then to align the verbal and nonverbal communication to relay the same message hence making communication to be effective (Blake, 2009).

For the teacher to be able to effectively communicate to the students, he or she requires to employ a strategy that will be effective. Strategies involve various things such as the subject concerns, time aspect of carrying out a lesson, physical resources to use during a lesson and the style of teaching among others. These are essential elements that a teacher uses in the teaching process to make learning effective. Teachers have used ICT resources such as the internet to enable them make a proper teaching strategy that will assist them in the classroom. This will help them to be prepared for a lesson and in the long run build their confidence. This will in the end help the teacher to properly communicate to the students as he or she will know what to say and when to say it (Blake, 2009).

8.12. ICT HELPS TEACHERS PASS INFORMATION TO STUDENTS IN A SHORT TIME FRAME

Time is a very crucial element in the learning process. For most of the subjects, there are very large syllabus and topic content that needs to be covered within a given period of time. Time has to be properly managed so that the teacher will cover all the topics and ensure that all the teachers will teach their lessons. This gave rise to timetables to manage the school time. Though there is a presence of a timetable, teachers also need to know how to manage their time so that all the content is covered.

This is why it is important for them to be able to pass information within a short period of time. ICT has been used as a tool to facilitate it. In the initial teaching processes, it would involve teachers dictating notes to the students which would take large amount of time making the teachers take long time in passing information. Through the use of ICT resources such as the printers, teachers have been able to change that. They print notes for all the students and while in the classroom they are able to discuss on the topic for some time. This has enabled them to pass the subject information within a short time (Unesco, 2011).

For teachers to pass on the information to the students within a short time, they need to know the important information that will be required by the students. Take the example a subject in history, there is plenty of knowledge that is given to explain on various things and if the teacher uses all that knowledge in teaching then he or she will take a long time in doing so. Through the use of the internet, the teacher has been able to know and identify the major points and use them for teaching enabling them to pass information within a short time.

Teachers can also pass on the information to the students through the use of videos or animation on the given topic. Rather than giving stories about the concept, teachers make their own videos or even use the once available in the internet to relay information. For instance, if the topic is of the third world war, the teacher can give the students a short clip concerning it. It will enable the teacher to pass information within a short time and in the long run it is beneficial as it will improve the students' ability to retain knowledge (Unesco, 2011).

For the teacher to be able to pass information to a student within a short time, they need to effectively relay the message to that the teacher may not end up repeating statements to enable the students to understand the concept. This is made possible through the use of ICT tools such as the smart boards that enables the teachers to illustrate what he or she is saying. This will enable the students to easily understand and the teacher would have passed the given knowledge within a short period of time. The teacher also needs to apply the right teaching methodology to enable him or her to pass information within a short period of time.

The methodology needs to be effective for that matter. The use of the internet will enable the teacher to learn of different teaching methodologies that are effective. If the teaching methodology is effective the teacher will be able to share good quality of information in an effective way. It will enable them to relay the information within a short period of time. The same case applies to the teaching strategy. It is essential for the teacher to have good communication skills for the information to be relayed in a short period of time.

This is because if the teacher has language barrier among other communication barriers, they the teacher will have a hard time giving information to the students within a short period of time. Teachers use tools such as the internet to gain more knowledge that will enable them improve their communication skills. ICT has also been used in improving the class environment making it learner friendly. This will assist in eradication of the environmental barriers to communication improving the learners' interests and hearing ability while in the classroom. With the environmental and language barrier removed, the communication process in the classroom will be effective and with the teachers' improved communication skills, the teacher will be able to relay information to the students within a short time (Kadijevich Angeli, & Schulte, 2013).

8.13. ICT HELPS TEACHERS TO DESIGN EDUCATIONAL ENVIRONMENT

Educational environment refers to the physical location, culture and contexts in which the students learn. This mostly refers to the classroom environment in which all the learning processes occurs. It is not limited to the physical attributes of the classroom alone. It also involves other aspects such as the culture of the classroom and also the context of the classroom. The culture of the classroom refers to the characteristics and ethos of the class which involves the interaction that occurs in the class. For learning to be effective it is required that the learning environment to favor the learning process (König, 2012).

The teacher is therefore tasked to design an environment that will favor the education process. They have involved the use of ICT tools to make the designing process smooth. For the teacher to design the educational environment, he or she requires to know the characteristics of the students. The teacher needs to know the learners' prior knowledge, their goals and learning context among others. ICT makes it easier for the teacher to gain all this information. For instance, the students' goals. There are computer programs created for learners where they can make their portfolios (König, 2012).

For the learners' prior knowledge, there are programs created to enable the teacher acquire information on this. The programs test the students by giving them questions related to the topic. With the aid of such programs, the teacher will be equipped with information on the students' characteristics.

This will enable the teachers to design the learning environment that will meet the learners' needs. Students' assessment is among the information that a teacher will require while creating the learning environment. With such information the teacher will be able to identify what resources such as books that will be required to be added to in the learning environment (Unesco, 2011).

In addition to that, they will be able to know what techniques and methodologies to use in the learning process. ICT tools have been of major help in carrying out the students' assessments. This has been through the use of online portfolios for students (e-portfolios) and online tests among others. The information acquired after students complete their test is given to the teacher who will analyze it. The results will guide the teacher as he or she designs the learning environment by adding and changing various aspects of the classroom environment.

For the teacher to design the learning environment, he or she requires to know the learning context. This refers to the context goals, the structure of the context, the quality and depth of the context, sources of the context as well as the activities in the context. These are all elements that evolve around the learning process. They will give the teacher insight on what to add in the learning environment. For instance, the activities in the context. This will enable the teacher to identify the type of learning materials to have in the classroom environment among others (Unesco, 2011).

ICT has been a useful resource in this aspect. Teachers have used e-books on teaching that enable them to have more knowledge of the context thereby enabling them to understand more on the learning contexts. The information will then be incorporated by the teachers as they design the learning environment. For the teacher to design the learning environment, they are required to know of the skills that will be incorporated during the learning process. For the teacher to develop various skills in the students, they may be required to incorporate various activities in the learning process. They may include thinking activities, discussions and practical activities in the classroom. Through the use of search engines like google they are able to acquire this information.

The resources that are available in the classroom will help the teacher in designing the class environment. Resources include the technology available, facilities and time among others. Designing the classroom accordingly may change physical aspects. For instance, the number of books in the classroom and the technology available will affect the arrangement of the students in the classroom. Most institutions use computers to keep a record of all the facilities that are available in the institution. The teacher is able to use this information to design a classroom layout that will ensure that all students will be able to access all the available resources. If there are limited resources such as books, the teacher may print out some of the available e-books that are available for the school (Sharma, 2002).

8.14. ICT HELPS TEACHER TO IDENTIFY CREATIVE CHILD IN EDUCATIONAL INSTITUTION

Creative children are those that are able to use imagination and critical thinking skills to come up with new and meaningful forms of ideas without being taught. These students are able to nurture this ability as they learn where they are able to create various solutions to problems without the teachers' assistance. In majority of schools these students may skip other classes which may not be right. It is therefore very important for the teacher to identify such students so that they may be able to further nurture the child's creativity.

ICT has become among the major tools in which teachers are able to identify such students. Teachers are able to identify such students through various ways. This include the use of students' evaluation. In this case, the evaluation process should majorly focus on the students' understanding abilities. By knowing the students' understanding abilities they are able to know how creative they may be in aspect of application of knowledge. Computer scientists have come up with programs such as Diagnoser that enable the teacher to know the students understanding abilities. This involves asking the student a series of questions and the evaluation will be on the basis of how they answer (Sharma, 2002).

It may also involve asking the student questions on a context that he or she may not have learnt but they have learnt something that is related to the topic. To answer the question, the student will be required to apply various skills. It may also entail the teacher creating a program that contains questions in which the student will be required to have critical thinking skills as well as creativity in order to answer the questions. The advantage of using ICT is that the student will be able to do the tests at any place and time.

The programs are designed to carry out and give an analysis of the students' performance. Depending on the outcome of the results from the programs, the teacher will easily be able to identify a creative student in his or her classroom. Creative students usually tend to make unusual associations or connections with remote ideas which may come from unrelated illustrations that the teacher gave in the classroom. This is why teachers have taken up the use of student podcasts. The teacher may give students a topic to discuss in the podcast. The students will then elaborate on the topic giving out illustrations among others.

As the teacher will be listening to the podcast, he or she will be able to identify a creative student depending on how they will be able to explain the given topic and more so the illustrations that they will use. The teacher may identify a creative student by giving them challenges such as projects that sought out to solve a certain problem in the school. ICT comes in handy when the projects as formed on its basis. For a creative student, he or she will be able to use various skills when creating the project (Blake, 2009).

He or she may modify some of the technological ideas that were initially present to come up with a project. For some of them, they take-up initially existing programs, identify their downfall and later on they come up with a related program but will even more features that are better than the initial program. This will enable the teacher to easily identify the creative student based on the approach they had in making the project. Also, the behavior the student will have when creating the project as creative students tend to want to complete the task.

The teacher is able to identify creative students by monitoring their behavior. How they interact with other students and how the behave when the teacher is not present may be crucial pointers for the teachers. For the creative students most of them tend to read books a lot and most at they are experimental. ICT helps teachers identify such students through the use of CCTV cameras. These devices have been installed in majority of the modern classrooms. With the use of the CCTV cameras, the teacher is able to identify the creative students (Blake, 2009).

Through feedback from other students, the teacher will be able to identify creative students. For a majority of them, they are not liked by other students because of the crazy ideas and their passion for coming up with ideas. Through the use of social medial platforms, the teacher can obtain such information and there by identifying creative students.

8.15. ICT HELPS TEACHER TO MOTIVATE STUDENTS AND GROW INTEREST IN LEARNING

For students to effectively learn, they need to have interest in what they are learning and also to be motivated so that they keep on seeking knowledge (König, 2012). Both the teacher and the student need to be motivated so that they can achieve their goals. If the students have interest and they are motivated to learn, it will reflect on their achievements whereby they will be able to attain the goals that they set at the beginning of the educational year. The use of ICT has paved a way so that teachers are able to motivate and grow interest in learning.

For instance, teachers can use videos to motivate the students. By using videos, both the teacher and the student will be motivated. Take a case of a history class where the teacher explains a topic such as the third world war. If the teacher will be explaining about the war by just reading the story in the textbook, it may not motivate and interest the learner to learn more about the third world war. Use of videos may be a better approach for this situation. Use of video material has been known to motivate students to learn (König, 2012).

By using video material, students will learn a lot and also it will spark an interest for the students to want to know more about the topic. ICT has also come in handy as very many of the educational videos are found on the internet more so in platforms such as YouTube. The advantage is that the teachers can use their creativity. They can make their own videos or animations for the students to watch. This enables the teacher to incorporate relevant information of the topic into the video for the students.

Research is a key aspect in the education industry. In the current system, learning is student oriented therefore the students are required to do most of the hard work. The teachers use this as a way of motivating and growing interest for learning. Majority of them incorporate the use of ICT tools such as the available e-resources when encouraging their students to carry out independent research. By giving them access to carry out technology based independent research, students will be motivated to learn more as they will easily be able to carry out research on any topic (Yadav, 2014).

Teachers can boost student motivation by incorporating the use of ICT devices in the learning process. Children love gadgets and teachers can use this to their advantage. For instance, the teacher can decide to use computers for a given lesson. This will make the students to have more interest during the lesson as they will be interacting with the computers. It is also a good approach when trying to change the method of teaching. It has been discovered that for teachers who tend to frequently use gadgets during their lessons, the students usually tend to be motivated to attend the lesson.

For most of the subject that are taught in schools, there are various apps that have been developed based on the contexts on the subject. In order to motivate and grow interest in the students, the teachers incorporate the use of such apps in the learning process. A majority of teachers tend to explore various apps related to their subjects that will make it easier for them to transfer knowledge to the students. They also look at the aspect of the ability of the app to appeal to the students. They then introduce the apps to the students which they can use during personal study time.

This will help in establishing interest for the subject by the students. Teachers can also use the available ICT tools to create interest and motivation for learning in students. For example, the use of smart boards has proven to be effective. It enables the teacher to visualize the concept through use of pictures and also creating 3D versions of the objects drawn on the screen. This will enable the students to relate to the given subject and improve their knowledge retention ability (Yadav, 2014). The teachers should enable the students to interact with such devices like allowing them to illustrate a concept on the smartboard. This will create interest for the subject by the student and also motivate them to learn. The teachers can also in a creative way make good use of the smartphones that the students have and incorporate it in the learning process.

8.16. ICT HELPS TEACHER FOR ORGANIZATIONAL PRECONDITIONS (VISION, POLICY, AND CULTURE)

A precondition refers to a condition that must be true before a section of a given code is implemented or executed. In the learning process, there are various preconditions that help the school to attain its goals. The preconditions may include having a vision, policy and a school culture. These all work together to ensure that the school is able to improve the quality of education for the students. These preconditions will create a sense of guidance for the learning institution so that they know their future aims. Therefore, teachers are tasked with the role of organizing the school vision (Unesco, 2011).

Vision as a precondition is a goal that is created by the teachers as well as the school leader. It is usually accompanied by a school mission. It usually outlines the goals and the direction the school will be taking. It is used to clarify the objectives and to identify ways in which the goals can be attained. ICT has been used by teachers in the organization of the vision of the school as well as the teaching process. This entails using ICT in the formulation of school goals.

For the teacher to develop the goal (vision), he or she requires to have records of information that will enable them to come up with a vision. They require knowledge on the quality of education that the institution offers to the students. Knowing the level of technology that is used in the learning process may enable one to easily identify it. Also, the students' performance in which the teacher may use computer programs such as spreadsheet to track the progress rates of the students. Also knowing the position of the institution when ranked with other schools may be important (Unesco, 2011).

Such information is usually present in the internet when the ministry of education ranks the schools according to performance. With all this knowledge, the teacher is able to formulate a vision for the school and also the teaching process. For the teaching process the teacher will carry out a teachers' evaluation that is usually a program created for teachers to asses themselves. Also looking at the learning environment that he or she designed as well as the students' performance, the teacher will be able gauge him or herself and come up with a vision for herself. But since it is based on an organization, the school vision is what matters.

Policy is also part of the organizational preconditions. For a school to effectively run there are policies that should be put in place to ensure that. It is also necessary to ensure that the learning process is effective. ICT has been a useful resource or formulating the school policies. Through the use of the internet, the school is able to identify some on the policies that a school is required to have. For instance, schools are required to have a school security policy, medicine administration policy, anti-bullying policy, anti-cyber bullying policy, e-safety policy and educational visits policy.

The school keeps records of all the cases and the challenges that have been experienced within the school premises. These records are usually kept in the school heads' computer. With such records, the teacher is able to come up with a variety of policies for the school. For instance, if there was a case of bullying, it will be shown in the school records. This will guide the teacher that there is need for a bullying policy within the school. ICT tools have been useful in recording and also printing of the policy for all the entire school (Willmann, 2017).

Culture is also a precondition for the success of a learning institution. School culture refers to the way in which teachers as well as other school staff members work together and also the values and beliefs that they share. ICT has been used by teachers to create a good school culture that aims at improving learner education. For instance, tools such as computers which are used during interactions are used by in facilitating communication between the teachers and other staff members ensuring that there are no problems between them.

In the classroom, the teacher can use ICT to make the learning process to be learner-oriented therefore students will be encouraged to research and read on their own. This will create a reading culture for the students. Also, ICT has been used to help teachers to interact with students. This will create a school culture of students being able to interact with their teachers (Willmann, 2017).

8.17. ICT IS HELPFUL FOR TECHNICAL PRECONDITIONS (INFRASTRUCTURE)

Technical preconditions are the technological conditions that are to be present for something to be achieved. In this case, it is necessary for learning to effectively take place. In education, the technical preconditions are referenced to the infrastructure that is available within the learning institution. There various infrastructure that is used in learning institutions. They include classrooms, laboratories, and electricity among others. Infrastructure may also be in terms of services offered in which in schools there are teaching and learning services that are offered to the students. ICT has been useful in improving and maintaining the infrastructure within the school so that learning may be effective.For instance, in the classroom. ICT has been used to improve the learning conditions in the classroom through the use of equipment such as smart boards. Smartboards have facilitated the easy sharing of information from the teacher to students. It is an improvement as before in its place were chalkboards. The chalk dust would create a hindrance to learning as some students are allergic to dust. This would, therefore, limit the teacher to dictation notes and illustrating using of objects available in the class (Cartelli & Antonio, 2013).

Using smart boards is a way in which ICT has been used to improve the classroom and make it more technology-oriented. The library is part of the school infrastructure and is a useful resource in giving students good quality education. ICT has been useful in making the libraries in various school to be more advanced. Initially, librarians would give out books to some students but they would end up getting lost or the student would not return it to the library. This has changed with the use of ICT in the library. It has enabled the generation of library cards which is useful student identification in the library.

Also, computers have been used to store information on all the books that are present in the library. They contain information on the number of books available and the specific location of the book. This has enabled the libraries to come up with library catalogs that gives students knowledge on where they can access the book they require. Additionally, librarians have been able to come up with a system where every book contains their unique bar codes. It will be easy to identify the book that was borrowed and then the student returns it the information is given to the computer (Cartelli & Antonio, 2013).

Teachers have used ICT to improve the status of the labs. They have used the knowledge in the internet to identify the type of equipment that are required in the labs. With the current digitalization of the world, even the equipment that is used in the labs is also being digitalized. Technology is being used to make advances in the technology being used. For instance, the anemometers and voltmeters have been digitalized so that the students can directly obtain information from the device. The teacher is able to know of these changes through the use of the internet and they request the school management to purchase the devices.

Computers have been used in schools to keep records on various infrastructure that is in schools. This include the study tables, chairs and furniture available in the school. These records are important for the teacher when planning on the class layout so that it will favor all the students. It is also important in identifying the number of desks present compared to the number of students available. This will be useful in determining whether more of the chairs or desks have to be bought. It also useful in determining which of them will be required to be repaired (Cartelli & Antonio, 2013).

Infrastructure may also be viewed in terms of the service that are offered.

This is in regard to teaching as the service that is rendered to students. ICT has been used in improving the teaching aspect of education. It has enabled teachers to gain more knowledge through the use of e-books and the internet making them to be more knowledgeable content wise. This will enable them to teach the students effectively. It has also been able to help teachers to know how to apply their skills in a real classroom environment. For instance, skills such as communication enable them to effectively relay information to the students. This in the end will enable the teacher to improve their teaching services hence facilitating effective learning. This are some of the ways in which teachers can use ICT to improve the infrastructure of the school (Cartelli & Antonio, 2013).

8.18. ICT IS HELPFUL FOR BOTH VOCATIONAL EDUCATION AND TRAINING OF FUTURE TEACHERS (IN THE TEACHERS TRAINING INSTITUTES)

Vocational training is the provision of education and training in order to provide knowledge and training. It is important as it equips the students with practical experiences as well as the skills required in a particular field. Many ministries have introduced vocational training of teachers to enable various students to access this service. With the recent modernization of the world, it has required the incorporation ICT in the teacher training institutes for them to be able to facilitate a better learning experience for the teachers.

ICT has been greatly used in teacher training institutes in various ways. For one it has been used to teach attitudinal and practical skills in the training institutes. ICT has been used in teaching the students the attitudes the teacher should have while in the classroom. It is also used to teach them the practical skills that they should have and those that will be used in the classroom. It has also been used to teach them on how they can apply the acquired skills while in a real classroom situation so that the learning process will be effective (Kadijevich, Angeli, & Schulte, 2013).

ICT has also been used as a curriculum in the teacher training institutes as it involves the use of technology. As ICT has been incorporated into the education system, it will require the teacher to have ICT literacy skills. ICT tools has been used in the teacher training institutes to equip the future teachers with the literacy skills. Therefore, tools such as computers have been used in the training institutes for the future teachers to obtain hands on skills such as keyboarding, using of databases, word processing, using spreadsheets, desktop publishing and how to be able to access the internet. This will also enable them create their own software to use in the teaching process.

ICT has also been used in the teachers training institutes as a research material. For the students in the training institute, research is part of the education process. For them to carry out extensive research they may be required to draw content from a variety of sources which may not be readily available. Therefore, ICT has been used to provide such limited resources. This is through the provision of resources such as e-books and the internet that has been used to facilitate research.

ICT has been used in teacher training institutes as a learning resource. It has been used to compliment the learning process. The trainers in the training institutes use resources such as videos that are available in the internet to elaborate various concepts to the students. This is to enable them effectively relay information to the students and also as it involves visuals, the students will be able to recall all that they learnt. It therefore enables the future teachers to have a high knowledge retention ability which is essential for them as they will be in future required to relay the information to their students (Yadav, 2014).

ICT has been used in the teacher training institutes to offer virtual internship to the students. Internship is important for the students as it will enable them to acquire work experience and they will get to know how to apply the knowledge that they have. ICT has been useful in creating a simulation of classroom scenarios where the teachers will be required to offer teaching services to the virtual students. The simulations are created by computer specialists for the use of the training institutions. As teacher offers the teaching service, it becomes a form of virtual internship.

ICT has major uses in teaching. Apart from that, ICT has also been useful in the program support of the teacher training institutes. Or instance it has been used for administrative purposes where tools such as computers have been used for storing records like financial records of the institution which may be useful in future when making strategic plans. The information is also useful in planning on how to manage the resources that are within the institution. It has also been useful in providing labor market information. This information is important to the students as after the learning process they will be required to know available teaching opportunities in various schools.

ICT tools such as computers and fax machines have been used to facilitate communication within the teacher training institutions. The institutions have also used ICT to control the technical systems as well as carrying out information search (Yadav, 2014).

Chapter 9 Bridging the Computer Science Education Gap

CONTENTS

9.1. Introduction 240
9.2. Imparting The Youth With Skills For A Digital Economy 241
9.3. Understanding IT And Computer Science 241
9.4. Filling The Gap For Computer Science Learning 242
9.5. Improving K-12 Computer Science Standards 243
9.6. Computer Science: Things Learners Should Know 244
9.7. Choosing Standards-Based Syllabuses And Teaching Resources 244
9.8. Introducing Elementary School Pupils To Computing 245
9.9. Involving Mid-Grade Pupils In Interdisciplinary Learning 246
9.10. Promoting High School Learners' Appreciation of Computer Science 247
9.11. Enhancing Enrichment And Investigative Learning Experiences Among Students 248
9.12. Further Actions That Local Governments Can Take 249
9.13. Preparing Competent Computer Science Educators 250
9.14. Obstacles To Educator Certification In Computing Disciplines 251
9.15. Techniques For Equipping And Supporting Cs Educators 252
9.16. Sreb States' Techniques For Equipping Computer Science Educators 254
9.17. Access To Technology and Modern Learning Methods 255
9.18. ICT Planning 256
9.19. Computer Science Investment In Schools 258
9.20. Children's Coding Academies Seek To Fill Up Computer 'Skills Gap' 260
9.21. Interdependence Between Education Technology and Other Systems 261

9.1. INTRODUCTION

Within the international job industry, computational reasoning abilities and knowledge of computing are necessary in almost all career fields. Moreover, careers in computer science, IT and other relevant fields represent a massive and expanding segment of the economy. Come 2020, it's estimated around 4.6 million jobs from the 9.2 million careers in science, innovation, engineering and math sectors will be computer-based, centered on statistics from the Computing Machinery Association. It's further believed that around 70% of these careers will need a bachelor's qualification or higher. Besides most will pay decently. The standard median salary of careers in IT and computer science was around $81,430 in 2015, based on research from the American Labor Statistics Bureau.

Nevertheless, the U.S. still lacks sufficient traction to meet growing labor market needs in computing disciplines. Code.org estimates that, come 2020, the U.S. will have roughly 1 million more computer-related jobs than competent persons to fill them. Fulfilling demand in these technology-intensive fields shall require countries to significantly expand and broaden their college-trained computing workforce. Recently, between 2015 and 2016, stakeholders in the education sector met to discuss how they could help low income communities get access to computer science courses, especially among young girls, Afro-American and Hispanic communities.

Figure 9.1. Computer science can help expose young girls to STEM subjects in school.

Source: http://www.adeanet.org/en/blogs/bridging-the-gender-equality-gap-in-stem-to-fully-transform-africa.

They came up with certain recommendations that states should adopt to help more youngsters learn CS and build computational thinking abilities, not only those pupils considering STEM careers but everyone. Computer science (CS) provides students with more than just expertise of how computers function or the skills required to develop a device, script a code or handle data. It develops high-level literacy, arithmetic, problem-solving and technical skills while promoting productivity in almost every discipline, market sector and profession.

9.2. IMPARTING THE YOUTH WITH SKILLS FOR A DIGITAL ECONOMY

Kids born after the early 90s have never witnessed a world where computing and IT aren't crucial to nearly every area of their lives. Cumulative knowledge of humankind may be retrieved with the simple tap of a button. Advances in computer science assist us in improving, healing, transforming and comprehending ourselves and the world that we live in (Strickland & Alvermann, 2004).

Even so, these technologies are also susceptible to misuse, going at the expense of the security of our private data. CS education is significant to steering through the exciting and occasionally risky digital world. But way too many youngsters, especially low-income and marginalized youth, lack sufficient opportunities to examine the impact of computing and IT on their livelihoods and to become shrewd consumers, designers and inventors of computing technologies.Presently, computing can't be considered as some optional aspect of K-12, or provided only to pupils considering fields in science, innovation, engineering and mathematics disciplines. Computer science provides students way more than the information of how processors work or the abilities needed to develop a device, script code or handle data. It creates lifelong learning abilities that hold credence in every academic field, industry and profession. CS knowledge further enhances our national productivity as well as wealth (Strickland & Alvermann, 2004).

9.3. UNDERSTANDING IT AND COMPUTER SCIENCE

Despite being entrenched at the postsecondary stage, both IT and computer science are occasionally combined at the K-12 stage with other frequently used education phrases. Such phrases include academic technology, the application of PCs as an educational tool in teaching; and computing or digital literacy, which is the understanding of how to apply computing technology in a knowledgeable way.Computer science refers to research on PCs and algorithmic procedures, including their philosophies, their firmware and software designs, uses and impacts on society." CS combines theoretical knowledge and practical programming abilities to develop software, create new uses for PC technologies and resolve computing problems. IT emphasizes the applied use of technology, particularly the "choice, creation, application, assimilation and management of computing technologies" for purposes of meeting the users' needs. Computing professionals in every sector manage and preserve applications, networks, communications and networking media, plus support those who use these particular technologies (Cartelli & Antonio, 2013).

9.4. FILLING THE GAP FOR COMPUTER SCIENCE LEARNING

To help the youth from low-income homes appreciate computer science and discover and choose occupations in computing fields, stakeholders must carefully plan and underpin their actions with research. Countries will be prudent to involve several stakeholders in checking the projected and unintended outcomes of increasing access to computing education.

Providing equitable access to CS education is a mutual responsibility of both high school and postsecondary teachers, state officials, economic and staff development agencies, education partners, caregivers and community members (Cartelli & Antonio, 2013).

By applying clever planning and smart strategies, stakeholders can help close the CS opportunity gap and guarantee that the students have necessary skills they require to flourish in the digital world. Computer science knowledge can assist in launching pupils on paths toward college qualifications and degrees, decent jobs and safe economic futures. CS fosters creativity, inquisitive thinking and reasoning which allows individuals to solve various challenges in their communities.

Increasing access to CS will necessitate a whole lot of changes in education. Countries will have to formulate rigorous policies which determine the design of syllabuses, instruction and trainer preparation plus professional development. Likewise, elementary and midgrade schools must teach literacy, mathematics and problem-solving abilities in the perspective of CS in all classes and grades.

Both high school and midgrade learning institutions need to reorganize around building engaging assignments which foster students' educational, technical and technological abilities as they grow their professional and college horizons. Moreover, interdisciplinary early instructor teams may help in co-planning and cooperatively teaching lessons.

Post high school, community and employer associates should foster career trails leading to qualifications, degrees and workplace achievement. Colleges and universities can also improve registration, retention and completion by incorporating their CS and technology programs with secondary schools. Change is usually brought at a cost, besides most states, districts and individual schools have limited resources to invest in new initiatives. Stakeholders and educators recognize that when a fresh curricular content is introduced, other matters may be set aside. Considering the significance of computing technologies in our day to day lives, incorporating CS across K-12 or further ahead makes great academic and financial sense. The era of computer-science is right here. Stakeholders in education are urging countries to start making computer science learning a priority (Cartelli & Antonio, 2013).

9.5. IMPROVING K-12 COMPUTER SCIENCE STANDARDS

Regardless of the overwhelming requirement to generate more graduates who have the credentials and certifications needed in computing disciplines, computer science still continues to be a "marginalized" subject in many American schools. Countrywide in America, only three states—which are Texas, West Virginia and Arkansas, necessitate all secondary schools to provide computer science.

Still, no state requires pupils to take CS to graduate from secondary school. Regularly, pupils' choices are restricted to low-level technology programs like keyboarding and PC applications, or even a program in coding—what a recent study calls simply a portion of what actual computer science involves. Currently, only Indiana, Massachusetts, Arkansas, Florida, Texas and New Jersey have totally established such standards. Besides, most state computing syllabuses aren't streamlined with the K-12 CS standards developed by the CS Teachers Association (Kumar & Turner, 2006).

Meeting the objective of helping learners access superior computer science training starts with promoting computer science standards, besides many states are stepping up to cover this need. Some U.S. states are engaging in a mutual effort to build a K-12 computing learning framework that schools may use to develop their personal grade-level standards, syllabuses, lessons, evaluations and professional development.

9.6. COMPUTER SCIENCE: THINGS LEARNERS SHOULD KNOW

The K-12 CS structure outlines 5 key concepts and 7 practices which teachers and experts believe learners should understand as they leave grades two, five, 8 and 12. Various models and activities highlight the physical and theoretic fundamentals of CS. The framework also provides guidance on building standards, developing and implementing syllabuses, entrenching computer science education opportunities in various subject areas, and guaranteeing equity, diversity and availability. Regions can use the structure to develop a measureable principle for a particular grade by merging a core model with a particular practice.

Instructors in any discipline can apply the framework to generate assignments through which learners come to comprehend the concepts by participating in the practices. For instance, an 8th-grade art instructor might design a project whereby students develop personal virtual art galleries after deciding which image type—be it png, jpeg or gif—provides the best photo quality while occupying the least space (Cartelli & Antonio, 2013).

9.7. CHOOSING STANDARDS-BASED SYLLABUSES AND TEACHING RESOURCES

States can apply the CS standards they adopt to create or implement curricula that is relevant to pupils of different races, genders, socioeconomic settings, and ability levels. Organizations like Code.org have a responsibility to review 3rd party elementary, mid and secondary school courses for quality, convenience, outcomes, cost-effectiveness, and completeness.

Education providers need to enter into mutual partnerships with other stakeholders, in order to establish scale and backing, quality programs and skilled development. The rubric for assessing third-party courses include computing concepts and ideologies; involving literacy, mathematics and problem-solving abilities which pupils require for achievement in computing fields; plus, the fundamentals of solid career pathways.The CS Teachers Association regularly evaluates third-party learning courses for conformity with CSTA principles, and performs syllabus reviews for local education departments following request. Organizations like CS.org have compiled tools and facilities for K-12 learning institutions which are seeking to provide CS education. Specific regions may consider reviewing international models, like the UK's curriculum, which is among the best education systems in the world (Cartelli & Antonio, 2013).

9.8. INTRODUCING ELEMENTARY SCHOOL PUPILS TO COMPUTING

In elementary class, students may learn computing concepts and develop problem-solving abilities through practical activities involving art, languages, mathematics, science and sociological studies. The younger pupils can develop computational reasoning skills by resolving puzzles, sorting and organizing data, using virtual media to build and illustrate stories, plus developing games using drag-and-drop coding tools.

Learners in the higher elementary grades may work together to build apps, explore professions and evaluate the social and moral issues of computing. Intended for kids between ages 4 to 10yrs old, Code.org's CS Fundamentals is a cost free virtual four-course syllabus conforming to CSTA's K-12 guidelines. Teachers can provide each 20-lesson learning course as a module or throughout a semester. A virtual learning application allows pupils to develop and debug video games at their unique pace; other activities don't need a PC. Code.org provides educators with free supplies and daily career growth workshops in around 60 cities. Built by the Harvard Graduate Education researchers, with assistance from NSF, the Creative Computing app is a 6-part introduction to coding in Scratch, a graphic programming language. Accessible for free within the Creative Commons licensing umbrella, Creative Computing exposes elementary learners to concepts such as loops, sequences, conditionals, and operatives. The program also applies practical activities to train students on problem-solving skills. The ScratchEd's website further provides teachers with news, consultations, workshops, and resources structured for education level, content type, and language improvement.

9.9. INVOLVING MID-GRADE PUPILS IN INTERDISCIPLINARY LEARNING

Mid-grade students thrive when their courses are challenging, helpful and individually relevant. During these years, learners must comprehend computing instruments and networks, determine how computing promotes communication and apply computational reasoning abilities to solve societal problems. Project-based studying, group activities and multidisciplinary approaches mostly appeal to midgrade students (Kadijevich, Angeli, & Schulte, 2013).

Authorized by NSF, the standards-regulated Bootstrap syllabus teaches mathematics and coding by utilizing students' normal interest in gaming. Delivered across a set of 20- to 25hr courses,

Bootstrap allows students to design complex computer games through models derived from geometry, algebra and computer science. Studies show that Bootstrap enhances student performance in mathematics.

Its developers provide reasonable curricula, educator resources, dialogue forums and downloadable learner workbooks on their site. Cooperating schools and districts obtain 2- to 3-day workshops, consultations and assistance from Bootstrap instructors. Recently, Bootstrap in conjunction with Project GUTS (Grow up Thinking Scientifically) entered into partnership with Code.org for purposes of developing an interdisciplinary CS module for midgrade students. In the project, Computer Science in Algebra comprises around 20 hands-on courses which utilize algebra and geometry in game design.

As for CS in Science, there are over 20 lessons which educate on computer science within the framework of humanistic, physical and earth sciences. Study frameworks, lessons, instruction manuals, pupil activity books and recordings are free to access from the Code.org site. Educators in partner districts should participate in skilled development to provide either of these courses.

The state of West Virginia in particular is building project-based programs for students in public schools in various subjects, such as informatics and computer science, which prompt midgrade students to learn complex texts, prepare written modules, maintain engineering notebooks, understand science and math principles, and use technology (Kadijevich, Angeli, & Schulte, 2013).

9.10. PROMOTING HIGH SCHOOL LEARNERS' APPRECIATION OF COMPUTER SCIENCE

Figure 9.2. Students keenly following a computer science lesson.

Source: https://www.esd112.org/news/computer-science-at-sunset-ridge-intermediate-and-view-ridge-middle-school/.

Education stakeholders urge individual states to require that high schools provide students with access to thorough, standards-based computing courses. This will help relieve the common burden of effecting such programs statewide, furthermore, states may allow districts to provide them in varying settings, such as regular or local high schools, tech hubs, community and mechanical colleges, or instructor-facilitated online courses.

Exploring CS is a broad subject that focuses on main ideas and 6 computational reasoning practices pertaining to the "creative, collective, multidisciplinary and problem-solving aspect of computing. Students can be presented with feature project-based roles that highlight the global impact of computer technology on people and the society at large. States, regions, and schools can get a free review sample of the curriculum for purposes of implementing it, they should acquire a license and offer ECS teaching career development. Instructors who lack local government backing may use the syllabus for absolutely free.

9.11. ENHANCING ENRICHMENT AND INVESTIGATIVE LEARNING EXPERIENCES AMONG STUDENTS

It's advisable for local states and wards to avail early and regular computer science learning opportunities for K-12 pupils to explore CS through institutional clubs, contests, camps, summer engagement programs, job experiences and other programs. Parents, civic organizations and companies can assist schools in promoting such opportunities to pupils. Since the original CS Education Week that was initiated in December 2013, well over 282 million individuals have tried their hand on Code.org's Hour-of-Code, an hour-long self-guided seminar whereby students develop games that feature Star Wars, Minecraft and Disney figures by applying Blockly coding language.

Schools may protract learning beyond the initial hour through Code.org's Code Studio, which is a virtual hub in which instructors and learners can choose from a variety of 20-hour programs for learners between ages 4 to 18 yrs old.

When providing such opportunities, local governments should consider helping boys and girls differently, in mixed-gender groupings and their specific families. Organizations like Girls Who Code provide clubs and summer courses that minimize the intimidation factor related with CS for many girls. Roughly more than 10,000 young women served claim they intend to major or even minor in computing in college.

Maryland County in the U.S. implemented an after-school software development course for young girls in midgrade classes, appealing to the various styles of gaming which young girls enjoy. Donation funding also permitted Maryland municipal libraries to support family programming nights to get caregivers and kids excited about computing studies.

Key players in education encourage local governments to track involvement in CS programs and extra-curricular activities. Sometimes, districts lack sufficient data on the entire scale of opportunities that are accessible to students. Plus many schools enrich their computer science syllabi with after-school courses that might not be available to the learners who require them the most.

Through tracking participation, districts can take active steps to ensure fair access to post-school activities and connect more students to the learning process (Kadijevich, Angeli, & Schulte, 2013).

9.12. FURTHER ACTIONS THAT LOCAL GOVERNMENTS CAN TAKE

By working in conjunction with high school and postsecondary educators, professionals and industry frontrunners to build K-12 CS standards which include the fundamental concepts and skills students must understand in elementary, midgrade and high school levels. It's also fundamental to align CS standards and projects so that they underpin foundational literacy, mathematics and problem-solving abilities, while further helping pupils to meet certain grade-level literacy and arithmetic benchmarks (Mittermeir, 2006).

Furthermore, key players should build or implement standards-based, age appropriate computer science courses that appeal to different pupils in elementary and midgrade. Elementary school students can be introduced to computing through practical activities rooted in vital content areas, like art, math, language arts, social studies and science. It's also significant for schools to implement project-based, interdisciplinary computing courses or syllabi modules in midgrade classes that are enticing to adolescents' requirements for challenging, appropriate studies.

Furthermore, it's important to assess the efficacy of CS-related syllabuses by tracking learner outcomes and utilizing data to adjust curricula, pedagogy and evaluations to meet learner needs and reflects the standards of the discipline. High schools besides need to offer pupils access to thorough, standards-based CS courses, like AP Computing Principles and Exploring CS. Following a preliminary period of applying CS programs throughout K-12, high school students must either finish a rigorous computing course or showcase competency in CS in order to graduate (Mittermeir, 2006).

Additionally, districts and schools must be given the opportunity to provide computing courses in public or regional secondary schools, at technology hubs, on college grounds or through virtual courses. Encouraging high schools to reposition crucial computer literacy abilities, such as keyboarding and simple computer applications is also recommended, especially in elementary and midgrade school. This further covers fair distribution of resources for career development, syllabus implementation, firmware, software and web access. Recently, funding has also been availed at state, local and school levels for purposes of supporting increased CS learning prospects in schools.

Resources dedicated to computer science staff within the state and regional levels will help schools to reinforce computer science curricula. Schools should charge these professionals with promoting the development and execution of standards-based courses, professional development, public outreach and co-curricular activities. Supporting schools through equitable funding of IT systems and educational technology stakeholders is necessary for expanding computing learning opportunities for all students.

Stakeholders must encourage postsecondary, civic and employer associates to provide funds, materials or mutual support to schools which offer computer science training. Not to mention extending early and regular opportunities for K-12 pupils and their families—particularly girls, Afro-American and Hispanic students, including learners from poor families—to explore computing and computer science-based professions (Mittermeir, 2006).

Equally, it is recommended to provide learning institutions with resources and release period for instructors to support CS clubs, contests, camps, summer immersion courses, job experiences and various other education experiences for students. It is also significant to provide learning prospects to single-gender plus mixed-gender grouping and families, this can be accompanied with student participation tracking in CS learning experiences within and outside school to guarantee increased participation.

9.13. PREPARING COMPETENT COMPUTER SCIENCE EDUCATORS

Good instructors are essential to spark student interest in computing subjects and placing more youngsters on a track to professions in computing fields. Competent teachers not only convey the crucial knowledge, skills and abilities needed to learn CS, they also enable pupils to use computing to solve various issues in their local communities. No matter their background, good computer science instructors are creative, passionate and insightful about their practice. Experts believe that the most ideal way to recognize prospective computer science educators is by recruiting problem-solvers—educators with a keen and passion interest for digital innovation who learn beside their students (Mittermeir, 2006).

Computer science educators need strong early training, continuing professional development and prospects to collaborate with instructors in other subject fields. Even though many fresh Exploring Computer Science educators have no formal CS training, they develop confidence during 2yrs of professional development. During their original summer institute, instructors focus on ECS' initial two units and fashion inquiry-based learning. Educators receive training on the other 4 units throughout the year, then participate in learning communities together with new and experienced ECS educators. During the subsequent summer institute, interdisciplinary educator collaboration is necessary to promoting academic accomplishment in all fields, not just computer science. For this, principals should provide sufficient time for educator teams to cooperate or co-teach programs in CS and other subjects (Mittermeir, 2006).

9.14. OBSTACLES TO EDUCATOR CERTIFICATION IN COMPUTING DISCIPLINES

Many regions are experiencing scarcities of skilled educators in most subject fields, not only computer science. Nevertheless, instructor shortages in computing and related disciplines may have severe and far-reaching impacts on the country's economy and security. According to one estimate, the U.S. requires around 10,000 extra computer science instructors to bring high-grade computer science subjects to all secondary schools (Sharma, 2002). Without the capacity to appeal to or prepare competent instructors, schools and districts can't provide computer science. For a recent survey, it was found that 44% of principals as well as 57% of superintendents mentioned an incapacity to find trained educators as a key reason for not providing computer science.

Nevertheless, 40% of principals from learning institutes not providing computer science mentioned that an educator at their school can teach such courses, which is an indication that other barriers—such as funding or certification needs, for instance—may prevent institutes from providing computer science. Concerning both new and experienced teachers, getting a CS certification may be challenging. Many states lack postsecondary educator preparation courses in computer science, besides many offer a puzzling array of certifications, commendations and licensures that may vary depending on which K-12 educational department provides computer science. Nonetheless, these certifications may not cover CS content or pedagogies.

A few state certification structures require educators to complete programs not available at state colleges or lack a substitute for instructors from industry. Presently, only the states of Wisconsin and Arkansas require computing teachers to finish the CS Praxis test as a degree of their willingness to teach. Initially, established by the Educational Exam Service for Texas, computer science Praxis evaluates the knowledge, talents and abilities of grades 4 to12 educators in technology software, computational thinking abilities and programming (Sharma, 2002).

In 2015, only 26 teachers countrywide took the CS Praxis test. Education commissioners urge stakeholders, computer science systems, policy groups, business leaders and others in collaborating with ETS to create a new multistate computing Praxis concentrated on higher-level coding and computational reasoning skills for grades 7 to 12 teachers.

9.15. TECHNIQUES FOR EQUIPPING AND SUPPORTING CS EDUCATORS

Generally, more states in SREB regions are meeting the need of clarifying the accreditation process and backing computer science instructors with continuing professional development. By October 2016, it was found that 11 out of SREB's overall16 states provide upfront paths to computing certification that cover options for new and veteran midgrade and secondary school teachers. For supporting these efforts, it is advisable that states develop multitier certification, introductory and professional advancement systems which assist new and experienced teachers gain computer science content understanding and learn the pedagogical abilities needed to involve diverse learners.

Education stakeholders advise states to entrench computer science material in pre-service preparation courses for elementary and midgrade teachers. There are two popular university-based STEM instructor preparation courses that can be adopted by schools:

- North-Carolina State University's bachelor's elementary education course, for instance, prepares educators in all fields to deliver STEM-based instruction. Students must complete roughly 27 full credits of STEM-based courses and double pedagogical methodology courses.

- The UTeach STEM learner preparation course at the University of Austin permits students who're taking degrees in computing, engineering, mathematics or science to obtain a secondary education certification without including more time to their courses. UTeach incorporates STEM material with inquiry-based, problem-solving and project-based education pedagogies.

Education players recognize that these multifaceted structures may take several years to formulate and implement wholly. On a short-term basis, states can provide 2- to 4-week, whole day summer institutes, directed by a master educator, whereby new computer science educators learn their syllabus by doing the same programs and assignments like their students. Day to day activities comprise time for members to contemplate on the expedition strategies demonstrated by the master educator. Teachers planning to teach any of SREB's Progressive Career pathways, for instance, attend a 2-week summer institute whereby they learn every course's mechanical content, technology, application and embedded mathematics; practice integrating literacy abilities in instruction; handle the course's practical projects; and learn strategies for directing classrooms and evaluating student learning (Mittermeir, 2006).

Educators who successfully finish the summer institute course usually obtain a state endorsement for teaching the AC syllabus. Continuing support covers in-service training, specialized learning communities plus additional summer lessons. States require the support of authorization and certification groups to increase the computer science educator talent pool.

Education consultants advise that states cooperate with the Board for Accreditation of Teacher Preparation to upgrade teacher preparation courses to include computing content knowledge and teaching practices. Equally, states can work together with the Nationwide Board of Practiced Teaching Standards to include computing among its group of 25 certificate fields for Country Board Certified Educators.

Federal and state bodies, computer science and learning organizations, statewide and district leaders, plus global technology businesses—for instance, Facebook, Google, Apple and Microsoft—are focused on supporting educator preparation as a component of multistate CS for all program. Furthermore, the National Science Group is presently investing $120 million throughout the next 5yrs for supporting educator professional development, plus AP CPS and ECS syllabus implementation. From this investment, around $5 million shall go into pilot-testing other teaching career development approaches (Mittermeir, 2006).

9.16. SREB STATES' TECHNIQUES FOR EQUIPPING COMPUTER SCIENCE EDUCATORS

Currently, Arkansas is reviewing its teacher accreditation and licensure procedures to conform with its fresh K-12 CS standards and is engaging several strategies to expand the teacher skill pool. In 2016, the Arkansas Education Department focused around $1 million towards supporting two key professional development zones. The first one is preparation for computer-science Praxis for secondary school teachers, plus training for master educators on the region's K-8 standards and programming course for grades 7 or 8. The sector's three-pronged method of teacher preparation includes various aspects. Among them is retraining tutors through full-week boot camps and continual engagement in simulated professional learning communities. Including working with postsecondary institutes to develop computer science tutorial education pathways, like the CS Education for Trainer Licensure course at Arkansas Tech, plus providing a nontraditional means to attaining computer science licensure (Donohue, 2014).

The Arkansas Career Education Department chose a unique licensure approach for its new 3-year Virtual Applications Development strategy to attract teachers. Regardless of whether they are coming from fields in art, corporate or STEM subjects, any instructors who participate in the state's preparation program may obtain a licensure for teaching the MAD system in grades 7 up to 12.

In addition, the Alabama State Education Department is working together with Code.org as well as A+ College Ready for purposes of preparing around 50 new AP computing educators in 2016 to 17—expanding the number of skilled computer science tutors in the state. Within the coming few years, Code.org shall provide roughly $500,000 in syllabi and professional development. The A+ College Ready program is recruiting educators to engage in training, which comprises a 5-day summer workshop, plus 10 days of preparation during the schooling year, and accessibility to virtual facilities and weekend study programs.

Likewise, Maryland provides two ways to computing teacher certification. A comprehensive secondary content area accreditation for those in conventional teacher preparation programs, plus Standard Professional Certificate provided by a Maryland Certified Alternative Preparation Course for teachers who're going to the class as career-shapers. State universities and colleges are organizing regional summer institutes, whereby K-12 and college staff work jointly to integrate computational thinking abilities into mathematics, computer science, science and different other subjects (Donohue, 2014).

Applied Kentucky instructors who hold a CS certification for grades 8 to 12 are qualified to teach AP computing courses, as are licensed teachers with a concentration in mathematics. AP computer science instructors in the Progressive Kentucky group of schools—a state-based math and science collaboration between Kentucky Science & Technology Corporation, the Kentucky Board of Education, National Mathematics and Science Initiative plus other organizations—where they engage in 5-day summer programs and 2-day fall trainings during their initial two years. Generally, support entails mentoring, teaming up across midgrade and high schools, plus resources for professional development.

9.17. ACCESS TO TECHNOLOGY AND MODERN LEARNING METHODS

Figure 9.3. Schools should make technology accessible to students so as to equip them for the future job market.

Source: https://www.globalgiving.org/projects/vhfinc/.

Significant investment has been done to promote technology use in schools and they have indeed caused many "success stories." Nevertheless, there are two particular gaps in educational applications of technology which should be looked at. The first one is usage gap. In comparison to how and the total number of today's learners who use innovation outside school, in-school innovation usage is way less intensive and expansive. The other is a results gap. Put against the outcomes attained through investments in innovation in fields outside education, the achievements in terms of minimized costs and increased output realized by schools is quite reduced (Donohue, 2014).

Moreover, in many regions, there isn't any clear sign or broadly used measurement of effectual teaching. While some researches have tried to use students' scholarly performance results as a considerable indicator of the efficiency of teaching, these findings have been contentious and open to deliberation. It is contentious since it is considered a vehicle for promoting an education system which has been forming imbalances of social and academic capital. It is debatable since effective teaching is among the many variables which might affect students' school performance. Additionally, there isn't any agreed-upon description of effectual teaching. This is particularly relevant in the conversation of the application of technology, plus how it can improve the success of teaching.

9.18. ICT PLANNING

Another reason for the disparity between technology developments and use in schools is poor technology planning. When making a technology policy design, a school defines its expectations, objectives, content and activities regarding the incorporation of ICT in mainstream education.

It includes elements like vision building, career development, and assessment. Although schools have been acquiring modern equipment with the goal of introducing the newest tools in teaching and education, the outcomes aren't clearly noticeable either in regards to approval by the educators or in pupils' learning outcomes. Experts note that technology assimilation is a complex procedure and an arduous task for instructors and school administrators. In their research, it was discovered that even instructors and supervisors who felt themselves experienced in using ICT stated that there was general lack of guidelines which would lead them to effective integration. This further furthered confirmed the significance of technology-based planning in schools (Donohue, 2014).

Additional surveys revealed that ICT planned along with ICT support as well as training has a considerable effect on general classroom usage of ICT. It is also been pointed out that education policies (in conjunction to ICT) are not well developed and underutilized. The outcomes lead many to assume that a mutual and school-wide edition of ICT is required to thrive in technology incorporation.

Furthermore, it is been realized that innovation planning is a procedure of developing, renewing and implementing technology policies in order to direct organizations to attain their objectives. A technology design also defines the learning goals, how the innovation will be applied and evaluated as well. According to some scholars, technological policies are the boundary between research and expansion in learning technologies plus their specific usage in schools (Cartelli & Antonio, 2013).

They are certain fundamental characteristics of effective planning for technology. The primary one to be contemplated is applying technology usage as a policy paper. Typically, a technology design is devised at various levels of administration. Within the highest level, this plan might be regarded as a draft for all stakeholders comprising educational organizers, mid-level managers, and school level supervisors. Furthermore, this policy plan would go down to educators at the class level. A technology policy then occurs at several levels and has various purposes. Even more, a technology plan can never be static. Since technology changes fast, the intention to use it also has to be elastic and conform to the circumstances. Researchers note that one common error done by schools which have designed a technology policy is the notion that the planning paper is the conclusion of the process.

Instead, the changing nature of technology needs regular modification to and reexamining of the plan. These adjustments and reviewing not only allow educators to make greater alignment with fresh technologies, instead also assist in adjusting the shifting learning environment plus social context. Another characteristic is that most successful technology plans require commitment, backing and cooperation at varying levels. It's important to develop a connection with schools plus outside organizations like teacher preparation institutions, including the corporate division. Much needed assistance can be gained through having close relations with these organizations (Cartelli & Antonio, 2013).

9.19. COMPUTER SCIENCE INVESTMENT IN SCHOOLS

Technology adoption in schools internationally has improved a hundredfold over the past two decades. Most of this venture has been done based on the supposition that technology-based learning environments offer opportunities for learners to seek for and analyze data, solve problems, connect and collaborate, hence furnishing them with a group of abilities to be relevant in the twenty-first century marketplace.

Nevertheless, the history of using innovation in schools has revealed that teachers would abandon technology which doesn't fit the social structure of schooling. Following a century or so, schools are still principally reliant on educators and textbooks. However, there have been several "success stories" to prove that when utilized properly, technology indeed leads to improved teaching and learning conditions (Strickland & Alvermann, 2004).

Researchers have proved that technology has largely been altering classroom practices plus learning procedures. These transformations comprise a change in the function of the tutor from being the only source of knowledge to a more significant role of exchanging lesson goals with students, availing varying levels of assistance to different students, assessing students' advancement, and providing reflection on class-based activities.

Learners have also assumed a more active practice in their individual learning process through using technology to look for and organize information, besides recording and sharing their findings. They are currently more involved and are capable of making improved relations between their earlier learning experiences, plus the new principles or theories being taught. A recent analysis has further revealed low to the modest effect size of innovation on students' accomplishments.

Nevertheless, these "success stories" aren't a prevalent factor in schools. Different from hardware, networking, and software, the activities and their socio-cultural frameworks that have caused these affirmative teaching and learning results have experienced a difficult period being sustained and transmitted across classrooms and learning institutions to foster the needed transformation in schools. Even though technologies haven't changed schools in a range as some people may have projected, they have caused irreversible variations in how people work, live, interact and play (Strickland & Alvermann, 2004).

Essentially, they've led to the growth of new industries, new regulations, and new fields of research. Organizations like Google, eBay, Amazon, Microsoft, Apple, and Facebook are but a few instances of the scale of the significance of these technologies.

When properly utilized, technology can serve as a basis and facilitator for the improvement of activities in schools. This transformation is getting particularly crucial considering that the practices the students follow in their day to day lives have gotten distinctly withdrew from the training and learning activities found in their schools.

Once this happens, learners may find classroom practices meaningless and become detached in school.

Computer technology isn't just a traditionally conceived concept, but rather a new tool which can be applied to improve our everyday lives in the real world, plus has inspired a whole new virtual world. Nowadays, we use various technologies to look for and deliver resources and information, convey our thoughts, communicate with others, develop and even play, typically assuming new and several identities. The scale of the virtual world is equal to the physical world in some regards; from virtual gaming to e-learning and many more applications (Unesco, 2011).

No matter the sector, most modern technology investments are accompanied by administrative investments and the ultimate product and service improvement related with it.

When there is insufficient organizational changes being done in respect with technology investment, then there could be substantial productivity losses since the advantages from the technological investment might be overshadowed by the negative relations with existing administrative practices. Thus, the effectiveness and application of these technologies rely on the people, procedures, culture and framework of the context where they are situated.

The virtual world is also starting to enter the physical world, since more and more actions are committed to and done by means of online resources. We nowadays learn, work, get entertained, and keep connected with family members, coworkers and friends within a system that's facilitated by technology which has become an indispensable part of our everyday lives (Unesco, 2011).

9.20. CHILDREN'S CODING ACADEMIES SEEK TO FILL UP COMPUTER 'SKILLS GAP'

In the modern age, there are lots of schools that have computers, though finding an instructor having tech industry experience is still rare. Some K-12 education improvement programs, nevertheless, are promoting a number of summer tech-based workshops across various U.S. cities to train high school pupils on programming fundamentals, app creation, front-end web designing and ways of getting a start-up running.

Increasingly at the nationwide level, there is a perception that computer science should place emphasis on public education systems. Educators are now seeking to attack the issue head on. They simply don't have a channel to produce talent domestically, despite most employers actively looking for IT solutions right now (Guzdial, 2015).

Recruiters and CEOs point out that they are unable to find skilled individuals to fill the increasing number of technology jobs. A few economists believe companies are however, hiding behind the skills gap argument to avoid hiring staff.

K-12 summer computing workshops in cities like New York, Boston, Chicago, Miami, Texas, and Austin are taking students further into industry-needed computing skills and giving them some sense of how significant coding and designs abilities are to various modern professions.

These student coding academies employ the same syllabus organizations like Flatiron use to assist unemployed adults switch into new careers. Learners will not just gain insight on CSS, HTML and JavaScript programs, but actually use the languages to develop a web app being part of the general coursework.

A great idea is never enough to make a change. Therefore, the academy pupils will also learn business essentials such as sales, finance, program management and marketing through the computer skills development courses. To keep students involved, stakeholders often ensure high commitment and energy levels are maintained through intense cooperation and project-based training. It does not matter whether one has never programmed before. There is no issue either if you never used a computer before. The programs have limitless material to challenge children at every level (Guzdial, 2015).

The executive of a leading tech incubator company called 1871 recently mentioned that, he doesn't need complex statistics to recognize there is a difficulty with finding qualified individuals for the technology industry. He mentioned his business's recruiter can't seem to find enough computing specialists, engineers or programmers to meet the requirements of the present-day companies.

Stakeholders have so far seen positive results in cities like Chicago. The area's Mayor Rahm Emanuel requires that every child in Public Schools should be exposed to primary coding skills, whereas new governor Bruce Rauner requires that education financing is reserved for technology. There is some basic yet outdated equipment in schools. Educators believe that programming should be the new language subject in schools. The current age is the most suitable for being exposed to coding since they are the most open-minded to learning this type of content (König, 2012).

9.21. INTERDEPENDENCE BETWEEN EDUCATION TECHNOLOGY AND OTHER SYSTEMS

Technology as an invention presented to schools isn't autonomous or isolated; it's closely linked to the ecological structure of the school plus connected to its wider systems.

A recently introduced innovation typically requires concurrent inventions in pedagogy, assessment, syllabus and school organization. Furthermore, it affects the relations within and without the school, plus the ongoing interaction facilitates changes in social interactions. Similarly, changes instigated by the connections between a technology and the school administration not only determines how the technology is adopted, though also affect the functioning of the school program.

Thus, the versatile co-adaptation and concurrent evolution of learners, educators and school directors with technology plus the system determines if the prospects of innovation for instruction and learning may be attained in schools (König, 2012).

The gap existing between modern trends and application of technology in public schools is quite evident. The effective co-adaptation of innovation and the schooling system is determined and constrained by various conditions. These factors may be associated to school technology facilities, school culture, preparedness and experiences of tutors and students concerning using technology, besides the dynamics of social connections in the school program are also shifting. These factors are interdependent of each other, plus their influence on innovation application is beyond the simple or linear one. Contrarily, they are entwined with one another, their influence differs from situation to situation, their connections and relationships differ as the school setting changes with the technology execution, plus the changes are based in local frameworks.

The school setting gradually evolves, altering the roles of teachers, learners, and various technology uses are further changing the school environment. Since technology usage in schools continuously changes alongside other aspects of the ecosystem -users, the education system, and relations between these substructures – there really isn't any all-encompassing solution to technology application in schools (Cartelli & Antonio, 2013).

An innovation implementation plan which works once may not necessarily function at another, therefore a dynamic plan which reflects changes shall work better compared to a static policy. Even for instances when a technology program has been successful, continuing its effective implementation, fresh policies must be made, more cash needs to be put on upgrading applications and updating firmware, more appropriate assistance should further be availed to both instructors and students, besides more investment must be invested into sustaining and enhancing adequate technical support—whereas all these changes are reliant on strong leadership.

Therefore, it is vital to provide continual technology planning and assessment, to regularly revise and refine modern practices, and give timely support. Nevertheless, even if the essential factors are put in place, it is still challenging to judge the impact of technology implementation since there's still lack of definite goals or concepts to emulate. Even though researchers have frequently suggested that effective policy implementation needs clearly defined objectives directly linked to student learning, there are no exact educational objectives described in educational innovation policy documents apart for solid intermediary goals like amount of firmware, pupil-computer ratios, and networking rates. Still, investing in educational technology is important for preparing kids for a digital world (Cartelli & Antonio, 2013).

Chapter 10 Factors Influencing Students' Choice of Computer Studies in Schools

CONTENTS

10.1. Introduction 264
10.2. An Overview of Computer Studies In Secondary Schools 264
10.3. Students' Aspirations on Their Choice of Computer Studies In Schools 265
10.4. Availability of Computer Facilities In Schools 268
10.5. Parents' Influence on Students' Choice of Computer Studies In Schools 270
10.6. Teachers' Readiness to Use ICT In Schools 273
10.7. Prior Computer Training 275
10.8. ICT Infrastructure 278
10.9. Internet Accessibility And Computer Usage by School Teachers 280
10.10. Computer Competence And Computer Usage by School Teachers 282
10.11. The Influence Of Gender Differences On Computer Usage by School Teachers 285

10.1. INTRODUCTION

There are not many students that are joining the workforce of today with the skills in technology that are required. This is due to a couple of factors such as low levels of enrollment in the disciplines that are related to computer by students in college. There has been some progress in enrollment that has been seen after the major decline between 2001–2008, and there are certain steps that been integrated so as to improve enrollment. There is still, however, a lack of understanding on the factors that are influencing students in choosing to do disciplines that are related to computers.

There are many countries that are facing challenges in the preparation of a workforce that is educated in technology. There is a need to ensure that there are enough students finishing with the knowledge required in computer-related issues. Many workers are required to meet this demand. There is a belief that there will be an increase in the number of people pursuing mathematical and computer occupations, as others also grow, such as engineering and architecture.

There are however, a couple of concerns in the growth of the number of people taking thus discipline. These include: the quality in the preparation of the students to use computers to solve issues in different aspects, the low number of students that are currently doing computer-related studies as of now, and whether the students and workers that are from other countries are enough to meet the demand of the specific country.

10.2. AN OVERVIEW OF COMPUTER STUDIES IN SECONDARY SCHOOLS

One of the optional subjects that are offered in secondary school level of education is computer studies. It was initially developed in the year 1997 and it has shown to be a very important subject that needs to be reviewed constantly due to its dynamic nature.

There are very many reviews that are done to the syllabus of computer studies due to the many different breakthroughs and developments in the information and communication technology sector, making it important to ensure that the syllabus is always up-to-date. The computer syllabus is expected to be independent of time and it should also be able to accommodate the current technology, which is contemporary (Kumar & Turner, 2006).

The syllabus has objectives on what the students should have learned by the end of the whole syllabus. This syllabus is aimed at equipping the student with the basic skills that will allow the student to use the computer to do different tasks no matter the environment, for example, home, school, etc., on a daily basis. The syllabus is created in a way that allows the learner to acquire the skills, knowledge and motivation to adapt to the computer world that is always changing and advancing, and also accept the computer as a tool that helps in the daily solving of problems.It also ensures that the students apply these skills in a manner that allows them to grow mentally, spiritually, morally, and also socially. There are also very many different career opportunities that the students will be able to appreciate, also allowing them to have a solid foundation for majoring in computer-related studies.

The use of Contemporary technology is advised of all teachers, as well as materials and resources that are contemporary, which will help in the exposure of the learner to the different developments that occur in the computer field. The trainer should always look out for any new hardware and software that have developed and be able to keep up with the new innovations (Kumar & Turner, 2006).

The syllabus also helps in teaching the students and keeping them aware of common global issues such as drug abuse, HIV/AIDS, human rights, environmental problems, etc. The time that is normally given to one topic in the syllabus is always set. In the Kenyan system, there is normally allocation of 3 to 4 lessons a week, depending on the level of education. It is important for the teacher to ensure that his/her work is well planned according to the allocated time, so as to ensure that the entire syllabus is covered in the time allocated. It is also necessary for the teacher to find different ways of relating the information to the students. The teacher will need to foster creativity and an environment for innovation, so as to make sure that the subject is interesting (König, 2012).

10.3. STUDENTS' ASPIRATIONS ON THEIR CHOICE OF COMPUTER STUDIES IN SCHOOLS

A study showed that students in public schools tended to appreciate computer studies more than those is private schools. This is seen because the students choose their technical subjects due to their preferences as well as what they want to do in the future. This is seen especially with computer-related studies, because they fix the subject to their future career options.

One of the reasons that many students in private schools may not prefer to do computer studies is because they have a wider variety of technical subjects to choose from. They may have other options such as music, art, etc. that many other public schools may not be able to afford. In both public and private schools, most of the students choose computer studies because it is something they might have gotten an introduction to in primary school. They find this easier than having to start from scratch on a different technical subject.

Figure 10.1. There are many different reasons why students choose to do computer studies. The main reason has been due to their career options after secondary.

Source: https://www.timeshighereducation.com/student/news/why-do-students-go-university-and-how-do-they-choose-which-one.

Another reason for students to choose computer studies is because they do not like the other options that are provided. There are many students who choose computer studies from their own volition, but there are also many who choose it because nothing else offered to them is interesting. There are some schools that may offer just three technical subjects, for example, agriculture, home science, and computer studies. Of these three options, it is very likely to find more people choosing computer studies, as it is more modern and seems much more interesting.

There are also other students who choose computer studied because they were forced to do it by their parents or teachers. Before students finally choose their main technical subject, it is common for them to do all the subjects for one year, then drop the ones they do not like. If students do not perform well in one of the subjects, it is common for teachers to discourage the student from choosing that subject. This may lead to the student choosing a subject that he/she doesn't like, just because they do better at it. This happens a lot in computer studies. This can also end up being a forceful guidance.

These students who may have chosen computer studies due to forceful guidance, may end up performing poorly in the subject. These students may also not have been ready to take the subject, or may have been guided poorly or with poor orientation.

Students also make decisions on the technical subject to do on a short-term focus, instead of thinking about their time after school. Despite having different career choices, there are many who chose computer studies just because it is the only interesting subject, or they didn't like the subject. Computer studies, however, has shown to be very important, no matter what career choice one has made. Computers are used everywhere for our daily tasks. Choosing computer studies should not only be on the basis of one's career, but also for anyone and everyone (Cartelli & Antonio, 2013).

The main factor that influences the choice of the students to do computer studies in their career aspirations. Many students choose computer studies because it relates to something they would like to do in the future. There are other students who choose to do computer studies due to peer pressure. They do it just because their friends and peers are doing it. Other factors that influence the choices of the students include, acquiring skills for one to employ themselves, interest in the subject as an individual, the job markets, etc.

There are many students these days who understand that is important for one to have basic computer skills in today's workforce. Almost all tasks and activities are completed using computers. This is the reality of today's workforce, and students being able to understand this allows them to choose computer studies as a means of building and realizing their future career plans. It is true to say that is one does not have computer skills, they are doomed in the workforce. Lacking the basic computer skills can lead to major consequences in one's career (Cartelli & Antonio, 2013).

Computer studies are important, and school orientation should be able to discuss on how important the basic computer skills are. Students should not be coerced to choose the subject if they are not interested, because it will affect the student's performance. All in all, despite the fact that it is important for students to know the basic computer skills, it is also important for the students to choose the subject they are more comfortable doing. This being said, it may be important for schools to consider making computer studies a compulsory subject, because without it, it is definitely hard to survive in the workforce.

10.4. AVAILABILITY OF COMPUTER FACILITIES IN SCHOOLS

It is important for all secondary schools to have computer laboratories that are well equipped. These labs are important for both teaching and learning. It is possible for students to fully master the concepts of computer studies by the practical use of computers. There is a study that shows that the availability of well-equipped computer facilities influences the decision of the student to study computer studies. This is seen in both public and private schools.

Being able to provide and improve the infrastructure for being able to teach technical subjects, including computer studies, in secondary schools, helps to improve the participation of students in these subjects. Schools that may have 10 computers may discourage students from taking the subject, as it means that they will be having to share one computer amongst many students. Schools that have many computers, as well as Wi-Fi, are much more motivated to choose computer studies, because they know they have the opportunity to be much more comfortable while doing the subject (Willmann, 2017).

Despite the fact that computer science is critical in allowing the students to have basic skills that they can use in today's workforce, there are not many public and private schools that provide the lesson to the students. This is because computers are expensive to obtain, install, and maintain. If there are enough computer facilities in the school, the students are equipped with the necessary materials to learn and teach computer studies. It is not possible for the learning and teaching of computer studies to be meaningful without the presence of computers. There are many students who prefer not to choose the subject, because of the lack of enough computer infrastructural facilities. When schools improve the computer facilities, it lowers the ratio of computers to students, thus allowing more students to choose computer studies as their technical subject.

Private schools may be able to provide well equipped computer laboratories; however, public schools have a hard time doing so, due to the inadequate funds that hinder them from providing modern computers and their equipments, Wi-Fi installation, expenses in subscriptions, etc. This also influences the choice of computer studies by the student (Willmann, 2017).

Most of the public schools are found in areas with low income minority communities. These areas do not have efficient internet connection and also lower resources, therefore preventing the school from offering the whole curriculum, preventing students from picking computer studies. Private schools are mostly situated near town or in areas with middle or high income. These areas are also equipped with an internet connection, promoting the accessibility to information that is educational, and thus pushing students to choose computer studies. It is true to say that the availability of computer facilities in any school, influences the choice of the students to study computer science.

Figure 10.2. A computer laboratory requires to have proper facilities that will help in the maintenance of the computers. These include proper electrical wiring.

Source: https://siu.edu.so/computer-lab/.

The lack of computer facilities that are adequate and efficient has proven to affect the choice of studying computers in secondary schools. Public schools are advantaged, being able to have adequate facilities, books for studying computer studies, as well as the internet connection. So as to enhance their computer skills, students in private schools are able to undergo exposure to different activities and projects that allow then to enhance their basic computer skills, in comparison to those students in public school.

There is a need for the government to work towards equipping all public secondary schools with enough computer facilities. This helps in increasing the number of students that take computer studies, therefore improving the skill quality, allowing students to be well equipped with these skills when joining the workforce of today. Students that choose to do computer studies should always be exposed to a variety of practical activities, allowing them to get used to the electronic environment of today, which is dominated by information technology (Willmann, 2017).

10.5. PARENTS' INFLUENCE ON STUDENTS' CHOICE OF COMPUTER STUDIES IN SCHOOLS

All parties related – students, parent's teachers and administrators-unilaterally agree that learning computer science in this day and age is of prime importance. Parents have always been a major key when it comes to identifying and influencing what students study, and with computer science it is no different. Knowledge and perceptions of computer science according to parents is what influences and gives encouragement in placing it as an educational priority.

A study that explored perceptions, access and barriers to computer science education in the United States, showed that perception and exposure play important roles in participation and interest, whereas students fell for the stereotypes of computer scientists being nerdy and lacking social skills, parents seem to encourage the study of all sciences and mathematics in middle or High School and therefore actually contribute to the increased likelihood of a young adult pursuing and persisting in computer science careers (Willmann, 2017).

The growing influence of computer science has represented itself in the manifestation of additional resources. Parents recognize the wide impact and applicability the subject has in the real world and therefore guide their children to schools that invest in the same and in turn schools place a priority on offering unique computer science curriculum to appear attractive to both the students and the parents.

Making sure that parents are part of their children's learning, especially in the house, is known ensure a huge difference and also ensures a greater change on the success of a child in class than anything else. When the parents are involved, it is possible for it to be affected by certain factors that may be social or economical, such as socioeconomic condition and some negative school experiences. One of the main factors that leads to the level of parents being involved is parental educational background.

One of the examples includes parents that have a higher college degree have much more when it comes to attending the activities or meetings that undergo organization at the school, talk more often about issues to do with education with their children and later on expect their children to have more success in their education. At the same time, parents who have lower levels of educational tend to be less involved, because they are not confident enough to contact or talk to the school staff (König, 2012).

Figure 10.3. Parents are an important part of children's lives, and it is important for them to play major role in guiding their children.

Source: https://theconversation.com/amp/how-parents-and-teens-can-reduce-the-impact-of-social-media-on-youth-well-being-87619.

In addition, the income levels of the parents tend to also have an effect on the levels of their involvement. The study found that parents that made a higher income tend to take part more often in the activities that are planned by the school in comparison to low-income parents. In addition, parents with that a high socioeconomic status try to ensure effective involvement in comparison to parents that have a low socioeconomic status. The parents that are from a socioeconomic class that is low tend to not be able to give their children of what they require in supporting their growth and as well as welfare. The academic skills that are initially acquired are seen together with the environment at their homes, where the low levels of involvement together with high levels of stress negatively affects the academic performance of the child. Parents from low socioeconomic background are less likely to have the financial resources or time availability to provide children with academic support.

Parents are important in shaping the perception and approach of learning that the child takes. Parents are also important in the determination of whether or not the child is aspiring to learn and achieve, behaves well within school and has good attendance. You may find, however, for some reason, some parents do not get involved in driving and influencing students' choice of computer studies in schools because they do not see their involvement as a parental duty. To a number of the parents, it is the school's responsibility to educate students (König, 2012).

To add onto this, the structure of the family also has an effect on parental involvement. Any disruptions that are marital, in the family, can lead to low levels of involvement by lowering the amount of time that parents spend with their children. This normally happens mainly with fathers, because there are many children who end up living with their mothers after the father and mother have divorced, is significantly higher.

It is not only the gender of the child, but also the gender of the parent that is a factor that contributes to the level of involvement. An example includes how mothers tend to spend more time helping their children with homework in comparison to fathers. Being able to increase the participation of mothers in computer science is important for the workforce and also the concern on equity. There has been a commitment by the technology field to ensure reversal of the negative trends for women in computer science as well as engineering and information technology fields of computing.

An important angle to explore as well is how are adults learning to use technology? Chances are if you are a parent, your child is teaching you. Many parents are being taught how to use computers by their children. Even the smallest ones know much more about it than most of the older generations. This means that there is a symbiotic relationship between parents and students in relation to computer science that cannot be ignored (König, 2012).

Overall, despite the positive image of CS careers and work, we still see a need for broader education on what Computer Science/studies is and is not among all populations, including educators. And, despite the high value and demand for Computer Studies from parents, the education infrastructure does not equitably provide all students with the desired exposure. This may be due to the perceptions across populations that computer studies are only for certain types of people, as well as a lack of awareness of parent demands.

10.6. TEACHERS' READINESS TO USE ICT IN SCHOOLS

It is possible for the teachers to record student marks as well as their records, both personal and academic, on pre-formatted documents, and still be able to keep them up to date.

They can also use thus method for recording of all school administration data. What is more important, is for teachers to be able to maintain their lesson, evaluations and exercises, in digital formats.

This will make it easier for them to update, share with their colleagues, and also ensure their enhancements over time.

For inexperienced teachers to accept training on computer studies, it is necessary to explain to them the many advantages that a computer, or any other computer device can be very advantageous to the teacher in their administrative task.

This is a factor that needs to be carefully considered during the planning of training the teachers, because many of them nay prefer to be aware of how the computers work outside the classroom, instead of inside.

This can be achieved by allowing the teachers to start with software applications, or the easier devices to use such as handhelds that they can learn to use almost immediately.

It is easy to learn how to use these machines to store texts, in the construction of spreadsheets, or to use the word processor to create documents (Cartelli & Antonio, 2013).

Despite a significant body of research that shows that information and communication technology have major influence on how school principals operate, and it important that we do not forget the role of principals as leaders of technology. Principals normally have a main position in the creation of successful changes in the school.

This is in relation to the improvement of schools and the effectiveness of schools. They are also the major key in implementing information and communication technology in school, for both teachers and students.

Figure 10.4. It is important for teachers to learn how to use computers, so as to allow them to use them in improving student engagement in the classroom.

Source: https://www.thetimes.co.uk/article/school-where-pupils-give-teachers-lessons-in-how-to-use-computers-wb77qf2fq.

Principals are left with the responsibility of ensuring that ICT is well integrated into schools, by making the complicated and difficult decisions that they are required to make. Teachers should be able to support their principles in implementing these changes, as they know that they are important in establishing a proper learning system.

One of the greatest challenges has been the incorporation of information and communication technology in school, as it has made the teaching and learning process complicated. Teachers are required to have knowledge on these systems and this has also proven complicated. It is harder to integrate computers into the learning system, in comparison to the provision of computers and installing of secure internet connections in the school. It involves a shit from the instruction to construction philosophies of learning and teaching (Strickland & Alvermann, 2004).

This means that will take time to fully involve the teachers into the use technology to teach. This is due to the level of innovation in this sector, as well as the time it takes to be fully prepared for its use. So as to implement these changes, principals need to apply strategies such as lifelong learner, change agent, and the provider of these resources. This means that they need to identify and push for a vision, ensure provision of a model that is appropriate, support the teachers individually, provision of stimulation that is intellectual, and foster the acceptance of these tools.

Teachers need to be equipped with the skills, knowledge, and positive attitude towards the integration of information and communication technology in schools. This will help in the creation of change, as well as the conversion of the teachers into leaders that are willing to become agents of change, and for this to happen, the teachers need to be committed and able to manage themselves (König, 2012).

Governments need to ensure that principals, teachers, and computer personnel are well trained on the use of computers and other equipments that are related to information and communication technology through workshops, seminars, and in-service training. There should also be an emphasis that aims at the development of long-term programs that are effective for the continued commitment in training and using of technologies that are instructional. Governments also need to show that they are interested in the integration of ICT and therefore provide the equipments that are necessary for this to all secondary schools, through improving the funds for buying these equipments. For teachers to be able to develop and utilize materials and methods together with their students, it is important for there to be proper instruction delivery that is site-based over a long period of time. Local schools should be well supported and there should be a distance delivery that is reliable for this to be achieved. This includes both hardware and software support (Strickland & Alvermann, 2004).

10.7. PRIOR COMPUTER TRAINING

Due to the increased need and trend in the integration of information and communication technology in teaching and training of students, it is important for teachers to have prior training on these aspects. There are many new and different technologies that are providing teachers and other education staff with many different tools and possibilities in teaching. These, however, have some challenges. Information and communication technology can be quite hard to understand and integrate, and approaching this task without the proper training and guidance can consume many hours.

There are many information and communication technology training courses that have been designed for teachers and the educational staff, which will allow them to gain knowledge on the best ways to utilize information and communication technology to promote and support education in schools. Teachers and other educators are able to develop strong information and communication technology skills, as well as be able to discuss and exchange the best practices for this technology through hands-on approach and also learning by doing methodology. This also allows them to reflect together on how this technology can best be used to promote education and the learning process (König, 2012).

The teacher training course gives them a chance to improve on their information and communication technology skills in a manner that is practical and concrete. It also allows them to do this together with other teachers throughout the country, allowing them to gain knowledge on the different learning systems in the different schools. This can also help in brainstorming for new ways to integrate computers in schools. Prior training helps to foster excellence in education by making sure that the teachers, trainers, principals, and other educators are empowered, somas to properly integrate these tools into the education system (König, 2012).

Figure 10.5. Training is important if the teachers are to be the stakeholders on computer integration in classrooms.

Source: https://www.globalgiving.org/projects/enhance-education-of-girls-through-technology/.

These trainings need to be flexible, so as to ensure that the teachers' and educators' needs are catered for in terms of the learning outcomes and the current skills of the people participating. Some of the things that the teachers and educators will gain include:

- They will be able to gain information on the main new innovations in technology that will promote the learning and teaching experience for the students and teachers respectively.

- They will also know the major applications, web platforms, and information and communication technology solutions for teachers and other educators.
- They also gain knowledge on the creation of multimedia content and presentations that are engaging and interactive for the students.
- They will also learn how to make assessments of the students' knowledge and understanding in a digital manner, which is in real time.
- They gain the main and basic concepts of learning online with e-learning and also the flipped classroom.
- They will be able to create blogs as well as websites.
- They will be able to use information and communication technology tools to ensure that education is much more motivating, engaging, and innovative.
- They will gain a whole new perspective on these tools and be able to know the best ways to integrate these tools into the education system.
- They will be able to share their knowledge with other educators and teachers allowing them to discuss on the best ways to go about the integration of these tools in their respective schools.
- They will attain different contacts that they can use to refer to and also to continue gaining knowledge on new innovations in the ICT sector.

There are many countries that are aiming at transforming their education system to be knowledge based, led by technology and in turn ensure that their societies are all middle income. ICT will help in energizing students as well as improving the socioeconomic development of many different countries (Kumar & Turner, 2006). One of the main strategies in achieving this is by enhancing the capabilities of teachers and educators in and through information and communication technology, so as to ensure development of high-quality skills and knowledge base.

Training teachers in information and communication technology will help in the increment of the resource base, as well as improve the delivery of education at all levels. This shows the need to make the use of ICT institutional as well as make sure that all teachers are well trained. Countries need to come up with ICT essentials for all educators, which will help in providing benefits for both the students and the teachers in the teaching and learning processes, therefore leading to better learning outcomes, led by student engagement and proper communication. All in all, ICT in schools can help in improving the socioeconomic state of any country.

10.8. ICT INFRASTRUCTURE

So as to access ICT in our schools, there is a need for consideration of infrastructure. Africa has limited access to ICT infrastructure, which can act as a hindrance for its integration in schools today. Many developing countries have many different shared accounts and there is also a possibility of public access. In comparison to developed countries, the technology penetration is low. Statistics in Africa in 2001 showed that:

- Only one out of four people owned a radio.
- One out of thirteen owned a television set.
- One out of thirty-five owned a mobile phone.
- One out of forty people had a telephone line that was fixed.
- One out of thirty people at the time owned a personal computer.
- One out of one hundred and sixty people were able to use the internet.
- One out of four hundred people had pay-TV.

There are many reasons why the statistics were like this:

- There was a low level of economic activity, which made it hard to afford technology.
- There are many countries in Africa that do not have a consistent electricity supply, making the integration of ICT complicated.
- There was limited infrastructure, such as rail, road, and air transport, which is important in the implementation and support of ICT, together with the activities, both social and economic, that ICT should stimulate.
- There are many tax regimes that define these devices, such as phones and computers as an item of luxury, which leads to the process of these goods increasing, especially because most of them are brought into the countries using imports.
- There is a decreased level of skill together with the brain drain, which has made it had to adopt the new technology.

These issues have not only made it hard to integrate ICT in the continent, but also in the schools. There is a need to strengthen the basic education curriculum reform and actively facilitate the application of ICT in education. This is however, harder due to the achievement gap of information and communication technology infrastructure as well as its application in schools in both the rural and urban areas. There is a gap that exists between the need for construction of information and communication technology infrastructure and the patterns that are set to promote the application of ICT in schools.

Figure 10.6. ICT infrastructure is paramount in computer integration in the classroom. It is not quite helpful for one to use the hardware without other factors such as internet.

Source: https://sidmach.com/solution/ict-infrastructure/.

For there to be full support of the integration of information and communication technology in schools, the is a need for hardware infrastructure to be set up together with the elements that support this hardware, such as maintenance, electricity, and even the technical services. It is impossible for the leaders to expect the educators to assume the technical responsibility for the hardware, considering the fact that they will still be dealing with the new role of technology in the education system.

There is a need for rooms and buildings that are appropriate for this technology to be housed. There may be a need for extensive renovation in schools that have old rooms and buildings, so as to make sure that the ventilation and heating and cooling systems, the electrical wiring, as well as the safety and security of these rooms is sufficed to house the technology (Willmann, 2017).

Another main requirement for ICT integration is to ensure that electricity and telephony is available. There is a need for all the schools to have electricity, so at to ensure the proper use of ICT in the classrooms. This is not a problem in some countries, but it is in others. There is also low telephone network and low access to internet in many developing countries, which also makes it difficult to incorporate these tools into the education system.

The internet is very important for there to be proper integration of ICT in schools. This is, however, expensive for some schools, especially in the rural areas, to maintain. Education has had a problem when it comes to keeping up with the digital society and economy. This means that we still have not seen how much technology can do for us when added into the education system fully. Many schools are still without access to digital equipment, high internet connections and fast broadband in schools. It will not be possible to achieve this without the appropriate equipment, tools, and networks. These are not accounted for in many schools, and it is up to the government to improve funding for many schools, especially in the rural areas. It is important to adopt the use of ICT in schools at an early age, and the government needs to take this up and equip schools with the infrastructure (Kumar &Turner, 2006).

10.9. INTERNET ACCESSIBILITY AND COMPUTER USAGE BY SCHOOL TEACHERS

Since more than 10 years ago, the National Center for Education Statistics (NCES) has been able to document the great increase in access to computers and the Internet in the public primary and secondary schools. This growth has led to a necessity to promote awareness, promote education and therefore understand the level and types of use of computers as well as the Internet, together with the teachers' perceptions of their own readiness to utilize these tools in their classrooms. To talk on these critical information needs, there has been commissioning of a survey using the Fast Response Survey System that was done in the year 2000. This survey showed that most of the teachers who teach full-time in regular public school, stated that they were able to access these computers or the Internet at some point in the schools.

One of the main questions involves how teachers utilize computers and the internet at schools. There are many teachers globally who were asked the level at which they utilize computers or Internet services in the preparation of schedules, managing and teaching their classes. Roughly thirty-eight percent of teachers in public schools that were able to access computers as well as Internet in their classes or somewhere else in the school, stated that they were able to use computers or the Internet many times a day in the creation of materials that are instructional, at the same time, around thirty-five percent stated that they used computers mostly for keeping and tracking administrative records. Less than 9 percent of teachers stated that they used computers or the Internet for the accessibility of model lesson plans or research and best practices (Unesco, 2011).

Teachers who were newer in the school are much more likely to utilize computers or the Internet to convey various teaching objectives. Teachers that had less teaching experience of about 8 to 11 years were more likely to utilize computer and internet usage in their schools many times to talk to their colleagues and also in gathering information for lessons, in comparison to those that had 15 or more years of experience.

Figure 10.7. Being able to access the internet is important for teachers, considering there any many software's that can be integrated in the school curriculum, and they all mostly require the internet.

Source: https://www.gordonlawltd.com/internet-law-website-accessibility/.

Statistics on computer and Internet usage showed that a high percentage of teachers use Internet frequently for day-to-day communication. Also, teachers with 3 to 10 years of teaching experience were more likely to report they used computers or the Internet many times for the creation of instructional materials than those teachers with 21 or more years of experience (Unesco, 2011).

The use of computers or the Internet at school by teachers varies for different types of uses in terms of school poverty level. Teachers that teach in schools that have a school poverty level of less than 10 percent are much more likely to utilize computers or the Internet many times to create instructional materials in comparison to those teachers that teach in schools that have a school poverty level of 69 percent or more. This sequence is also seen in teachers who normally utilize computers for administrative record keeping.

There are many factors that affect the use of computers in schools. As a classroom tool, the computer has been able to capture the attention of the education community.

This is because of how versatile computers are, their ability for their storage, manipulation, and retrieval of data. Computers are also able to engage students at a level that humans are not able to achieve, in activities that allow for the increase of their learning experience, and also in being able to solve problems, therefore improving their cognitive skills (WANG, 2017).

Internet use in schools is important, as without it, it is impossible to access data from the web, which is also important in the classroom, so as to be able to access certain online apps that can help in student learning as well as teaching. E-learning is also normally done on the internet. There are many different applications that can be found on the web and to access them, there is a need for internet. Internet is considered one of the main infrastructures that is needed in the integration of ICT in schools.

10.10. COMPUTER COMPETENCE AND COMPUTER USAGE BY SCHOOL TEACHERS

Computer competence has a couple of definitions. It involves the ability to understand both software and hardware or being familiar with the languages if computer programming. In addition, it can be considered the knowledge of the characteristics, applications, and capabilities of a computer, together with the ability to use this knowledge in a skillful and productive manner. It involves being able to understand as well as have the skills and attitude, that are required in performing roles socially that involve the computer, both directly and indirectly. For one to be computer competent, they need to have the collection of knowledge, understanding, skills, relationships and values that will allow them to comfortably function as a member of the community who is productive in this society that is oriented on computers.

There are three main objectives in computer competency instructions:

- Knowledge of the terms, applications, components, and ethical issues that are found socially.
- Skill in the use of the major applications such as word processor, the spreadsheet, and even doing other functions such as retrieving information, publishing desktops and solving problems.
- Attitude in accepting of the tools as valuable, and also appreciating them as being productive.
- There are three stages in computer competency for teachers:
- The basic level – this includes being able to operate a computer, be able to manage data, do tasks on the processing of data, troubleshooting of basic storage, usage of both output and input devices, be able to use external components to manage content and data, create emails, surf the web, etc.
- Intermediate level – being able to create and manage content with the help of software applications, use devices that are digital, use search engines and websites, etc.
- Advanced Level – the use of database applications, perform research, be able to use audio-visual communication, utilizing collaborative-cooperative learning, dealing with copyright issues, etc.

These stages account for the set of competencies that the teachers should be equipped with.

Educationalists have been able to explore the education potential of computers in schools over the past years. It is therefore important for every teacher to be ready to adopt and utilize computers, and also know how these tools can help in supporting the learning of students. The teachers have the larger responsibility of learning how to use these tools. This approach is constructivist, and it requires for high levels of computer competency to work.

Actually, there are many teachers who know how to and use computers in their daily work to support the educational practice, however, only a few use computers as a tool in the classroom for teaching and learning. There are many trends that are being developed in the developing countries. One of the major issues that is affecting the computer competency levels of teachers in most African countries is the lack of enough research in these matters (Unesco, 2011).

Figure 10.8. There are many teachers that do not have the literacy that is required for one to use computers in classrooms. This is up to the government to provide training for the teachers.

Source: https://helpersaide.org/donations/education/.

There is no comprehensive and inclusive definition for assessing teachers in terms of their computer competence. Even more important, it is hard to ascertain the level at which the teachers are in terms of computer competency currently. It is also hard to design remediation plans that are suitable for the teachers due to these issues, which ends up affecting the integration of computers in schools.

Governments should create questionnaires that will help in the assessment of teachers' competency levels, which should include questions on three main areas: technology, pedagogy, and integration. These questions would help in giving a detailed appraisal on the current levels on computer literacy within the teachers of today, which will help in creating the measures that will help in improving the computer liter of teachers. This study can help in many of the countries that are in Africa.

Some of the competencies that the teachers require include pedagogical ones such as being able to select computer tools as well as pedagogy that with help in the integration of computers into the education system. They also need to cater for the students' needs as well as the learning objectives of the students. They need to help the student in the management of their learning, as well as allowing the students to in charge of their own learning so as to ensure the update of the knowledge and skills of the specific subject. The technological competency requires one to be able to restrain from intrusion that is not authorized, manipulating other people's data together with hacking, etc. The integration competency requires one to know how to use a computer to evaluate and assess the students in term of their performance, being able to design learning experiences that are personalized, evaluation and adaptation of software that is instructional, and even being able to write courseware for the lesson the teacher is conducting.

10.11. THE INFLUENCE OF GENDER DIFFERENCES ON COMPUTER USAGE BY SCHOOL TEACHERS

Recent research focused on low female participation in computer science courses and the information and communication technology industry. This leads to women missing out in the many career opportunities in today's market, due to the high need of people who are skilled in the information and communication technology sector. This also means that the information and communication technology industry is also missing out of the many different perspectives and talents that could have been advantageous if there were more women participating in the industry (Sharma, 2002).

The number of women who do degrees and courses in information and communication technology deceases almost every year in the last decade. This directly shows in the same manner in the education system. Most of the female teachers did not have the opportunity or interest in studying computer studies. Weirdly enough, the number of women in the science and engineering field has increased as it decreases in the computer field. The fact that women are not interested or are not given the opportunity to study computer-related studies has led to a lower computer competency among the female teachers in schools.

The ability of female teachers to participate in the integration of ICT in schools depends on their willingness to learn at least the most basic computer concepts. This is considering the fact that classroom technology is not difficult to use and it is developed in a manner that suits the teacher. Most female teachers lack the interest and perceived ability in computer-related studies, and this mentality continues to persist. It is important to understand how we can increase the interest of female teachers to achieve knowledge on computer science, and even be able to study it so as to teach it in both primary and secondary schools (Sharma, 2002).

Socialization has negative effects that has also hindered female teachers from learning computer-related issues. There has not been much research on how different genders have different leaning preferences. This research would help in understanding the matters that discourage and encourage different genders to pick or not pick computer as a subject of study. There are, however, studies that can help in this understanding, including the views of learning held by feminist pedagogy, etc.

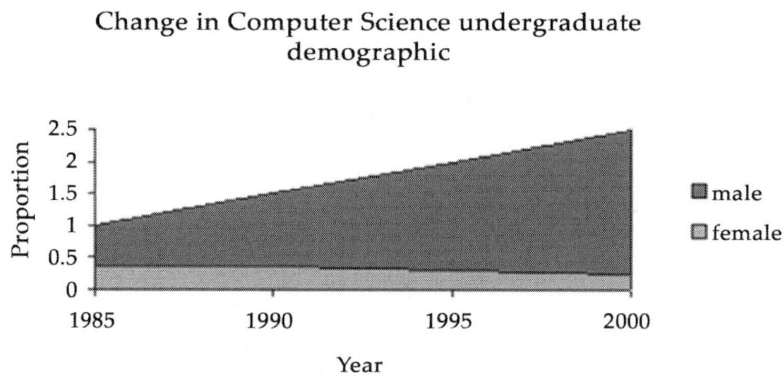

Figure 10.9. Above is an example of the demographic that shows the difference between women and men in computer science.

Source: https://www.cs.kent.ac.uk/people/staff/jec/gdp/Gender_issues.htm.

When it comes to computer studies, different studies have shown that male teachers prefer to start their process of learning using concepts that are abstract, while the female teachers prefer to use learning styles that are concrete. Those of men were found to be much more similar to the traditional methods of learning, in comparison to those of the women. This is probably because most education systems were created for the learning purpose of the men, which was initially socially constructed by white males. This has made it harder for women to study computer-related sciences.

It has been proven in the past years that the way that women develop and learn has different emphases and attributes. The females prefer to have a relationship, connection, collaboration and understanding in the learning approaches that they prefer. This is similar to female students who may prefer to play games that have a storyline, relationships, and even being able to have learning that is attentive to the physical, social and cognitive space (Unesco, 2011).

One of the main reasons that female teachers may take longer to learn computer-related studies is due to the fact that they are an underserved population. There is a need to change from the traditional methods of education to a method that shows the necessary and intimate relationship between education and the actual learning process. These thoughts have change and grown from the previous framework. Of different thinkers who were aiming at ensuring that education serves the diverse learning community. It is important for the education system to accommodate female teachers in a manner that allows them to find an interest in taking up computer studies.

INDEX

A

Academic capital 256
Academic diary 149
Academic performance 96, 98, 100, 108, 271
Actual learning process 287
Administrative computer information system 149
Adolescent advancement 6
Algorithmic thinking 53
Amazon web services (AWS) 173
Analytical skills 23
Aptitude test 59
Arithmetical skills 152
Artificial intelligence 191, 195
Assembly language 35, 38
Automatic migrating tools 199

B

Basic education curriculum 279
Batch processing system 147
Behavioral beliefs 183, 185, 186
Bibliographic information 149
Biohazardous materials 71
Blended classrooms 105
Block-based coding 64
Block-based graphical programming language 66
Block programming 64, 69, 70
Bookkeeping 76
Brainstorming 276

C

Card catalog system 149
Central memory 147
Central processing unit 34
Childhood education 93

Childhood schooling 76
C language 32
Classroom management tactic 213
Classroom scenarios 208, 211, 212, 215, 236
Cloud-based learning 221
Cloud computing 171, 172, 191
Cloud migration 198
Cloud services 171, 173, 196, 198
Cloud technology 192, 193, 194, 195
Coding languages 84
Coding procedure 79
Cognitive maps 62
Cognitive systems 51
Collaborative online tools 119
Collaborative search engines 119
College-trained computing workforce 240
Common global issues 265
Communication 23, 28
Communication barriers 226
Communication process 177, 181, 223, 224, 226
Communication system 147
Compiler 33, 38
Complex problems 52
Computational artifacts 78
Computational intellect 50
Computational problems 77, 78
Computational reasoning 50, 51, 54, 58, 59, 67, 91, 240, 245, 246, 247, 252
Computational science like algorithms 82
Computational thinking 48, 49, 50, 51, 52, 53, 54, 57, 58
Computational thinking systems 48
Computer application 175
Computer applications 49
Computer architecture 41, 42
Computer-assisted instruction 153, 155
Computer augmented learning 153
Computer-based learning 162
Computer competence 282
Computer games 8
Computer literacy 156, 157, 160
Computer machines 150
Computer network 36
Computer occupations 264
Computer-related actions (CRA) 165
Computer science 2, 4, 5, 14, 15, 16, 17, 18, 21, 22, 26, 29, 30
Computer science-based professions 250
Computer science education 82
Computer science tutorial education pathways 254
Computer scientist 2, 3
Computers function 241
Computer skills 267, 269
Computer studies 264, 265, 266, 267, 268, 269, 270, 272, 273, 285, 286, 287
Computer technology 80
Computer world 147
Computing devices 80, 81
Computing professionals 242
Computing system 147
Computing technologies 241, 242, 243
Contemporary technology 265
Continual technology planning 262
Conventional algorithms 54
Cost analysis 24
CPU architecture 43

Creative computing 245
Creativity 23, 24, 26, 27, 29
Credit analysis 24
Critical reasoning 50
Critical thinking 3, 10, 11, 12, 24, 28, 29
Critical thinking abilities 10
Critical thinking skills 26, 28, 228
CS technology 82
Cumulative knowledge 241
Curriculum system 151

D

Data analysis 23, 24
Data-based issues 53
Data collection 24
Data dictionaries 198
Data entry 24
Data management tool 105
Data privacy 194
Data processing 37, 42
Data protection 195
Data structures 39, 43, 44, 45
Data values 43
Decision-making process 177, 178
Decompositional practice 54
Decomposition procedure 54
Descriptive analysis 24
Designer language 34
Digital literacy 242
Digital machine 146
Dimensional reasoning 60

E

Ecological elements 7
Educational games 108, 130, 210, 217
Educational practice 283
Educational system 118
Educational technologies 98
Educational technology 250, 262
Educational tutorials 216
Education community 282
Education process 226, 236
Education sector 204, 206, 211, 217
Education stakeholders 247, 252
Education system 117, 137, 138, 140, 141, 148, 151, 152, 204, 211, 216, 235, 276, 277, 279, 280, 284, 285, 287
Emotional knowledge 76, 77
Environment frameworks 181
Evidence-based reading 101

F

Face-to-face communications 94
Feminist pedagogy 286
File organization 41
Financial records 219, 236
Fundamental language 32

G

Game-based learning 108
General data protection regulation (GDPR) 195
Generation technology 171
Global organizations 181
Google earth 124
Google's searching algorithm 54
Government agencies 37

H

Hardware and software resources 39
Hardware infrastructure 279
Hardware management 71
High-level language 38
High school academic system 148

Human interfaces 70
Humanoid machine 72

I

ICT programs 210, 216
Information and communication technology 264, 273, 274, 275, 276, 277, 279, 285
Information science 160
Information system theory 170
Initial teaching processes 224
Innovation planning 257
Innovative teaching 207
Instructional materials 281, 282
Integrated circuits 34
Integrative learning projects 107
Intellectual progress 63
Intelligent algorithms 71
Intelligent communication appliance 81
Inter-organizational systems 183
Interrupt processing 41

L

Learning computer-related issues 286
Learning environment 96, 226, 227, 232
Learning experience 105, 117, 135, 136
Learning institutions 17, 18, 21, 22, 148, 211, 219, 220, 233
Learning management system 101, 135, 136
Learning materials 214, 227
Learning methodologies 206
Learning organizations 253
Learning outcomes 113, 276, 278
Learning process 204, 206, 207, 208, 209, 210, 211, 212, 214, 218, 220, 223, 224, 226, 227, 230, 231, 232, 233, 235, 236, 237
Learning programs 204
Library catalogs 234
Linguistic arts 51
Local area network 37
Low-level language 35, 38
Low-level technology programs 243

M

Machine language 33, 34, 35
Management institutions 219
Management skills 96
Mapping skills 63
Markup languages 115
Mathematical calculations 157
Mechanical thinking 49
Media gadget 9
Memory management 39, 40
Metropolitan area network 37
Microcomputer 146
Microcontrollers 33
Microprocessor 34, 35, 36
Minicomputers 147
Mobile technology 110
Modern computers 268
Multiple programming languages 65
Music synthesizer 152

N

Negative behaviors 98
Networking 37
Non-verbal aptitude tests 59
Numbering system 159

O

Online digital services 193
Online information 105
Online learning 103, 104, 105
Online program 63
Online programming 68
Online research methods 116
Operating system 39

P

Parallel instruction computing 35
Pattern recognition 53, 57
Perceived ease-of-use (PEOU) 188
Perceived usefulness (PU) 187
Personal computer 171
Physical activity 61
Physical progression 5
Positive learning outcomes 92
Practiced teaching standards 253
Problem-solving procedures 55
Problem-solving process 52
Problem-solving skills 15, 23, 25, 26
Process management 39
Professional development 19, 20
Professional skills 18
Programming 4, 14, 17, 22, 24, 30
Programming language 32, 33, 34, 38, 42
Programming resource 70
Programming skills 85, 88
Programming system 82, 84
Project-based activities 107
Project-based learning 105, 108
Project-based programs 246
Pupil activity books 246

R

Racialized systems 100
Real classroom environments 18
Real-time spatial language 60
Resilience skills 29, 30
Response system 110
Robotic equipment 72
Robotics systems 71
Robotic structure 70
Robotic systems 70
Robotic technology 71
Robot locomotion 72

S

School administration 261
School administration data 273
School vision 231, 232
Scientific knowledge 96
Scientific methodology 85
Scientific thinking 49
Scripting languages 115
Service level agreement (SLA) 200
Skilled development 244, 246
Small machines 147
Smart devices 110
Social circumstance 8
Social-emotional learning 88, 90
Social influence 188, 189
Social networks 174, 190
Social service 107
Socio-cultural frameworks 258
Socioeconomic status 271
Socioemotional learning 88
Socio-emotional skills 90
Sociological studies 245
Software engineering 3, 5, 32, 33
Software programming 196
Sorting algorithms 57
Spatial reasoning 59, 60
Spatial thinking 58, 59, 61
Standards-based computing courses 247

STEM subjects 55
Storybooks 7
Structural decomposition 55
Student behavior management 99
Student evaluation 220, 221
SWOT analysis 24

T

Task technology 178, 179, 180
Teacher-preparation programs 17
Teacher's teaching techniques 205
Teacher training program 18
Teaching critical reasoning 79
Teaching industry 212
Teaching practices 207, 211
Technical support 37
Technological century 2
Technological innovation 81
Technology acceptance model 170, 180, 187, 188, 191
Technology acceptance network 188
Technology adoption framework 184
Technology-based methods 124
Technology integration 96, 97, 98, 103, 106, 140
Technology skills 101
Time-shared network system 147
Traditional learning 104
Traditional text-based coding languages 64
Training services 20

U

Unreal engine 66, 67
User interface 84
UTAUT model 189

V

Video games 8
Virtual machine 34, 172
Virtual version 68
Visual programming system 66
Visual representations 78
Vocational training 235

W

Web-based systems 8
Web projects 115
Wireless device 10
Word progressing systems 97